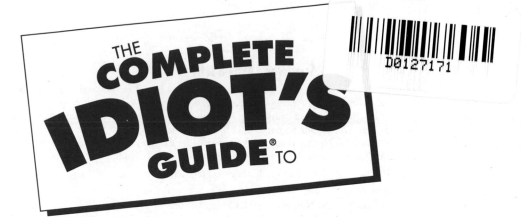

THE COMPLETE IDIOT'S GUIDE® TO

Beating Debt

Second Edition

by Steven D. Strauss and Azriela Jaffe

ALPHA

A member of Penguin Group (USA) Inc.

To our wonderful families.

Publisher: *Marie Butler-Knight*
Product Manager: *Phil Kitchel*
Senior Managing Editor: *Jennifer Chisholm*
Acquisitions Editor: *Gary Goldstein*
Development Editor: *Jennifer Moore*
Production Editor: *Billy Fields*
Copy Editor: *Jeff Rose*
Illustrator: *Chris Eliopoulos*
Cover/Book Designer: *Trina Wurst*
Indexer: *Heather McNeill*
Layout/Proofreading: *Becky Harmon, Mary Hunt*

Contents at a Glance

Contents

Foreword

Economics is a topic that often eludes even the best and brightest.

Most individuals have read about finance in school or learned a little along the road of life, but soon realize that the knowledge they have is not enough to cope in today's financial world. Many of us are stumbling in our own personal finances and need a helping hand.

The Complete Idiot's Guide to Beating Debt, Second Edition, brings the world of economics and personal finance down to the level of the average person's understanding. In easy to read chapters it lays out the basics of debt, credit, and budgeting. With these basics, each of us can gain an even better understanding of the mistakes we have made in the past. This valuable book also gives us the tools to help us make sound decisions for our futures.

The Complete Idiot's Guide to Beating Debt, Second Edition, explains ways to avoid bad debt and demonstrates that some debt is considered an asset. It also demystifies the world of credit, giving us the edge we need in today's challenging climate. Perhaps the most important tool it gives us is knowledge and sound advice when it comes to our own personal budgets.

Sidebars in the chapters give quick economic hints that are readily understood. The sidebars "Two Cents" and "Money Talks" give advice that can be quickly read and put to use, eliminating the need to drudge through mountains of material to get the information you need.

By reading this book, you will come to understand the basics of personal finance, giving you and your family the edge you need to stay debt-free.

By following the simple steps set forth in this book, almost anybody can pull themselves out of debt and into fiscal independence.

Best of luck in your financial endeavors,

—JoyChristine Hollins

JoyChristine Hollins is the administrator for American Family Debt Counseling Centers, Inc., a national nonprofit consumer credit counseling service (www.creditamerica.com).

Introduction

It's no wonder that debt is a four-letter word. Financial problems are among the most stressful problems a person can have. Psychologists say that money problems are one of the main causes of divorce.

There are a host of stuffy books out there that will tell you that all you need to do to get out of debt is tighten your belt and budget better. If that's what you're looking for, then put this book down, because we take a different approach.

First, while we certainly offer many budgetary ideas, more important, we are determined to help you figure out why you've gotten into debt in the first place, and to offer plenty of practical advice to help you out of debt that goes beyond just putting together a budget. Also, we don't portray debt as an entirely horrible problem. Your authors appreciate the debt that has allowed each of them to start businesses, provide for families, and purchase homes.

Further, although you'll find plenty of fairly technical information in these pages, the tone is light, sometimes funny, and always easy to understand. Finally, although the title for this book may be *The Complete Idiot's Guide to Beating Debt, Second Edition*, we don't treat you like an idiot. We carry no judgments, regardless of how much of a pickle you've gotten into.

What's in It for Me?

Part 1, "Money and Debt," covers the basic problem of why people go into debt and begins to offer some solutions. This section looks at common mistakes that get people deeper into debt than they want to be.

Part 2, "Changing Your Relationship with Money," looks at your beliefs about money and helps you begin to change any negative money attitudes you may have. This section also looks at budgets and helps you formulate some ways to cut back (if you want to) and begin to repay your debts.

Part 3, "When Cutting Back Is Not Enough," offers suggestions that go far beyond what most financial books offer. Find out the best way to get out of credit card debt. Learn how to negotiate with your creditors and reduce your debts. Beat the IRS at its own game. Handle business debt.

Part 4, "A Last Option: Bankruptcy," explores what bankruptcy is, how it works, and shows you when bankruptcy may make sense. As one of your authors is a bankruptcy attorney, we certainly understand that bankruptcy is sometimes a necessary evil.

Part 5, "Getting Ahead of the Game," helps you see that a life of financial prosperity may not be that far away. Here we show you several methods that you can use to make more money, whether it's for getting out of debt, getting ahead, or retirement.

Throughout this book we've provided information and advice in the following sidebars:

Over Your Limit

There are many financial traps that are easy to fall for. Heed these cautions and avoid the traps.

Two Cents

In these boxes you'll find insider tips and ideas for getting out of—and staying out of—debt.

Money Talks

Stories and statistics about money and debt.

Check It Out

The jargon of money can sometimes be confusing. "Check It Out" boxes define money terms clearly and simply.

Acknowledgments

Thanks to my co-author, Azriela for her help, encouragement, insight, and friendship. Thanks also to Jillian, Sydney, and Mara for their assistance. Special thanks and love to Maria for her patience, love, humor, and support.—Steve Strauss

Thanks, as always, to my husband, Stephen, who tolerates and mostly embraces my whole-hearted commitment to being a writer and columnist, and all of the time that this profession requires. Thanks to Deb Haggerty, friend and "Aunt" to our family, who has been generous to our family in times of need. Thanks, Deb. You are family to us and we appreciate knowing that you are there for us. Thanks to Mom and Dad: For being there for me, in good times and in bad. I love you.—Azriela Jaffe

Special Thanks to the Technical Reviewer

The Complete Idiot's Guide to Beating Debt, Second Edition, was reviewed by an expert who double-checked the accuracy of what you'll learn here, to help us ensure that this book gives you everything you need to know about beating debt. Special thanks are extended to Warren J. Ladenheim.

Trademarks

All terms mentioned in this book that are known to be or are suspected of being trademarks or service marks have been appropriately capitalized. Alpha Books and Penguin Group (USA) Inc. cannot attest to the accuracy of this information. Use of a term in this book should not be regarded as affecting the validity of any trademark or service mark.

Part 1

Money and Debt

This part goes over the basics: We define the terms and introduce some simple concepts. But the basics also involve being honest with yourself: How did you get into debt? What do you need to do to get out of debt? Part of the solution lies in examining the problem closely—and honestly.

For most people, getting out of debt simply involves looking around. That's why we say, "Take that paper bag off your head when you drive."

Chapter 1

Not All Debt Is Bad Debt

In This Chapter

- ◆ Why you went into debt
- ◆ Debt that hurts, debt that helps
- ◆ Debt you may want to keep
- ◆ Debt you may want to get rid of
- ◆ The first rule of holes
- ◆ Thinking long term

So you are in debt—who isn't these days? We live in a society that encourages people to go into debt. Credit card commercials tell us that a trip to Jamaica is just what we need, regardless of whether we can afford it. (That's what your gold card is for, right?) Loan brokers want us to borrow up to 125 percent against our home equity. Even the federal government just had its first balanced budget in a generation and now faces the enormous task of paying off over trillions of dollars in debt.

Yet not everyone is in debt. Many people know how to deal with money. Their debts are manageable, and they have money in the bank. That sounds nice, doesn't it—money in the bank? That is what you deserve. In order to get there, however, you are going to have to change some of your thinking about money and learn a few new methods of dealing with it.

Why Are You in Debt?

People who are not in debt think about and treat money differently than the rest of us. They know a few things about money and debt that escape the rest of us. Let's call them the "financially literate." If you can begin to relate to money as they do, you will be well on your way to a life that is not only debt-free, but also prosperous. What we hope to do in this book is to show you some of their secrets so you can adapt a few of these ideas and tools to help you get out of debt.

> **Money Talks**
>
> The average millionaire in the United States drives a used car that is several years old and owns his own business. Rich people are rich simply because they do not squander their money.

Do not feel too badly if you are not good with a dollar, a lot of people aren't. Money literacy is not taught in schools, and too often parents are too busy trying to dig themselves out of their own financial hole to help much either. Yet, unfortunately for many of us, we learn more about money from our parents than anywhere else. The good news is that learning how to get out of debt and become more financially literate is not all that complicated.

The first step in the process is to figure out how you created so much debt, because if you don't figure out how and why you got yourself into this pickle, you might get out of debt, but you certainly won't stay out. So the first question to ask yourself is: Why did you go into debt in the first place?

Sometimes going into debt is unavoidable, but often it is not. When money is tight, you have several options; going into debt is just the easiest. Instead of choosing more debt, you might have decided to work overtime and make more money, or possibly you could have tightened your belt and spent less money. Debt was not your only choice.

There are many reasons people go into debt: Some are good reasons, and some are bad. It doesn't matter. Did you buy luxuries you could otherwise not afford? Did an illness or a divorce set you back financially? Was debt your way of dealing with some other sudden, unexpected expense? When you look at the reason why you went into debt, the important thing is to notice whether your spending habits follow a pattern. If you can see a pattern, you need to address that pattern as much as the underlying debt. Part 2 will help you break your debt pattern.

Consider Mark and Diane. They both make a good living: He's a psychiatrist, and she's a psychologist. They have two kids to whom they are devoted. They send both to private school, which costs a total of $15,000 a year, and both kids go to summer camp. These expenses adds up.

Mark and Diane don't buy luxuries, they don't travel much, and, except for the kids' expenses, they are very frugal. Yet the only way they can pay for everything is by going into debt. They use their home equity line of credit and credit cards to stay afloat. Although they would like to move to a less expensive neighborhood, they can't because they have no equity in their home, so they are stuck.

What are they to do? If they are going to get out of debt, something in their lives is going to have to change. The private school is going to have to go, camp may be out, or they are going to have to start making more money. The same is true for you. If you want to get out of debt, you are going to have to identify why you went into debt and change that behavior or pattern.

> **CAUTION**
>
> **Over Your Limit** _____
>
> The average credit card cash advance is $1,600. Given normal interest rates for credit cards, if it takes you a year to pay back that advance, it will cost you $1,808.

Good and Bad Debt

Debt in and of itself is not a bad thing. Both of us (the authors) were able to start our own businesses because of debt; Steve began his own law practice, and Azriela began her own entrepreneurial consulting business. So we understand what debt is and why some debt is great debt.

Debt allows you to do things you otherwise normally could not do, such as start a business, go to college, or pay for a home. Debt constructs buildings and funds investments and entire corporations—even the government is funded by debt. The trick is to foster debts that help the cause and banish the ones that don't. Not all debts are bad debts.

Good Debt

Debt that helps you, enriches your life, is manageable, and is not a burden can be called good debt. For example, student loans are good debt if they enabled you to get through school and further your life goals. They are bad debt if you dropped out of medical school after one year to become a writer. A good debt helps; a bad debt hinders. We want to help you get rid of that bad debt.

Other examples of debt that may be considered good include:

- ◆ **Home loans.** A mortgage can be a great debt. Not only does it permit you to own your own home, but it also allows you to build home equity. It is an asset.

As Chapter 25 explains, people who are financially savvy earn interest and equity. People who are not financially savvy pay interest and create money for others. For example, charging groceries means that you will pay about 17 percent interest on items that will be consumed within a week. A financially literate person would never do that.

Money Talks

In 2003, 68 percent of all families owned their own home, the highest rate of homeownership ever.

Two Cents

Businesses use credit cards in a positive, responsible manner all the time. According to the Small Business Administration, 47 percent of small and midsize businesses used credit cards for financing in 2002, and 38 percent paid their balances in full each month.

- ◆ **Car loans.** A car loan can be a fine debt because you get something long-lasting out of the debt. If you need a nice car for your job (if you are a real estate agent, for example), a car loan may be considered good debt because it helps you in your career. However, a car loan that you cannot afford is a bad debt because it only gets you deeper into debt.

- ◆ **Business loans.** If you can service the loan, and it helps you make more money, the loan is good debt, but if the loan is nothing but a source of problems for you, the debt is bad.

- ◆ **Credit cards.** Credit cards can be both a blessing and a curse. They can help finance a business or even medical emergencies. The problem with them, as you probably know only too well, is that it is too easy to fall under their siren spell and get in over your head very easily. That's when they become a curse.

Bad Debt Blues

How do you know if your debt is good debt or bad debt? Easy. Bad debts cause stress. You sleep poorly because of them. They cause fights and foster guilt. Supreme Court Justice Lewis Powell was once asked to define *obscenity*. Hard-pressed to come up with a definition, Powell uttered the famous line, "I know it when I see it." The same could be said for bad debt: You know it when you see it, and it certainly can be obscene.

Bad debt seems impossible to pay back. You create bad debt when you charge things you don't need or when you borrow for things that you consume quickly, such as clothes, meals, or vacations. The things quickly disappear, but the debt has a nasty habit of sticking around, seemingly forever. Bad debts can become very bad debts because of interest and penalties. For example, if you buy a CD player for $200 and don't pay it off by the end of the year, and your credit card company charges 20 percent APR (20 percent per year), you owe $220 by the end of the year. If you do this with five items, you owe $1,100 and that's a lot of money.

Money Talks
Tight for money? Here are some simple ways to save a little extra: Don't use ATMs at other banks and avoid $2 user fees; cancel your movie channels on cable and save about $20 per month; put all of your change at the end of the day in a jar and save about $50 a month; hold a garage sale and make about $200; cancel your cell phone and save $50 a month.

You can create bad debt when you agree to pay these crazy interest rates that some creditors charge, because the debt seems to grow exponentially. Credit cards are the prime culprit, but they are by no means the only one. High interest can also come with personal loans, business loans, or unpaid taxes.

You probably purchased this book because you have a lot of these bad debts, debts you are having a difficult time handling and that cause you anxiety. They are the debts you avoid thinking about, the phone calls you don't answer, and the bills stuck in a pile. Avoidance dances with guilt only to be tapped on the shoulder by your new suitor, fear.

You know what the bad debt dance looks like, anyone reading this book does: New bills are coming in before you've cleared out those from last month. You're surprised to find that the phone bill is still unpaid. Somehow the dentist was never sent his check. You know what past-due notices look like. Your Visa and MasterCard bills include late payment penalties. The hardware store sends a letter telling you you're past due and requests that you send a check at once. There is more month left at the end of your money, and payday seems far away. Worst of all, these things don't surprise you anymore.

Avoidance is a common coping mechanism to deal with a budget that doesn't balance. The problem is, it can create even more problems than you already have:

Your property could be repossessed. The finance company can seize your car. Likewise, the electronics store will take its TV back.

You could get sued. If that happens, your wages could be garnished, or your bank account could be levied upon. Imagine your surprise when you go to get that $1,000 out of your checking account to pay your mortgage and you find that it has been seized by one of your creditors.

A lien can be placed on your real estate. Failure to pay a bill now means that a creditor can get a judgment against you and force you to pay it later when you sell your house, only then you will pay it with 10 percent interest per year.

Over Your Limit _____

When someone sues you and wins, it is called getting a judgment. A judgment can be used to empty your bank account, garnish your wages, or put a secured lien on your house.

Yet, as much as you have been avoiding the problem, the truth is that your debts are neither crushing nor hopeless. They are simply a problem—one for which there is a solution. But no one ever eliminated a problem until he or she recognized and admitted that there was a problem. You began to do that the moment you bought this book. As you read it, you will need to begin to formulate a debt-reduction plan that will work for you. As you do, you need to determine which debts are necessary and which are not.

Debts You Want to Keep

Steve, one of the authors of this book, is a bankruptcy attorney. One day, an old acquaintance named Bill came into his office and said that he needed some help getting out of debt, but he also wanted to avoid bankruptcy if at all possible. They talked, came up with a plan of action, and Bill went on his way. About four years later, Steve ran into Bill again and asked how things were; Bill relayed the following story.

Bill had $30,000 in credit card debt and was behind two months on his mortgage when he left Steve's office. That day, Bill finally decided that something had to change. He wanted to pay everyone back, put some money in savings, and keep his house. His mortgage was his largest, and favorite, debt because he loved his house.

Bill's first order of business was to prioritize his debts. Wanting to save his house, Bill called his lender and found out that it had a program that would enable him to roll his mortgage *arrears* onto the end of his loan. He was therefore able to keep his most important debt and focus his energies on getting rid of the debts he didn't want anymore.

Check It Out _____

When you are behind on a debt like a car loan, home loan, or child support, it is called being in **arrears**.

Bill put together a credit card repayment plan. He started living a bit more frugally, making some extra money by moonlighting, and paying more on his credit cards than the minimum. He was diligent, but not always perfect. Although it took him several years, he finally did get out of debt. He also kept his house and even created a little nest egg. Bill did it, and you can, too.

Debts to Get Rid Of

If you want to prosper financially, there are plenty of debts that you will want to wipe out. The most obvious are those where you are paying high interest and penalties, things such as credit cards, lines of credit, taxes, or any other debt that is much higher than inflation. In Chapter 9 you will see how to formulate a plan that will enable you to get out from under these burdensome debts. But as you contemplate this plan, you also need to prioritize certain debts and pay them on time:

- **Rent or mortgage.** Make paying your rent or mortgage a top priority. Payments on a home equity line of credit or second mortgage are also essential because you can lose your house if you don't pay.

- **Car payments.** Make the payments. If you don't, the car will be repossessed.

- **Utility bills.** These services are important, and the bills usually have heavy late-payment penalties.

- **Child support or alimony.** Not paying these debts can land you in jail.

- **Taxes.** Taxes may be put off for a while if necessary, and we show you how to do so later on in the book, but if the IRS is about to take your paycheck, bank account, house, or other property, you should set up a repayment plan immediately.

The First Rule of Holes: Stop Digging!

The goal of this book is to help you get out of debt within the context of making your life work. You will not be asked to make radical, unreasonable changes in your life because doing so rarely works. Instead, important, sometimes gradual, small but significant changes can make a big difference.

If you are going to start getting out of debt, you have to stop going into debt. One way to start is to begin to wean yourself from the credit card teat if you think that is part of your problem. You don't have to cut up all your credit cards; that would be impractical and unreasonable. Start slowly, but build up to it and get strong. You can do it. The only way to stop going into debt is to stop going into debt. You might as well start now because the sooner you start, the sooner you will get out of debt. The longer you wait, the longer it will take.

Two Cents

If you were able to put $2,000 a year away in a tax-deferred IRA beginning in your 20s, you would have over half a million dollars by the time you are 65.

In subsequent chapters, we will show you how to easily trim your budget (well, almost easily) so that you need not incur more debt to stay afloat. But begin now. You are going to have to stop sooner or later. Down the road you will see that this is one of the most important steps you can take in getting out of debt. You will thank yourself for this gift. Remember the first rule of holes: Stop digging!

Long-Term Goals

Now is the time to begin to think about your long-range financial vision. What is it you hope to accomplish by getting out of debt? Changing some habits? Paying off your MasterCard? Probably what you really want is a less stressful life, one that's free from money worries. But you can have even more. Getting out of debt is one thing, but prosperity is another thing altogether.

You have read this once already, and you will read it again in this book: If you don't begin to do some things differently, to change the way you think and treat money, you might get out of debt, but you won't stay out of debt. If you do make some simple changes to your thinking and your behavior, not only will you get out of debt, but you also will get ahead. You will get what you deserve: a life of abundance.

The Least You Need to Know

- Going into debt for essentials makes financial sense; doing so for nonessentials does not.
- Not all debt is bad debt.
- You may want to keep debts that enhance your life and get rid of the rest.
- Stop adding to your debt right now.
- Cultivate a long-term plan of action.

Early Warning Signs of Trouble

In This Chapter

- ◆ Money signs
- ◆ Banking signals
- ◆ Evading the inevitable
- ◆ Emotional problems

How serious are your debt problems? The spectrum of possibilities ranges from negligible to severe. The fact that you bought this book indicates that debt is something you are obviously concerned about. As you read this chapter and review the most common signs of debt problems, consider that the more signs that apply to you, the more serious your situation is.

Where Have All the Dollars Gone?

The first sign that debt is becoming more of an issue in your life than it should be is the incredible shrinking bank balance. Although you make enough to pay your regular bills, more and more of your monthly income goes toward servicing your rising debt. It gets to a point where money is tight, and you feel like you are choking because there is never enough money. Unfortunately, this situation creates a negative domino effect upon the rest of your financial life.

But I Still Have Room on My Card

The first to fall is the credit card domino. Your lack of funds causes you to begin to take cash advances to pay your minimum balances or basic living expenses. You know that your gold card still has about $5,000 left on it, so you begin to use it to live on. Or, even worse, you begin to accept all of those credit card offers that come in the mail, and before you know it, you have 10 open credit cards.

Two Cents

"He who restrains his appetite avoids debt."

—Chinese proverb

You take out $100 here and $500 there. "No big deal," you think. After all, you are used to paying off your cards, or at least paying enough that the debt has not, so far, seemed burdensome. You begin to rationalize. You tell yourself that you're just in a temporary cash crunch, that this is why credit cards were invented. Feeling better, you take out another $500.

Money Talks

When you use your credit cards to withdraw cash, extra fees kick in. Cash advances carry an up-front fee of up to 4 percent of the amount advanced. There is a higher interest charge for cash advances than regular card charges, and many issuers also require you to pay down the balances for purchases before you pay down the higher-interest cash advance balance. Finally, cash advances carry no grace period; interest charges begin to mount as soon as the ATM spits out the money.

The Balance Transfer Shuffle

"Not to worry," you tell your spouse or yourself. You have a plan. These stupid credit cards can't outfox you. You will just transfer your balances from the card with the high balance or the high interest rate to a different card. You are smarter than the credit card companies.

Not only do you transfer balances, but you start to use those convenient checks the credit card companies are always sending you. You begin to pay one card with another card. In the meantime, not wanting to upset your precarious financial balance, you begin to use your cards more to pay for everyday things such as food.

The bills grow. Whereas you used to be able to pay more than the minimum, now the minimum is more than you can pay. In an effort to conserve your rapidly dwindling cash reserves, you decide you have no choice but to save money—by using your credit cards more!

Money Talks

Debt got you down? Consider these rules penned by Thomas Jefferson:
1. Never put off till tomorrow what you can do today.
2. Never trouble another for what you can do yourself.
3. Never spend your money before you have it.
4. Never buy what you do not want because it is cheap; it will never be dear to you.
5. Pride costs us more than hunger, thirst, and cold.
6. Never repent of having eaten too little.
7. Nothing is troublesome that we do willingly.
8. Don't let the evils which have never happened cost you pain.
9. Always take things by their smooth handle.
10. When angry, count to 10 before you speak; if very angry, count to 100.

Relief is in sight. Using your cards more and not spending your precious cash to pay off these credit card balances gives you a (false) sense of security. Your money situation is not that bad. For a few months, things seem back to normal. Anyway, those tiny classified ads you are going to start running all over the country are going to make you rich, and then you will pay off all of your cards, and this situation will be something to laugh about in five years.

Then the card with the low interest rate jacks up your rate to 18.9 percent. You have a $10,000 balance on that card! It's OK. Stay cool. You still have two more cards with room on them. All the while, you are getting deeper and deeper in debt.

What do you do? Eureka, you have a solution! You can apply for more cards, get some more low "teaser" rates, and transfer some more balances. So you do, and so it goes. Sound familiar?

Two Cents

When looking at credit card offers, check how long the introductory rate lasts, the annual percentage rate after that teaser rate expires, whether the teaser rate applies only to transferred balances, any annual fee, late fees, over-the-limit fees, and balance-transfer fees.

Dog Logic

Soon, the mailman becomes your enemy; all he brings is bad news. Maybe you're not smarter than the credit card companies after all. Every bill you get from them now is shocking. You can't afford to pay them. So you start to only pay some of the bills on time.

Paying some of the cards late frees up some cash, but now you are incurring late fees and extra finance charges because of your ever-increasing poor bill-paying habits. The problem is, you are so far in over your head that all of your bills begin to look like messages from the enemy. Soon, you start to create a pile of unopened bills.

In order to make it through until payday (if only that little ad had generated some phone calls!), you start to pay your other bills late. Late fees pile up on late fees. You begin to get threatening letters from your creditors. Soon, you get letters from collection agencies.

Finally, you become a juggler in a three-ring circus of your own making. The cable is about to get turned off, "I'll run down and pay it today!" "Yes, I know, I understand I am behind; I'll drop a check in the mail tomorrow." "Maybe," you think to yourself, "they won't get it until next week, and it won't hit my bank until next Friday." That's the ticket!

The small brushfire that began back home is beginning to burn out of control. The next indication that things are getting out of hand financially relates to your bank accounts.

Bye-Bye Savings

You might have entered this period proud of the fact that you had some money in the bank. Maybe you were saving for a rainy day or maybe for a special trip that you wanted to take.

Money Talks
Fee-mania is all the rage at banks. According to the U.S. Public Interest Research Group, customers are charged a fee for almost everything now. There are fees for opening an account, moving cash from one account to another, for not using your account enough (inactive account fees), missing a signature, inquiring about your balance, and depositing a bad check. In a final attempt to gouge you, banks have now started to charge you for closing your account.

Sadly, by this point, your savings are probably long gone. Despite the penalties, your IRA or 401(k) have probably been raided, too. Equally bad, your previous valiant efforts to do the right thing and consistently save some money have probably gone by the wayside as well. With money as tight as it is, you don't see how you can afford to begin to save some money again. Your pride is hurt, and your ego is wounded. You might begin to feel depressed over the sad state of your financial affairs. That rainy day has come.

What's My Balance?

Your checking account is in even worse shape. Maybe you've gotten into the habit of bouncing a couple of checks here and there. More likely, you have figured out how to just skate by.

It could be that you go to pay the phone bill at the last possible moment on Friday afternoon, knowing that the check won't get to your bank until probably Tuesday of the next week (but hopefully Wednesday!). That will work, because you get paid next Wednesday. Even if the check doesn't clear the first time, the phone company always puts a bounced check through a second time, so it will only cost you a $25 bounced check fee to keep your phone for another month.

Maybe you do what Tom does. When things get really bad, he pays the bills on time, but "accidentally" puts the check for the phone company in the Visa envelope and vice versa. By the time the mix-up is fixed, two weeks have gone by, and he's gotten paid again. He fixes the problem and makes it through another month.

Or, like Jessica, you just stop balancing your checkbook altogether. What's the point? After all, when you go to the ATM, you check your balance! Jessica can't bear to figure out how much she owes to whom and refuses to keep track of her ATM withdrawals, so she just continues to write checks and take out money, keeping a rough balance in her head and hoping that it will be all right. This is the next signpost on a debt-end road: evading, avoiding, and ignoring the truth of the situation.

Check It Out

Often, even if a check you write to a creditor does not clear the bank the first time, that creditor may try to deposit it again before deciding that the check is no good. These creditors are **putting the check through twice.**

How to reduce your ATM charges:

1. Keep your checking account at a bank that doesn't charge you for using its ATM machines.

2. Don't use an ATM machine belonging to an institution where you don't bank.

3. Consider using a credit union. Its ATM fees are usually lower.

4. If you use an ATM regularly, withdraw larger amounts of money to reduce the number of times you are charged a fee.

5. Avoid ATMs that surcharge.

6. Use a teller instead of an ATM, especially when lines at the bank ATM are long. Be certain, however, that you won't be charged a teller fee!

End of the Line

Creditors are now starting to close your accounts. Credit card companies, once your good friends, want nothing to do with you. Your accounts have been assigned to collection agencies. Sadly, they do want to talk to you.

You stop answering the phone. You get caller ID. Finally, you change your phone number, get an unlisted number, and give it out only to your friends.

At this point, you have a chronic debt problem. You know it, too, but you would rather ignore the problem or explain it away:

◆ **You are concerned only about today.** Although your debt problems are now constant, and every month is as bad as the month before, your only concern is this month. Getting the rent paid, paying back Dad, and keeping the heat on are your concerns. The fact that you have the tax bill or insurance payment due next month is of no concern to you today. You will solve that crisis when you get to it.

◆ **You have lost track of how much you owe.** You don't even bother to look at the balances on the statements you get; you can't pay them anyway. If you do have any credit cards left, you don't care what the interest rate is; all you know about your cards is how much room you have on any one of them with which to charge.

◆ **You have become the king or queen of rationalizations.** You refuse to take a good hard look at your financial affairs and instead have reasons for why things are the way they are. "The divorce killed me." "I'm too busy with my novel to worry about something as mundane as my bills." "I'm no good with numbers." "I'll deal with it after the first of the year."

◆ **You are in a state of constant worry, but do nothing.** You may be frozen with fear. The problem looms so large that you don't know where to start, so you start nowhere.

Your Money or Your Life

What began as an isolated skirmish in the outback of money country has now spilled over to the rest of your life. It could be affecting your health, your job, your relationship, and even your life.

Marriage and Money

Money troubles are the leading cause of divorce in this country, and now you know why. Your debt issues are now beginning to affect your relationship. Your mate is angry with you, scared about the well-being of the family, and concerned that your problems will affect his or her financial life as well. Here are some signs that you're in drastic debt:

Two Cents

Before they walk down the aisle, couples should have a money session to avoid surprises down the road. From student loans to car payments to credit card bills, it's best to come clean on every "I owe" before saying "I do."

- ◆ Your mate is afraid to apply for credit with you for fear that your problems will spill over.

- ◆ The constant phone calls from creditors cause pain and anger in your mate.

- ◆ The constant worry about money takes its toll on your sex life.

- ◆ Your mate is worried that the boss will find out.

Money Talks

Of all married couples, 66 percent have only one checking account, a joint account; 22 percent have a joint account and two separate checking accounts; 8 percent have two completely separate accounts; and 4 percent have no checking accounts at all.

Finally, you resolve to do something and face your money demons. Congratulations, buying this book is an important first step.

Test Yourself

As we said at the beginning of this chapter, debt issues can range from mild to severe. Take the following quiz to see how serious your debt situation is:

Are your debts making your home life unhappy?

Do your debts make you careless with the welfare of your family?

Are your debts a source of constant friction with your mate?

Are your debts affecting how people view you?

Do your debts affect how you view yourself?

Do your debt problems distract you from your work?

Do you fear that your employer, family, or friends will learn the extent of your total indebtedness?

Have you ever lost a friend because of your money habits?

Have you ever lied in order to obtain credit?

Do you expect a negative response when you apply for credit?

Have you ever borrowed money without considering how you will pay it back?

Have you ever borrowed money without considering the interest rate?

When faced with a difficult financial situation, is your first thought to go deeper into debt?

Have you ever lied to your creditors regarding payment of a bill?

Does the pressure of your debts cause you difficulty in sleeping, or cause you to overeat, undereat, or smoke, or otherwise affect your health negatively?

Has the pressure of your debts ever caused you to drink more than you should?

Do you think about your money problems a lot during the day?

Do you justify your debts by telling yourself that you are superior to the "other" people, and when you get your "break," you'll be out of debt overnight?

Have you ever developed a strict regimen for paying off your debts, only to break it under pressure?

Have you seriously considered bankruptcy?

Scoring:

1–5 yes answers: Your debt issues are not bad and are easily resolvable.

5–10 yes answers: Your debt issues are more serious, but not out of control.

10 or more yes answers: Your debt problems are very serious and deserve your immediate attention. You must begin to take corrective action now.

You see that you need to take action to resolve your debt situation, which is good news. Consider these ideas:

- ◆ Continuing to run from the problem will only get you into deeper trouble.

- ◆ Respond to your creditors and show them that you have an interest in working things out. (We'll show you how in Chapter 13.)

- ◆ Acknowledge to yourself that you have made some irresponsible decisions.

- ◆ Get professional counseling if it is warranted.

- ◆ Share your problems with a close friend or your spouse.

- ◆ Know that there is a way out and that this process and a debt-free destination are probably a better experience than the stress in your life today.

Today is a turning point in your life. There is plenty you can do to turn this situation around, and it may not be nearly as difficult as you think. The remainder of this book helps guide your way.

The Least You Need to Know

- ◆ The first signpost on the road to indebtedness is a lack of money and an increase in money worries.

- ◆ When you begin to have problems with your bank accounts, things are getting more serious.

- ◆ Evading and avoiding the problem make the matter worse.

- ◆ When your home life is affected by money troubles, it is time to take action.

Take That Paper Bag Off Your Head When You Drive

In This Chapter

- ◆ Paying bills late
- ◆ Falling for the credit card trap
- ◆ Not saving
- ◆ Believing in scarcity
- ◆ Working for others
- ◆ Overspending

There are many ways to fall into debt. One person may overspend while another blindly ignores the mounting bill pile, believing that the problem will somehow magically improve. The reason for your indebtedness could be poor planning, a spending addiction, or a combination of bad habits. Whatever the reason, it is important to identify what you are doing wrong so that you can begin to make some changes. (Of course, there are many reasons for going into debt that have nothing to do with anything you may be doing "wrong," such as a medical crisis or starting a business. These types of situations are dealt with in other chapters.)

The Check Is in the Mail

One reason why people end up in debt is that they were never taught basic financial skills, such as paying bills on time. Failing to pay your bills in a timely manner only compounds your debt problems because late payments can hurt you in so many ways. This problem should be easily fixed.

The first way comes from the costs incurred for the "privilege" of paying late. Say that you have a $139 credit card payment due on the 15th. If you end up paying that bill on the 20th, you will probably pay at least another $25 in late charges.

In and of itself, a lone $25 late fee is no big deal. Usually, however, we are not talking about a single late fee; paying late can be a bad habit. If you multiply this late fee times, say, six bills—a couple of credit cards, your mortgage, a car payment—you could be easily losing at least $150 a month. That is a big waste of money.

What's worse is that the late payment habit can cause you to fall even deeper into a vicious cycle of debt. Money is tight, in part because of late fees, and then you pay late because money is tight. If paying late has become a habit, it could cost you upward of $1,000 over the course of a year.

Over Your Limit

In 1983, 62 percent of disposable income went to paying off debt. By 1996, that figure had jumped to 84 percent. By 2002, the figure jumped to 86 percent.

Over Your Limit

Spending increases an average of 23 percent when credit cards are used instead of cash, according to *The People's Almanac*.

Paying your bills late hurts you in other, more insidious, ways as well. A history of late payments will ruin your credit rating, making getting other credit more expensive and, thereby, costing you even more money. (Note, however, that it takes 30 days from the date the bill was due for the negative remark to hit your credit report.) A bad credit rating can really kill you financially.

Suppose you went to get a $20,000 car loan with good credit. At 6 percent over five years, you would pay roughly $6,000 in interest for that loan. If persistent late payments have hurt your credit rating, you might pay 15 percent for that same loan. Interest on that loan would cost you up to $15,000.

The good news is that it is not that difficult to get off the late payment train. A month or two of budgeting can get you back on a normal payment schedule and save you a lot of money in the long run (and in the short run).

Congratulations, You've Been Approved

Credit cards can be a boon or a bust, depending upon how they are used and treated. The responsible use of credit cards makes living a lot easier for many people. They fund business startups and treats for your spouse. We have no problem whatsoever with the reasonable and responsible use of credit cards.

The problem is that being unreasonable and irresponsible with credit cards is just so darn easy. Convenient and fun to use, credit cards can too easily become more of a curse than a blessing. With an average 17 percent interest, credit card debt is easy to create but difficult to erase.

You must be especially wary of what we call in this book "the credit card trap." This trap is very easy to fall into and very difficult to get out of. You fall into the trap when

- ◆ You run up a card with, say, an 18 percent interest rate that you know you can't pay off.

- ◆ You use credit cards to buy easily consumable things like food, because you will be paying exorbitant interest for items that quickly disappear.

- ◆ You use credit cards for luxuries that you could not otherwise afford.

- ◆ You pay only the minimum payment due.

Once you have fallen for the trap, you have a card on which you owe a lot of money, on which you pay only the minimum payment, and on which the *principal* never seems to decrease.

Like so many of us, Nancy fell for the credit card trap. After graduating college, she moved to New York and got a job waitressing while she looked for acting jobs. She used her credit card overdraft protection to balance her checkbook every month. After a year, she was about $10,000 in debt.

Check It Out

The **principal** is the amount you actually borrowed. If you charged a $300 plane ticket, that is your principal.

She decided that she had to get rid of these debts before they got more out of hand. Although she used a method that we hadn't thought of before hearing her story, it worked for her, and that's the important thing.

Nancy took every extra cent that she made and started to pay off the card with the smallest balance, while paying the minimum on her other three credit cards (since the minimum amount due was a relatively small amount), until that card was paid off. She then did the same thing with the next smallest card, but instead of making only minimum payments on the other two cards, she made double the minimum payment, which she could afford to do because one card was paid off already. She then repeated this strategy with each of the last two cards.

It took her a little over a year, but at the end, Nancy was completely out of the credit card debt that had been overwhelming her. Also, and equally important, because none of the payments had been late or behind, her good credit remained good.

Of equal consequence, Nancy did not cut each card up as she paid it off or cancel the accounts as people are often advised to do. Instead, once each account was paid in full, she wrote a letter canceling it, saying that she was in the market for a card with a substantially lower interest rate. She was amazed when she started getting offers for cards with much lower interest rates from the very same credit card companies that had been charging her such horrendous rates.

Nancy then began teaching herself how to properly use credit cards. Instead of grabbing each offered card, she carefully read everything about each and selected two that offered the best overall terms, not just the lowest rates. She treated each one like an American Express card: It had to be paid off in full each month, unless she used it for an unexpected emergency. No matter what, her rule was, revolving balances had to be paid off within three months. So you see, there is a way out of the credit card trap and out of any debt if you make a few simple adjustments to your money habits.

Savings? Who Needs Savings?

Many people have no savings at all. Although we all know that we are supposed to have some money saved, between bills and kids, it just seems too hard most of the time. It's kind of like losing weight. We know it would be good for us, but it's awfully hard to do.

Two Cents

Between 1970 and 2002, the percentage of income earmarked towards savings dropped from over 8 percent to below 4 percent. Try to save for the unexpected.

Yet the great thing about having a little money in the bank is that you can use it for things that you would have otherwise have gone into debt for. Instead of charging that $400 trip to the beach, going further into debt, and paying more in interest, if you can save $400 you will be in much better financial shape. And it doesn't have to be that hard.

If you would like to begin to save, try these easy-to-implement ideas:

Realize that small steps can yield big results. Put 10 percent of your spending money away at first, even if it's just 10 percent of your pocket change. Over time, small amounts add up, and you probably won't even miss 10 percent of your pocket money.

Eat more cheaply. Eliminate a trip to a fast-food restaurant, make a cheap dinner one night a week, or bring your lunch to work. Save the savings.

Use 10 percent less. Stretch your shampoo, laundry soap, and dishwashing detergent. Just stretching by 10 percent will enable you to meet your weekly savings goal.

Change brands. Prices fluctuate, and without brand loyalty, you can get the best prices.

Applied consistently, these ideas and others you come up with can yield enough savings to make a difference.

I Believe in Santa Claus

Another way to get in debt and ensure that you will stay in debt is to pretend that the problem will somehow magically disappear. You will win the lottery or make so much money next year that you need not worry about your mounting debts today. Wishful thinking can happen to anyone, for any reason; it happens to all of us for different reasons at one time or another.

The problem with this thinking is that it allows you to avoid responsibility for your financial problems. You need not take any corrective action because there will be a magical solution.

Dangerous wishful thinking happened to Mitzi Schlichter, former wife of pro-football quarterback Art Schlichter. When she married Art, she knew that Art liked to gamble, but she didn't think he had a problem. She had her first inkling otherwise when, on the flight home from their honeymoon, Art told his bride that he had $10,000 in new gambling debts.

It took nine years of broken promises, debt, and heartache for her to realize that they had a serious problem with money and gambling. She divorced Art and now works at a treatment center for gambling addicts. Her ex-husband, once a number-one draft pick and a starter for the Indianapolis Colts, has been in and out of prison for forgery.

You may win the lottery, but most likely not. Getting out of debt takes work, being straight with your creditors, and being honest with yourself.

Over Your Limit
At the height of his career, Art Schlichter made over one million dollars a year.

Believing in Scarcity

Your beliefs have as much to do with your current economic situation as almost anything else. When you are in debt, it is easy to see the world as one of lack. But the fact is, there is a lot of money in this world.

The story is told of a famous movie actor (who shall remain nameless) who enjoyed making millions and then blowing it all, every single penny. This actor is said to have done this time and again. He apparently liked the challenge of having to create a new fortune over and over again.

It takes a lot of courage—or stupidity—to do this, and there is no guarantee in life, certainly not in the movie business where some new actor is always coming along as the latest flavor of the month. After blowing his fortune for the third or fourth time, there was no guarantee whatsoever that this actor would ever make millions of dollars again acting in movies. But he did it again anyway.

Besides *having nerve*, what this actor had was a belief in abundance. He believed in it so much that he put his money where his mouth is. If he believed in scarcity and were afraid that he would never work again, he never would have done what he did. He credits his bedrock belief in abundance for his ability to keep working and making money.

No, you are not a Hollywood actor, but the moral of the story still applies. As the saying goes, "As a man thinketh, so is he." In the next few chapters, we will look at how to change some limiting beliefs you may have about money.

Working for Others

Another reason you may be in debt, probably a big reason, is that you don't make enough money. If you are tight for cash, the usual solution is to borrow by getting a credit card advance or asking your brother for help. But the fact is, when the books don't balance every month, you have three options; it just seems like going into debt is the only one.

Instead of incurring more debt, you could cut back and spend less, or you could make more money. Either of these options would work. The important idea to realize right now is that you don't have to quit your job to make more money. There are plenty of ways to increase your income every month that have nothing to do with your job. As you will see in the last section of this book, an entrepreneurial mindset can go a long way toward getting you out of debt.

> **Money Talks**
>
> The Lillian Vernon company sells household items, has revenues of over $200 million a year, and is listed on the American Stock Exchange. Lillian Vernon started the company in 1951 from her small apartment while pregnant to make some extra money to help out the family finances.

Time for a Plan

Most of us have negative connotations when we hear the word *budget*, likening it to a financial diet. But budget does not have to be a bad word. Honest!

(We ask you to suspend your negative beliefs about budgets for a little while and see whether creating one might help you far more than hurt you. If, at the end of the next few chapters about budgeting, you are not convinced that a budget can help save the day, by all means revert back to your former budgetary beliefs. Just give us the benefit of the doubt for a little while. Thank you.)

A budget is a money plan. You can use it to organize and control your financial resources, set and realize goals, and decide in advance how your money will work for you. A budget allows you to know how much money you have to spend every month and where you are spending it. As such, a budget is one of the most important steps you can take toward maximizing the power of your money.

An architect would never start work on a new house without a blueprint. An auto manufacturer would never begin construction of a new car without a detailed set of design specifications. Yet many of us spend money without a plan to guide us. At the very least, a budget should allow you to find extra spending money in your paycheck every month.

Compare a budget to driving a car. In an automobile, you get plenty of feedback on how you're doing. When you drive, you use mirrors, speed limits, and the instrument panel to get information about your driving, and you know that a small mistake can cost lives. If you go too fast, you get a ticket. There is plenty of feedback from both within and outside the car to tell you whether you are doing a good job.

Think about what would happen if you took some of that feedback away. Suppose you didn't have a gas gauge, or an oil pressure monitor, or a rearview mirror, or a speedometer? What if you had no windshield? Driving would be beyond dangerous. You need feedback to know where you are going. Managing your finances without a budget is like driving a car with a blindfold on.

The Overspender

Compulsive overspending is a sure way to get deep in debt. Maybe you are the overspender, or maybe your spouse is (maybe you both overspend). An overspender is someone who loves to spend money to bring pleasure. Budgeting, saving, and investing are not part of the plan. The spending is such a problem that it gets in the way of paying normal bills.

Overspenders may use the spending of money for many different, and not altogether healthy, reasons:

- As a substitute for love
- As a way to avoid problems at work
- To avoid intimacy
- To relieve guilt
- To feel important
- To gain power
- To gain confidence

Over Your Limit

With the Internet adding to cable television, at-home shopping will top more than $100 billion in sales by 2005.

A compulsive overspender spends money whether he needs to or not. He celebrates an important event by blowing a wad of cash or running up a credit card. He does not stop to think whether he can afford something; if he wants it, for whatever reason, he gets it.

Compulsive overspending can ruin a relationship. The other partner may become so angry at the precarious financial situation the overspender has put the couple in that she pulls away. Or she might become an enabler, helping the overspender by making up the difference and then resenting it.

There are several things a spouse can do to help the overspender or that an overspender can do to help himself:

- **Realize that overspending is usually a symptom of a deeper problem that is not being addressed.** Counseling might be in order to help the overspender figure out what the real problem is and begin to deal with it.

- **Be honest.** An overspender may deny that there is a problem, thinking that he is just a misunderstood, fun-loving guy. The spouse must tell the truth. The overspender must admit the truth.

- **Come up with a financial plan of action.** You, or you and your spouse, need to set some financial goals and decide how you will begin to achieve them. (Read the rest of the book!)

- **The spouse cannot rescue the overspender.** She can help, she can love him, but rescuing him just makes the problem worse. She may even have to separate herself financially by opening up a separate checking account and getting credit cards in her own name. For example, Carol finally had to divorce her husband to avoid getting sued by his creditors, although she continued to love and live with him.

◆ **Try a role reversal.** Go to a department store and switch roles. The frugal wife should become the overspending husband, and the husband should be the one that constantly says no. Watch how your mate behaves and notice how it feels to act differently. You might be embarrassed to see yourself through your mate's eyes.

For Mark and Jean, this last simple exercise helped them see things just a bit differently. Mark was the overspender, and Jean was the practical one. He just loved to binge shop, and she loved to hoard things. She was in charge of their finances and paid all the bills. Needless to say, they constantly fought about money.

After their relationship took a turn for the worse because of money, they sought counseling. After a few sessions, they realized that Mark's overspending was rooted in his poor childhood; spending money helped him feel powerful. Jean also learned something; she learned that making money and not spending any was a way to make her husband feel guilty and gain some power in their relationship.

That was when they went on their excursion to the department store. That trip helped her see why Mark liked doing what he had been doing; it was fun to spend money. For his part, Mark didn't like what he saw when Jean acted like him. She looked out of control and irresponsible. Though it took time, both began to change and become a bit more like the other.

If you are an overspender, or know one intimately, there are solutions. If the problem seems out of control, you should also read Chapter 18 to see whether that group might be a solution.

The Least You Need to Know

◆ Paying bills late hurts you in many ways.

◆ Beware of the credit card trap.

◆ It is not that hard to start saving if you start small.

◆ Your beliefs affect your material world.

◆ Be open to the possibility of budgeting.

◆ Overspending is usually a symptom of a bigger problem.

Part 2 Changing Your Relationship with Money

Here we introduce the solutions to the problem. Not everyone is in debt. What do they do that you don't do? What did their parents teach them when they were growing up? These are some basic, simple ideas that everyone should know, but that many people don't know.

People don't avoid debt effortlessly, but it's simple. It just requires a little work every month. We lay the process all out step-by-step, and explain what we're doing at every point along the way. We'll teach you what to do and why to do it.

Chapter 4

A Frank Talk with Dollar Bill

In This Chapter

- ◆ Your family and money
- ◆ Your money history
- ◆ Uncovering hidden beliefs
- ◆ Money talk

Getting out of debt will take more than making more money or sticking to a budget. Money is an emotionally charged subject, and what you think and how you feel about money has as much to do with your level of prosperity as anything else, if not more.

If your debt problems were not caused by a sudden emergency, but instead because of a pattern, then we think that it is important that you discover your negative money beliefs so you can change them. Because unless you change your beliefs about money, change these patterns, and begin to relate to it like wealthy people do, you may get out of debt, but you won't stay out of debt. The first step in that process is to understand that you learn more about money from your family than from anyone else.

Your Money History

Like any relationship, your relationship with money can take many forms. It can be good or bad. It can be dysfunctional, or it can be healthy. Most people with chronic debt problems have some sort of an unhealthy relationship with money.

The key word is chronic. Many people who have a healthy relationship with money consciously choose to go into debt because it enables them to do things they otherwise could not, and these people have a plan for how they will service the debt. Debt becomes a symptom of an unhealthy relationship with money when debt is created unconsciously or when it is unmanageable. The fact that you bought this book probably, though not necessarily, indicates that you are probably no longer creating debt unconsciously.

Do as I Say, Not as I Do

As we grow up, we learn about money from our parents. Unfortunately, for many people, plenty of these lessons were negative. One reason is that our parents learned about money from our grandparents, many of whom were children of the Depression. As a result, a lot of people learned that money was a scarce item, and owning it was something to be afraid of or embarrassed about.

Sam learned this lesson in childhood. Sam's father was a successful entrepreneur who made a very good living. But he had always told Sam that he was "not made of money." Despite the fact that Sam's dad made plenty of money, money was still a constant point of argument and worry in the house.

When Sam's first daughter was four, he found himself one day telling her that she could not have a new toy because he "was not made out of money." Realizing that he was merely mimicking a family belief about the scarcity of money, Sam decided to buy her the toy, more for his own good than hers.

Two Cents

"When I was young I thought money was the most important thing in life; now that I am old, I know it is."

—Oscar Wilde

That experience was the first step in a long process of rethinking his money values and fixing his relationship with money. From that day forward, Sam would say to himself, "I *am* made out of money." Of course, he wasn't made out of money, but by using this statement to change the family belief that he had unwittingly learned and unconsciously accepted, he began to unleash himself from some of his family's suffocating beliefs about money.

Linda had almost the opposite experience. She was raised in a family that constantly tried to "keep up with the Joneses." Overspending was less important than appearances. As a result, the message she received from her parents was that budgets were bad and overspending was good. As an adult, she realized that she had some work to do.

What Were You Taught About Money?

Some of us adopt our family's attitudes regarding money without even realizing it; others knowingly and consciously rebel against their parents' money beliefs and actions. Either way, your parents are still molding your behavior. What you should strive for is to relate to money in a manner that reflects your values today and the values you want to pass along to your children. You begin this journey by noticing what you learned from your parents about money:

- **What were their actions regarding money?** Was it a source of constant worry? Did they avoid talking about it? Did they always argue about it? Did they blame each other or you and your siblings for money problems? Did they act as if they never had enough, or maybe as if they had more than they really had? What did this teach you?

- **Do you remember any traumatic incidents that may have affected your beliefs about money?** Maybe your parents had to close a business or were ashamed of having to file for bankruptcy. Maybe you didn't have enough money to go to the prom or felt ashamed of how you had to dress for school. How did this make you feel about money?

- **What did you know about your family's financial situation?** Was it ever discussed? If it was a secret, why do you think that was so? Was money a source of pride or embarrassment? What did you learn from this?

- **What was the main message you were taught about money?** You may have learned that the husband earns the money and the wife spends it. If your family was struggling financially, you may have learned that your family at least had love and that rich families do not.

Money Talks
As a general rule, families with healthy attitudes about money are not afraid to discuss financial matters with their children. Kids are brought up knowing how much dad makes, where the money is invested, and how much the monthly mortgage payments are.

When you were a child, you were likely told not to ask or talk about money. Now think about that for a second. What is the subliminal message being sent when a topic is taboo? If your family avoided talking about money, did that send you a signal that money is not only a forbidden subject, but also a bad thing?

We do not mean to suggest that all the things you heard about money were dysfunctional, but we would not be surprised if that were mostly true. What you need to do is look at what you were taught about money and see how that may be affecting your life today. The good news is that you can change this pattern with your own children and teach them to have a positive relationship with money so that they don't continue the debt cycle you've gotten yourself into.

Money Stories

How your family earned, spent, saved, wasted, thought about, and perhaps even fought about money has had a powerful role in shaping your financial attitudes and behaviors today. For example, it dawned on Laurie why she had grown up to be a compulsive overspender when she finally started to think about her family's money history. Her father was quite strict and always very tight with both a dollar and his emotions. Her mother, though, had been very loving and was rather extravagant with Laurie. Don't tell Laurie that money can't buy you love; she learned differently. Laurie grew up equating money with love.

Over Your Limit

According to one survey, 93 percent of all American girls say that shopping is their "favorite activity."

Two Cents

According to *The Wall Street Journal*, an average parent spends 40 minutes a week playing with his or her children and six hours a week shopping. Think about how much time you spend on each.

As an adult, Laurie realized that she had learned that spending money (even when she didn't have any) had become a way to feel loved. That simple realization began her process of financial solvency.

Not all families' money attitudes are bad. Born and raised in Boston, Michael learned what he considered to be "powerful lessons" about frugality, ingrained by three centuries of New England conservation, typified, he says, by the clean-your-plate admonishment that "children are starving in China."

He tells the story of walking down the street one day with a friend, when he watched "incredulously" as a man in front of him casually tossed the four pennies he'd just received as change onto the sidewalk. "With barely a moment's hesitation, I scooped up the discarded pennies. My friend was clearly embarrassed. She couldn't believe that I would literally and figuratively stoop that low." Michael did not care. He had been raised to believe that with four pennies here and a dime there, you would soon have some real money. It was a belief he appreciated.

Money Makes the World Go 'Round

Answer the following questions honestly. You might want to write your answers on a piece of paper. It is not necessary, but it could help. As you do, notice which questions tend to make you uncomfortable. Those are the important ones:

- If your family had a motto about money growing up, what would it be?

- Did you get an allowance growing up? Did you have to work for it or was it given to you? What did that teach you about money? Is that what you do (or plan to do) with your own children? Why or why not?

- Was money ever discussed in your family? If not, what do you think were some of the unsaid beliefs your parents had about money?

- Were you taught the value of a dollar growing up? Did you have a savings account?

- Did you have to work as a teen? What happened to the money you earned?

- When did you first go into debt to get something that you wanted? How did you feel going into debt? Was this the beginning of a pattern?

- When was the first time you remember losing money? What did that teach you? Was it helpful in some way, or did you learn to be afraid of money?

- Did money influence your choice of careers? Was that a good idea?

- How do you feel about money now? Is it your friend or your enemy? Do you love it or resent it? Do you pay too much attention to it or not enough?

Simply becoming aware of some beliefs and patterns helped Mara. Growing up, whenever she asked for a special treat, Mara was always told by her father not to be "greedy." She heard this again and again until it was finally ingrained. Making matters more difficult was the fact that Mara adored her father.

As an adult, Mara always deprived herself. To be kind to herself meant, on some level, to be a greedy, disobedient daughter. Her finances reflected this. She was always broke and always ended up in low-paying jobs. When she finally took stock of her money history, one of the first things she realized was that she would have to rethink her beliefs about "greed" and accept the fact that wanting something did not mean she was a bad person or daughter.

So, what were you taught about money? All of these lessons created your personal money belief system. This belief system is firmly established in most children by the age of 14. After that, because there is a cultural taboo against personal discussions about money, you probably accepted your money beliefs without question.

Your money belief system forms the basis of your relationship with money. It tells you whether to spend or save, whether to invest in stocks or to buy a new car, and even how to price your services. Your money belief system decides whether you will be a borrower, a lender, a saver, or a spender—even whether you will be rich or poor.

Do you doubt this? How can you ever expect to get rich if you believe that money is the root of all evil? Your actions, based upon that belief, would repel money away from you. You may assume others around you have the same beliefs and values about money, but guess again. It is safe to say that Bill Gates has different beliefs about money than you do. (Or than we do!)

Money Beliefs

Let's begin with the supposition that your beliefs create much of your life. If you believe that it is important to be a good Christian, you will behave accordingly. If you believe in sacrificing your own needs for the good of your children, you will make life choices based upon that belief. People who believe that they can drive after a few drinks make different choices than those who don't.

The funny thing about a belief is that it may or may not be true. How does anyone know whether money figuratively grows on trees? Is money the root of all evil? No one knows for sure. The great thing about a belief is that it can be changed, as you will see in the next chapter.

We all have money beliefs, and although you may not know it, many of yours may be quite negative. Just look at some of the most common sayings and beliefs about money:

- Money is the root of all evil.

- Money doesn't grow on trees.

- Money isn't everything.

- Money can't buy you happiness.

- Money can buy you happiness.

CAUTION

Over Your Limit

In her book *Money Demons*, Dr. Susan Forward says, "Conscious beliefs represent only a fraction of our personal belief system. Like the tip of an iceberg, the stuff that sinks ships is hidden beneath the surface, in our unconscious."

There are plenty of money slogans reflective of negative societal beliefs about money: blood money, drug money, dirty money, funny money, and so on. Is it possible that you may have unknowingly adopted some of these negative beliefs about money? Yes, it's possible. Actually, it is more than possible; it's probable.

How do we know? Look at the facts: You are deeply in debt. Being in debt is a symptom of unhealthy beliefs and attitudes about money. Becoming more aware of your money beliefs is your next step toward resolving your indebtedness.

Other Sources of Money Beliefs

You can receive money messages from many sources, not just your family:

◆ What did your religion tell you about money? Many religions foster a belief that money and spirituality are mutually exclusive. Were you given the message that to be successful financially meant you had to be a bad person?

◆ What did you learn about money from your friends? Was it cool to be struggling for money? Maybe it was cool to be driving a BMW. Did you unintentionally pick a money mode so that you would be like (or different from) one of your peers?

◆ What did you learn about money from society? Jeff grew up wanting to be an artist and became enamored with the "struggling artist" lifestyle. Although he was ready to finally make some money by the time he turned 40, he had a difficult time believing that he was not "selling out" by wanting to draw a cake and eat one, too.

You should begin to notice a theme in your life with regard to money; a theme that had its genesis in your childhood.

A Heart-to-Heart Talk with Money

You have a lot of strong feelings about money and your relationship to it that you probably have never before expressed. As you begin to become aware of these feelings (and in order to become more aware of your hidden beliefs about money), it might help to sit down and have a heart-to-heart talk with money.

We're serious here. Money has controlled a lot of your life, and if money could listen, you'd probably have plenty to say. So we want you to say it. It will help crystallize things for you and further elucidate what you have been taught about money and what you believe to be true.

Get over the silliness of this exercise, take out a twenty-dollar bill, go to a quiet place where no one can see you (hopefully!), and give money a piece of your mind. Tell money …

- What I want from you is:

- My biggest mistake when it comes to you is:

- What needs to change about our relationship is:

- The reason I haven't changed is:

- What gets me angry with you is:

- A secret I have about you is:

- My biggest fear about you is:

Go for it, have some fun, get it out, and don't stop here. You surely have plenty to say to Mr. Money. Tell him what you think. As you do, look for some beliefs you have that you may not have noticed before.

Conversations, by definition, are a two-way street. What do you think money might have to say to you if it had the chance? Consider the following:

- If money had one piece of advice for you, what would it be?

- If money had a secret to tell you, what would it be?

- What would money say about how you treat it?

- If money could sum up the main thing that needs to change about your relationship with it, what would it be?

- What would need to change for you to become best friends with money?

Two Cents

"Money is congealed energy, and releasing it releases life's possibilities."

—Joseph Campbell

We are asking you to do a bit of soul searching in this chapter. Some of these things may be uncomfortable, but remember, that is where the gold is. Stick with it. Choosing some positive new beliefs about money and getting out of debt and ahead of the game is far more important than any bad feelings that may bubble up.

The Least You Need to Know

- We learn more about money from our families than from anyone else.

- Many of the messages we get about money are negative.

- You probably have some negative beliefs about money that you may not be aware of.

- Becoming aware of your money beliefs is the first step toward changing them.

Chapter 5

Money Affirmations

In This Chapter

- Changing your belief system
- Visualizing and change
- Feeling and change
- Thinking and change

We've said it before, and we'll say it again: If you do not change the way you think about money, you might get out of debt, but you won't stay out of debt. In this chapter, we provide you with a variety of techniques and tools you can pick and choose from to change some of your money beliefs.

Fake It 'Til You Make It

One way to change a belief is surprisingly simple. You just change your thinking. If you have been conditioned to believe that money is hard to come by, catch yourself when you think that and consciously choose a different thought.

Jim used this technique. He was a struggling actor in Los Angeles, and his family was quite poor. At one point his dad was fired, and Jim's family ended up living in a van. Jim had every reason to believe that money was a scarce item.

Nevertheless, one day, Jim took out his checkbook and wrote himself a check for $20 million. In the little note section on the check, he wrote, "acting services rendered." He dated the check for 10 years in the future.

Every night, Jim would drive up to the hills above Los Angeles, take out the check, look at it, and believe it to be true. He tried to make his entire being believe that he was worth and had $20 million. Jim says that he would not leave and go back home for the night until he truly believed that the check was real.

Over Your Limit

A great majority of lottery winners eventually end up back where they began. The most common reason is that although they knew how to spend money, they knew very little about how to invest it. Their circumstances changed, but their attitudes and beliefs did not.

Money Talks

Jim Carrey was not even paid $1 million for the first Ace Ventura movie. The movie went on to gross over $100 million and established its relatively unknown star as a bankable actor.

Two Cents

"Repetition is the mother of skill." —Anthony Robbins

Ten years later, the day before the check was set to be "cashed," Jim inked a deal to be the first actor in Hollywood history to be paid $20 million for one picture. That picture was *Ace Ventura: When Nature Calls*. That's right, Jim is Jim Carrey, and now you know the rest of the story.

Jim did several things right, things that you can do, too, if you want to change a limiting belief you have about money. First, he made a conscious decision to change the way he thought about money. At the time he boldly wrote his check, he had no evidence that it would ever be real. He was an unknown, broke actor. Yet he made himself believe it was real. He changed the way he thought about himself and money.

Second, it was not just his thoughts Jim worked on. Mr. Rubberface says that it was a whole-body experience. He felt the emotions of having that much money, of believing that he was worth that much money. He says he made himself physically feel the experience and joy of being rich. He was so committed that he would not go home until he felt the feeling.

Jim also used repetition to his advantage. Think about it. Whenever you have had to learn something new in your life, wasn't repetition a key component of the process? How else did you learn your ABCs, geometry theorems, or how to shoot a 20-footer, if not by repetition? Alrighty then; if Jim can do it, why can't you?

Creative Visualization

Another thing that Jim Carrey did right was to use a physical object to change his belief. Holding an actual check made visualizing the check when he wasn't on his mountain a lot easier.

Creative visualization is the technique of using your imagination to change a belief or otherwise achieve a goal. With creative visualization, you create an idea or mental picture in your mind and regularly focus on it, thereby setting in motion the event.

Two Cents

A wise woman once said that worry is nothing but "negative visualization."

You use visualization every day of your life. Whenever you create something, you create it first as an idea in your head. A thought always precedes creation. "I think I'll make dinner" precedes the meal. "I want to write a book about getting out of debt" precedes the book. Creative visualization is using this simple concept toward purposeful ends.

The Process

Here is how the technique works: First, think of something you want or would like to change. Let's say that you want to create a new belief regarding abundance. Go to a quiet room and get in a comfortable position, either sitting or lying down. Relax your body completely. Breathe deeply and slowly.

When you are deeply relaxed, begin to imagine the belief you want to adopt: "I have more than enough money for anything I want. I am able to pay for whatever I want in cash!" Imagine what it feels like to truly believe that. What would you own? How would you feel? What could you give to those you love? How would *that* make you feel? Imagine yourself in the experience of abundance. What are people saying? What does it look like? How does it feel to be finally out of debt? Create a complete and thorough picture.

Check It Out

Positive statements made to yourself are called **affirmations.**

Do this for a few minutes. Have fun with the experience and make it enjoyable—having complete abundance should be enjoyable! Now, make some very positive *affirmative* statements to yourself. "I am so fortunate to finally have abundance in my life." "I love this new car!" If doubts arise, just let them flow on through. Don't fight them or resist them.

End your visualization with a statement, such as "This, or something better, is now mine in satisfying and harmonious ways, for the highest good of all concerned." This statement reaffirms that visualization works only when it is best for all concerned.

This exercise can take anywhere from five minutes to half an hour. Each time you do it, it may be different. Try to do your visualization as often as you can, usually two or three times a day.

> **Money Talks**
>
> Visualization has become commonplace in the field of self-improvement. Athletes use it all the time, imagining a knockout or a personal best. It is said that Mark McGwire used visualization as he chased the home run record.

Don't get hung up on the term visualization. It is not necessary to "see" an image. Some people do see a very clear image in their heads; others do not. The important thing is to feel the experience, to believe it is so.

Set a goal. Decide on something that you would like to have, work toward, or create. It can be a physical thing, a new belief, or even a relationship. Start with things that are achievable fairly easily in the near future until you get the hang of this technique and believe that it works.

Create a clear vision, idea, or picture. Create it in your head as if it already exists. "I love my new car!" Get a picture of the car you want. Write yourself a check for $20 million. Make your desire clear and specific.

Be positive. Think about your goal in a positive, energetic way. Make strong positive statements to yourself about it: that it exists, that it has come to you, that you appreciate it—that sort of thing. See yourself with it, feeling it and accepting your blessing. Don't be too serious.

Rinse and repeat. Bring your mental image to your mind often, both in quiet times reserved for this exercise and in the middle of your busy day. This repetition helps integrate the image into your life. Repeat this exercise until you have achieved your desired goal, or your desire for the goal disappears (which sometimes happens in life).

Money Affirmations

There are many things that you can say to yourself as you visualize the change you want in your life. Some good money affirmations that you may want to adopt are the following:

- I have abundance in all things; my needs are met easily and effortlessly.

- I now give and receive money easily.

- The more I have, the more I have to give.

- Every day, in every way, I am becoming richer and richer.

- I now have a perfect, satisfying, well-paying job.

- I now have enough money to do whatever I want.

- The world is abundant and easily shares its bounty with me.

- Abundance is my natural state of being.

- Every day I am becoming more financially prosperous.

- The more I have, the more I give, and the more I give, the happier I am.

- I am finally out of debt.

Two Cents

Use a notebook to serve as your money changes workbook. In it, write down exercises in this chapter that inspire you and record your thoughts and feelings. Write down some affirmations or old and new beliefs that you are working on.

As you say these things to yourself, your old beliefs will bubble up and tell you that you are a liar. The thing to do then is to acknowledge your past, accept these feelings, let the feeling fade away, and go on creating a new belief. Soon you will have a new belief and new feelings.

New Beliefs

Besides visualization and affirmation, emotion and experience can also change beliefs and money values. A bad experience changed one of Robert's money values in an instant.

Robert always used to pay his rent late. His landlord kept warning him to stop, his wife kept telling him to stop, but Robert ignored the warnings. After nine months, Robert had gotten very comfortable with this arrangement, until he came home one day and found an eviction notice tacked to his front door. The shame and embarrassment he felt having to see his wife's tears and tell his kids that they all had to move deeply affected Robert. After moving to a new place, Robert never paid his rent late again.

People want to avoid repeating negative experiences. Being mugged makes you more cautious. Getting hit by a car jaywalking probably means you will never jaywalk again. After losing World War II, Japan amended its constitution and disavowed war, searching for greatness through peace, which it achieved.

For our purposes in this book, the good thing about a negative experience is that it can change a belief in a hurry. Having a heart attack will shift your thoughts about diet and exercise in a flash, for example.

Money Talks

Frank Layden is the general manager of the Utah Jazz basketball franchise. An affable and funny man, Layden also happened to be very overweight for much of his adult life. That is, he was overweight until one of his best friends, umpire Norm McSherry, dropped dead of a heart attack. The very next morning, Layden woke up early, struggled, but walked around the block. He has walked more and more every day since and has now lost over 100 pounds.

You don't have to wait to be a victim of a bad experience. You can create a negative experience in your mind and emotions and thereby create a shift in attitudes and beliefs in a hurry. We are not talking about creating an actual negative event, just feeling the experience of one, like a sense memory. If you link actual emotional pain to your negative money beliefs, you can change these beliefs. Linking death to being overweight caused Frank Layden to change his belief system overnight.

The reason this technique works is that researchers have discovered what you inherently know: A highly emotional experience, usually a negative one, can have a lasting impact on what you think and feel. The following exercise uses this fact for your benefit instead of your detriment.

Go to a quiet place and answer the following questions. As you do, allow yourself to feel bad—really, really bad. Linking the pain to your outmoded money belief will create the desired change:

- What can't you do because you do not live in abundance? How has a lack of money damaged you? What would you have done with more money? Have you not traveled somewhere? Is there something you want to own that you cannot? How does that make you feel?

- How has your limited thinking about money negatively affected those you love? What were you not able to do for your family because of your money belief system? How many times have you told family members that they can get something they want or do something they desire "later"? How much pain has that caused them?

- Do you know someone who has needed your financial help, but you were unable to help him? Does someone you know need some medical help that you cannot afford to pay for? How does this make you feel?

◆ Would you like to be able to buy your parents a home, or send your sister on that vacation she always dreamed of? Is there a certain school you would like to send your children to? How does it make you feel not to be able to do these things?

Make yourself feel the pain. If your brain associates negative feelings with a lack of money, it will want to change your money beliefs.

To create a true change in a money belief with this system, you need to associate positive feelings with abundance as well as associating negative feelings with lack. Let's look at the abundance side of the coin. As you answer these questions, allow yourself to feel great:

> **Two Cents** _____
>
> "Affluence is the experience in which our needs are easily met and our desires spontaneously fulfilled. Affluence is reality. When we are grounded in the nature of reality and we also know that the same reality is our own nature, then we realize that we can create anything."
>
> —Deepak Chopra

◆ How would you feel and what could you do if you had financial abundance? What would you do if money were no object? What would you buy? Where would you go?

◆ Who could you help if you had an abundance of money? How would that make you feel? What would be said about you if you gave away as much as you wanted to?

◆ What experiences could you have if you were financially free? What could you learn? What could you do? Is there a dream you have that you have never been able to fulfill? How would you feel about yourself if you conquered your money demons?

◆ How would it feel to pay off all of your debts?

◆ How free would you be without money worries? Feel that freedom. Would you feel more secure? Would you have peace of mind? How would your mate feel if you created financial abundance for the two of you?

Try doing this exercise every day for a week and see whether you begin to feel differently about money. After doing this exercise, many people begin to create such negative feelings about their lack of money that they automatically adopt new, more positive beliefs about money. Others vow to take all necessary actions to get out of debt and get ahead.

A pattern emerges. Jim Carrey's trick, creative visualization, and the preceding exercises all require that you feel the feelings of abundance. Creating a physical change in your body causes an emotional change in your head.

Think and Grow Rich

Do you doubt that thoughts are things, that as you think so, too, you create? "As a man thinks, so is he" is one way of saying this. Even the Bible says (paraphrased), "As you sow, so shall you reap."

> **Money Talks**
>
> Among the people who used Carnegie's secret in their own endeavors are Henry Ford, Charles Schwab, Theodore Roosevelt, Wilbur Wright, John D. Rockefeller, Thomas Edison, Woodrow Wilson, and Alexander Graham Bell.

Probably the most well-known book about creating wealth also happens to be one of the best, if not *the* best. *Think and Grow Rich* was written by Napolean Hill in 1960 at the behest of Andrew Carnegie. Carnegie, who amassed his fortune in steel, is one of the richest people to have ever lived; the book contains his secret for creating wealth. *Think and Grow Rich* is one of the best-selling books of all time. It is now in its twentieth printing.

According to Carnegie, there are six steps by which a desire for wealth (or any change for that matter) can be transmuted into actual wealth:

1. Decide the exact amount of money you want. Be definite and state a specific amount.

2. Decide what you intend to give for that money. You cannot get something for nothing.

3. State a definite date by which you are committed to having the money.

4. Create a specific plan for carrying out your desire and immediately put this plan into action.

5. Write out a clear, concise statement of this plan. For example, "I will have $100,000 by January 1 of next year, and I intend to give _____ through my plan of action to get it."

6. Read your statement aloud, twice a day. Once upon waking up and once right before bed. As you read, see and feel yourself in possession of the money.

If these steps seem surprisingly similar to the other exercises in this chapter, you are correct. If you think these six steps could be used to create any change in your life, you are correct again.

What is interesting about Napolean Hill/Andrew Carnegie's recipe is that it requires action on your part. This aspect is important to realize. Changing your beliefs is only one part of the plan. In addition, you need to take action. In Part 5 of this book, we give you several different things you can do to make more money.

The confluence of positive beliefs and new actions creates different results. If you always do what you've always done, you'll always get what you've always gotten.

What you are doing with all of these exercises is messing with your own head. To the extent you have limited or negative beliefs about money, the more you begin to introduce some new ideas into your brain, the more you will begin to believe in, and thereby create, a more affluent life.

The Least You Need to Know

- Changing your belief system often depends on linking new feelings to new beliefs.

- Visualizing a new way works for many people.

- Forcing yourself to confront the negative effects of a lack of money can quickly cause a change in beliefs.

- Putting your plan to paper and rereading it daily has worked for some of the wealthiest people who have ever lived.

Chapter 6

Money Is a Family Matter

In This Chapter

- ◆ Marriage and money
- ◆ Children and money
- ◆ Teens and money

As we have seen, your parents were instrumental in the creation of your money belief system and debt problems. Your own family is an opportunity to put an end to this cycle and implement some new beliefs, although it may not be easy. Not only will you need to accommodate your mate's money beliefs and money style, but you will also have to teach your children some things about money that may seem foreign to you.

For Richer, for Poorer

When figuring out how to resolve your debt problems, you and your spouse must be on the same page. Getting to this point is a two-step process. First, you need to figure out what your different money styles are. Then, you need to merge those two styles to create a unified front and plan of action.

Who Are You?

That John Gray's book *Men Are from Mars, Women Are from Venus* is one of the best-selling books of all time is strong evidence that the sexes have inherent differences. This is as true for money issues as it is for anything else.

Compounding gender differences are other problems that make money peace a difficult thing to achieve at home. Even today, men usually make more money than their wives do and thus tend to wield the financial power in the relationship. In 1980, 88 percent of all women earned less money than their husbands; by 1990, that figure had dropped to 80 percent.

> **Money Talks**
>
> A recent survey found that 34 percent of women and 35 percent of men admitted to having a hidden stash of cash their spouses don't know about. Women reported socking away around $500; for men the amount was $1,000 to $5,000.

> **CAUTION**
>
> **Over Your Limit**
>
> In her book, *You Just Don't Understand: Women and Men in Conversation,* Deborah Tannen says, "Women speak and hear a language of connection and intimacy, while men speak and hear a language of status and independence, [therefore] communication between men and women can be like cross-cultural communication, subject to a clash of conversational styles."

Further, all people have different money styles based upon beliefs and backgrounds. The most common styles are …

- **The spender.** This person spends money regardless of financial circumstances. Going into debt is no problem for the spender.

- **The cheapskate.** This tightwad is so afraid of losing money or going into debt that he deprives both himself and those around him of the joys that money can bring.

- **The worrier.** This person worries so much about money that he has a difficult time enjoying it, even when he has it.

- **The free spirit.** The free spirit is the opposite of the worrier. Bounced checks, late charges, and too many bills? No problem, dude!

- **The dreamer.** "Don't you know that our lottery win will save the day?"

- **The planner.** The healthiest of all the styles, the planner plots out his financial future while trying to still enjoy the present.

The labels are not what matters; the important thing to realize is that partners have different money styles that must be accommodated. Maybe you and your mate are the same type, and maybe you're not. A union of different types can cause a lot of money problems. On the other hand, different styles can also give you a balance you would otherwise not normally have.

David was a classic spender; his wife Ellen was a worrier. Whenever they would get some extra money, his first thought was to go shopping. She wanted to save every penny. She wanted every bill paid on time (even if it meant doing without), and he thought the bills could always wait a while.

David and Ellen fought constantly about money. After several years, they finally had a talk that made a difference. They sat down, admitted and discussed their respective money styles, figured what their joint core values were with regard to money, and created a plan of action that met those values. A bit of each of them went into the plan.

He could spend some money (but not as much as he wanted), and she could save some (ditto). They merged their styles for the good of the whole.

David and Ellen's styles, like those of many couples, were practically polar opposites. Merging styles, values, and attitudes is no easy task. Yet it is a necessary one.

> **Two Cents**
>
> Most first-generation millionaires create wealth by combining money styles. Not only do they take risks and invest wisely, but they also live below their means and clip coupons.

When Worlds Collide

Although each of the money styles has its strengths and weaknesses, you and your spouse need to combine the best of both. Combining the styles will help you teach your children some consistent values about money and enable you to put together a debt-reduction plan that you both agree with.

You absolutely need to compromise and come up with an agreeable joint plan that will accommodate both partners' money needs. If you do not agree at the outset about how you are going to go about solving your money crisis, your chance of succeeding is quite poor. Solving this issue is critical to your financial health and may even save you from divorce. The number one reason for divorce is financial difficulties.

There are three key elements to this process:

Communication. Sit down with your partner and make an honest assessment of where you are financially and how both of your styles and family histories have contributed to the current state of affairs. Honestly admit what you have been doing right and what you have been doing wrong. Acknowledge both your and your partner's money strengths and weaknesses. Tell your spouse what you admire about his or her money style.

> **Over Your Limit**
>
> A serious debt problem can either be a symptom of trouble in the marriage or the cause of the conflict. Few things cause as much marital friction as money. Sometimes, it takes counseling to resolve these issues.

Get out whatever old grudges and resentments you have about money. Because this discussion will hopefully be the foundation of a new financial future, you had best get the past out of the way. Finally, tell your partner what the optimum result of your financial problem would look like to you. Lay it all on the table.

Compromise. Next, you must find some mutually agreeable middle ground. This is the negotiation phase of the discussion. Set some joint goals and agree in a general way on issues such as debt reduction, savings, investments, and bill-paying habits.

Two Cents

If you and your partner do not usually butt heads over spending versus saving, it is unlikely that your problem is a difference in beliefs or styles. Instead, a good talk about priorities is probably in order.

Money Talks

Worried that you do not have enough money to begin to invest? Check your beliefs! Henry Ford started Ford Motor Company without using a single penny of his own money.

Realize what you have been doing wrong and agree to what you will do differently in the future.

You need to set both short-term and long-term money and debt-reduction goals. Do you want to begin to invest a little bit of money in some mutual funds? Do you want to pay off two credit cards completely within a year? Where do you want to be financially in five years?

Often money matters are so emotionally charged that it is difficult to have a rational discussion. If you are in that place, it may make sense to see a counselor to work through these issues.

Plan of action. The remainder of this book will help you with this part. You need to create a plan based upon your goals. The plan should specifically state what you both want to accomplish financially and when you plan to have each item completed. Your plan may look something like the following plan.

Sample Action Plan

Goal	Completion date
1. Transfer all credit cards to card with lowest interest rate	1 month
2. Save 1,000 dollars	6 months
3. Send kids to summer camp	9 months
4. Pay off orthodontist bill	1 year
5. Buy a new car	1 year
6. Buy a rental property	3 years

A plan of action that is based upon a frank and honest discussion and mutual values and goals and that includes something for everybody is a plan that has a great chance of success.

Kids Are People, Too

The rich are different than the rest of us. Not only do they think about money differently than most people, but also, for the most part, they teach their children different values about money. Rich people tend to teach their kids about saving and investing; the poor and middle class usually teach their children about spending and debting.

Your children are your opportunity to break the familial money cycle of which you are an unwitting participant. Teaching your children to have a healthy relationship with money today means that you won't have to lend them this book tomorrow.

Money Talks

Dear Ann Landers: My husband and I have two sons. The oldest one calls me and complains incessantly about his finances and borrows money often, yet he and his wife dine out often and see several movies or plays every week. Our younger son has moved back home, still runs through money as fast as he earns it, and borrows from us whenever he needs cash. Where is it written that children have a right to expect such things from their parents? Had it in Kentucky

Dear Kentucky: You are making this possible by your actions. It's time you stopped being enablers.

—From "Dear Ann Landers," April 29, 1999

Teaching your kids the right way to deal with money has the added bonus of reinforcing what you are now learning. Showing them how to deal intelligently with money helps you do the same. Concentrate on three main areas when it comes to young kids and money: earning, saving, and spending. Teaching teenagers about money is a separate matter taken up at the end of this chapter.

Whistle While You Work

How do you teach your kids good money values? Remember what you were taught and do the exact opposite! We're just joking. Children need to learn that money is good and that it can be their friend if they treat it with respect.

For instance, it is helpful to show children that one of the reasons you go to work every day is to make money, which is good. They need to see the connection between work, the money it generates, and what that money can be used for.

Lily never saw this connection growing up. Her single mother struggled for every dollar. Lily recalls one particular day when she was about nine years old and her mom was complaining about a lack of money. "Mom," Lily said, "just go to the bank." "What?" her mother replied. "Just go to the bank, and they hand you money." Lily and her mother had a good laugh about this comment years later.

Probably the best way to teach children the value of money and work is to allow them to earn some money at home. We advocate paying children for jobs they would not normally do. This way, they learn that "fun" money comes from extra work. Children also need to learn that work is not just about making money, but that money sure is a great benefit of a job well done.

Two Cents

A recent survey found that 74 percent of parents give allowances, and 66 percent tie them to chores. Of the parents who give allowances, 54 percent require their kids to save a portion.

Jerry Seinfeld once said this about money and work: "I never consider the money. That's the most financially sound approach you can take in business. When you don't consider the money, then you can make the right choice. And the right choice always leads to money."

Consider the following ideas when you hire your children:

◆ Tell them what you want done, but let them figure out how to accomplish the task. This should foster independence, a desire to do a good job, and a better appreciation of the financial rewards of their work.

◆ Pay by the job.

◆ Evaluate their performance. Praise a job well done and consider a small "bonus" for exceptional work.

You Teach Best What You Most Need to Learn

After your kids have earned some money, the next trick is to teach them the value of saving some of it. The problem is that saving money for its own sake, or for a rainy day, or to invest is just too amorphous a concept for most young kids to understand. Instead, find something they want to buy that is too "expensive." Then show them that by saving their money, they could get it. Imagine the difference in what they will learn if you teach them to save and spend versus if you taught them to charge and spend! The idea, at least initially, is to just get them into the habit of saving. You have that habit, don't you?

For instance, your six-year-old daughter may want a special Barbie that costs $20. Put her to work and show her that if she saves some of her earnings, then she could buy that Barbie in three weeks. Saving money will then equal Barbie. Now that's a powerful connection for any six-year-old girl!

Imagine the difference if she has to work and save to get that special Barbie versus if dad pulls out the credit card and charges it to see the smile on his precious daughter's face. Sometimes, love means having to say no.

Although a piggy bank for savings is a nice idea, a savings account is better. A piggy bank is just too easy to dip into. A trip to the bank, though, is a special event. The feeling of importance and mastery your child will feel when she goes to deposit some money in her own account will surely pay dividends in more ways than one.

Two Cents _____

Experts agree that there are certain things you can do to teach your children to be financially literate. Among the things most often cited are: Start early, encourage saving, give allowances, pay for chores, teach them about shopping, buy them a good money book for kids, show them how to invest in the future by buying a stock, make finances fun, and remember to have family discussions about money.

No Lessons Required

Spending, the final frontier. "Teach them how to spend," you say. "Now you're talking, spending is the easy part." We agree. Teaching someone to become an intelligent consumer, one who respects his hard-earned and long-saved dollar, is easy compared to breaking a lifetime of bad habits.

Teach your kids the things about shopping that you had to learn the hard way. Always keep the receipt. Find out what the store's return policy is. Read the label. Compare prices. Look for sales. The most expensive item is not always the best. Name brands cost more. The picture on the box always looks better. Television commercials are not always 100 percent truthful. Read the fine print. There is nothing wrong with buying at a consignment or second-hand store.

Teen Time

It is never too late to begin to teach your children the right way to deal with money. It should help them to avoid some of the mistakes you have made and will also help reinforce your new ways.

Teens have special money issues that younger kids don't share. They need to be financially prepared to go out into the world. They need to be taught such simple things as how to write a check and how to balance a checkbook. They also need to be made aware of just how easy it is to go into debt but how difficult it is to get out of debt.

Over Your Limit

There are 400 million VISA cards and MasterCards in circulation worldwide.

Credit card companies target high school graduates with incentives and card applications. Make sure your teenagers know about the credit card trap and how to avoid it. Teenagers should be made aware of the following:

♦ They will be solicited with an introductory interest rate, but it will jump, and many credit card interest rates are well above 15 percent.

♦ Charging up a storm is easy, but maxing out the card and paying the minimum payment ensures that the card will never be paid off.

♦ Late fees and penalties make a credit card balance difficult to reduce.

♦ The smart way to use a credit card is to pay it off every month.

Teaching teens to be respectful of money and fearful of debt is one of the best parting gifts you can give them before they leave home.

The Least You Need to Know

♦ Everyone has a money style.

♦ Spouses need to learn to blend money styles and create a plan of action to get out of debt.

♦ Children are your chance to teach (and learn) correct money values.

♦ Teens need to be made aware of the dangers of going into debt.

The "B" Word

In This Chapter

- ◆ Budget is not a bad word
- ◆ Keep a record
- ◆ Make a plan
- ◆ Create a budget
- ◆ A sample budget
- ◆ Budgets and your computer

Most of us view budgets as a necessary evil at best and something to be avoided at worst. The traditional view is that a budget is a restrictive plan forcing you to deprive yourself of what you want.

The truth can be far different, if you want it to be. A budget should be a guide, not a constraint. A reasonable, good budget is a tool that allows you to do what you want. That's why you went into debt, right, to get what you want? And guess what? If you spend more than you wanted to one month, you don't go to jail. Your budget is your tool; it can be as friendly as you want it to be.

Budget Is Not a Four-Letter Word

Most people who go deeply into debt have no idea how much they spend on groceries, entertainment, clothes, or restaurants every month. As we said in an earlier chapter, not knowing the state of your finances (except for the fact that you are in debt) is like driving with a bag over your head. A budget allows you to take the bag off and get a good look at where you are going financially. If you don't like what you see, make some changes.

Maybe budget is the wrong word to use. A plan is more of what we are talking about here. You need to come up with a plan that lets you see what comes in, what goes out, and what you want to go out.

For example, maybe on September 1, after reading this chapter, you decide that you would like to spend $200 a month on entertainment (it is your budget after all). The first part of the plan would be to find out what you normally spend on entertainment.

Over Your Limit

Seen on a bumper sticker: "How can I be overdrawn? I still have checks left."

Two Cents

If you plan ahead and begin to budget accordingly, it is easier to save for a vacation, because you will be able to get the best rates by booking far in advance.

So for the whole month of September, you would spend money as you usually would, keeping close track of your entertainment expenses.

At the end of the month, you would add up those expenses and see what you spent. If the total were $300, that would be valuable information to have, would it not? You could then decide that you want to spend $300 a month the next month and cut back somewhere else, or you might decide to watch your entertainment spending more closely. Maybe you had no idea that you were spending $300 a month on entertainment. Either way, the budget, the plan, is working for you, not against you. It takes the blindfold off, see? (We will explain how to make this plan in a tad more detail.)

So the first of many benefits of budgeting is that you know what is going on. Planning (we will use the terms planning and budgeting interchangeably) is a tool that shows you how your funds are allocated, what your priorities are, and how far along you are toward reaching your goals.

Creating a budget has several other benefits:

> **You are in control.** A budget enables you to take charge of your finances. It helps you get a grip on your spending so that you can make sure your money is used properly. It will help you have enough for essentials, and actually allow you to create enough extra left over for "nonessentials." With a budget, you decide

what is going to happen to your hard-earned money and when. You can control your money, instead of having your money control you. Now that would probably be a welcome change.

You are more organized. A basic budget divides funds into categories of expenditures and savings. Beyond that, however, budgets can record all your monetary transactions. They can also provide the foundation for a simple filing system to organize bills, receipts, and financial statements.

You are more communicative. If you are married, have a family, or share money with anyone, having a budget that you create together can resolve personal differences about money handling. Your budget is a communication tool to discuss priorities for where your money can best be spent.

You don't lose opportunities. Knowing the exact state of your personal monetary affairs and being in control allows you to take advantage of opportunities that you might otherwise miss. Have you ever wondered if you could afford something? With a budget, you will never have to wonder again. You will know.

You will be more efficient. A budget means that all of your finances are automatically organized for creditor communications, for tax time, and for any query that may come up about how and when you spent money. Being armed with such information saves time digging through old records.

Most important, you will have extra money. Hidden fees and lost interest paid to creditors can be eliminated. Unnecessary expenditures, once identified, can be expunged. Savings, no matter how small, can be accumulated and made to work for you. A budget will almost certainly produce extra money for you to do with as you wish.

Two Cents

More money-saving ideas: Select a cheaper long-distance carrier; avoid impulse purchases; turn off unnecessary lights, heat, or air conditioning; get rid of premium cable channels; shop at consignment stores. Eat out less, car pool ... The list is endless, isn't it?

Even if you don't use the budget you draw up, just the homework involved in creating it can be instructive because you may find that you are spending more than you want to on various items.

There are three steps to creating a budget. The first step is to keep track of where your money goes in a normal month before you create your budget. After reviewing where your money is spent, the second step is to decide where you would rather see it applied. The last step is to create a budget and track your spending.

Keep a Good Record

Getting out of debt requires that you know how much you spend every month and where you spend it. Vicky was shocked when she began to keep track of her spending habits. She had no idea how much she was spending on lunches at work and on music. She didn't know where her money went every month until she kept track. Do you? If you don't, do you see how knowing this could be immensely helpful? That is the purpose of keeping a good record.

Spend a month writing down, every day, exactly what you do with your money. How much do you spend on food, cabs, gas, and magazines? Create categories, carry a little notebook with the categories listed, and keep a daily log of every expenditure. If you are not keen on the notebook method, many personal finance computer programs enable you to do the same thing. Either way, every day, you need to record every expenditure for at least one month. Yes, this process sounds like a pain in the rear, but what you discover will be worth the effort, and it's not as hard as it sounds.

Two Cents

Keeping your receipt from the ATM will help you keep track of where the money goes because you will know where and when you took out money.

List every little thing, to the penny: lunch, movies, books, dry cleaning, haircuts—everything. On days that you write large checks (your car payment, for example) enter those in one of your categories too. Having 20 to 30 categories is not uncommon. Every time you spend money, record it in a category or add a category.

This is not as much work as it sounds. You only need to create this list once, in the beginning. It will be the basis for any budget you create later on. Your categories, the more specific the better, should include …

- Rent.
- Utilities.
- Groceries.
- Insurance.
- Clothes.
- Fast food.
- Restaurants.
- Entertainment (be specific).

- ◆ Transportation.
- ◆ Medical.
- ◆ Child care.
- ◆ School expenses.
- ◆ Health.

At the end of the month, tally the results. Make sure that you also include all canceled checks and itemized credit-card statements so that all of your expenditures are accounted for. The picture should be illuminating. Maybe you never knew that you spent $30 a month on late video charges. Maybe those computer games added up. Whatever the case, this record will help you see where the problem lies.

Your Plan

Once you see where things are, you can decide where you want them to be, put yourself back in control of your finances, and begin to make more intelligent decisions. You can decide that less needs to be spent on vitamins, for example, or that more should be spent on clothes for the kids. Instead of blindly spending whatever cash you have in your pocket on whatever need you may have on any given day, you start your month by planning ahead.

Madeline decided that she could easily spend a lot less on fast food every month. Next to the $300 she had in that category's recorded total, she added a category called "budgeted" and listed $150. On the first day of the next month, she went to the market and loaded up on her favorite items and made sure to keep some with her each day as the month progressed. That first month, she spent less than the $150 projected, and for the first time in a long time, she ended the month without a money crisis.

This type of plan is flexible, can be changed, and does not control you; you control it. The whole idea of the record and plan is to enlighten you and enable you to make intelligent decisions. A budget is simply your plan for how you can best utilize your money. It's restrictive only to the extent that you want it to be.

Two Cents

Different stages of life require different budgets. A college student will have fewer categories of expenses and different priorities than a single parent of four will.

Creating a Budget

After you monitor your spending, the process of putting together a budget is quite easy. The simplest budget of all would consist of just adding one more column to the record you made and listing how much you plan to spend on each item the next month. You would then need to continue to track your expenses to see whether they meet your goals. *Voilá!* You have created the dreaded budget.

However, because a budget is a planning tool, it is wiser to create a more elaborate one. For example, you may have had no health-related expenses the month that you tracked your spending habits. That does not mean, however, that you do not want to budget some money every month for that purpose. What you should do, then, is to create a budget that covers everything that you plan to put money toward in any given month.

Although adding more detail into your budget plan will be time-consuming initially, doing so will give you more information and make your plan more useful in the long term. It will also enable you to put aside money every month for specific reasons and make paying bills quicker and easier because there will be no fights over priorities; you prioritize your discretionary spending up front. Your budget will be broken down into three sections: income, fixed spending, and discretionary spending.

Income

Whether you use a computer program to help you with your budget or do it by hand in a notebook, the first category will be your income. Before you can decide how best to spend your money, you must know exactly how much comes in every month.

Check It Out

The full amount of money you are paid is called the **gross**. Out of your gross pay, taxes, insurance, and other items may be withheld. The amount you actually take home is called your **net**.

Income will include your *net* paycheck, money from freelancing, tips, alimony, child support, trust funds, interest, dividends—everything. All revenue streams must be included. If your income varies every month, then the best thing to do is to use an average month calculated from income generated over the past year. Let's say that last year you took home about $30,000. Some months you made $2,000, and some months you made $3,000. Average it out. $30,000 over a year is an average of $2,500 a month.

Fixed Expenses

Fixed expenses are expenses that stay the same every month, month after month. You have no discretion when it comes to fixed expenses. This part of your budget will include …

- Mortgage or rent payments. Yes, your rent or mortgage may go up or down, but budgets change as your life changes. Whatever your housing costs currently are, put them here.

- Utility bills. These bills include gas, electric, phone, heating, water, garbage, cable TV.

- Car payments.

- Taxes. If you make ongoing payments to the IRS for past taxes, or if you are self-employed, you need to budget some money every month for this expense.

- Loan repayment. Student loans or other personal loans are included in this category.

- Child support or alimony payments.

- Insurance premiums.

- Any other fixed expense or regular monthly payment.

Discretionary Expenses

Your budget will make a difference in the area of discretionary expenses. What are your priorities? Upon reviewing your record, you will probably decide that you need to spend more in some areas and less in others. That's the whole idea. By reallocating these expenses, you will be able to refocus your finances. You can decide to spend less on food and more on saving or whatever works for you.

This is not how most people view a budget. Instead of something that is always telling you "no," we see a budget as something that says "yes" to your most important values. This kind of budget tells you to spend *more*, not less, on those things most important to you. If spending money on your children is important, then you can create a budget that reflects that desire.

This part of the budget will include …

- Food. Include all food and household goods spending at grocery stores, bulk-food stores, farmers' markets, and so on.

When making a budget, give yourself extra room in case you have to spend more because of inflation or an unexpected emergency.

♦ Eating out. Dinners, work lunches, breakfast meetings, and so on.

♦ Home-related expenses. Furniture, electronics, home improvements, the gardener or handyman expenses, and maintenance belong in this category.

♦ Clothes.

♦ Entertainment. These expenses would include concerts, clubs, movies, video rentals, and so on.

♦ Work. Any work-related expenses not covered in the clothing or food categories would go here.

♦ Accounting and legal. Even if you don't have ongoing expenses here, you might want to budget for that yearly trip to the CPA at tax time.

♦ Automobile. Gas and upkeep.

♦ Health and medical. Here you account for health items such as vitamins and your gym bill, as well as any potential expenses not covered by your insurance, things like prescription drugs or chiropractic treatments.

♦ Travel. Toll road expenses, airline travel, and so on.

♦ Taxes. Ideally, you will have enough money taken out of your taxes by your employer that you won't owe any at the end of the year. But if you normally owe taxes, account for it here. If you are self-employed, you probably don't need to be reminded to budget for taxes.

♦ Books and magazines. We can't forget to buy books!

♦ Vacation. If you spend $500 every summer taking the kids camping, you save a little for it every month.

♦ Children. Monthly child care expenses, baby-sitting, piano lessons, school expenses, and everything else.

♦ Saving. You said you were going to start saving, right?

♦ Debt repayment. As you will see in Chapter 9, it is very important to budget some money, whatever you can comfortably live with, toward repaying your debts.

♦ Fun. If this isn't in your budget, what's the point?

♦ Miscellaneous.

Although the goal here is to have your spending stay within the limits you've set, a concurrent goal should be to discover if some of your figures are unrealistic. If so, adjust them. There is no point in making a budget that you can't live with. You will probably have to change it two or three times before you come up with a useful, workable budget.

Optimally, your goal should be to reduce your spending to about 90 percent of your income. Why? That way, you will be saving 10 percent of your income and hopefully earmarking it toward investments (discussed in the last section of this book) and your other long-term financial objectives. If you reduce your spending and invest the savings, not only will you get out of debt, but you also can get rich.

Two Cents

Discuss budget items with everyone in the house. When it affects others, budgeting is a family affair.

A Sample Budget

Let's look at Chris and Amy's budget. Their problem was that, although both made a good living, they were running in the red every month and borrowing from their credit cards to make up the difference. Chris brought home $1,500 a month, and Amy took home $2,200 a month. They have two kids.

They bought a computer program to help them create a budget. Every day for a month, they each dutifully kept track of their normal spending habits, and every night for a month, they spent about 10 minutes entering it into their computer. They agreed up front not to fight over how the other one was spending money. At the end of the month, they had made $3,700 but had spent $4,000. Let's look at how they solved the problem.

Their fixed expenses included a mortgage payment of $1,100. Car payments were $600 a month, and utilities were $200 a month. Their fixed expenses totaled $1,900 per month.

Their discretionary spending broke down this way:

◆ Food: Chris and Amy spent an average of $800 a month at the market, although their record disclosed that they spent quite a bit at the convenient and expensive small market down the street. By shopping at a less expensive grocery store and making a run for bulk items once a month, they figured they could save about $100.

◆ Eating out: The family ate out or ordered in three times a week. They decided to cut back to once a week (if that), intending to save another $200 a month.

◆ Entertainment: Chris and Amy had a standing Saturday night date for movies and dinner. Between this and the baby-sitter, they spent $60 a week. They decided to cut out the dinner portion of their date sometimes and stay home once a month, saving another $100.

◆ Children: Both kids participated in activities such as music lessons, kung fu, and soccer at a cost of $200 a month. Each child had to cut out one activity. This saved another $100.

◆ Saving: They had no savings when they started but decided to allot $100 a month to start with.

◆ Debt repayment: They also began to pay $100 extra toward paying down their credit cards.

CAUTION

Over Your Limit

Have patience. Take your time when setting up a budget. It does not have to be done in one sitting. Also realize that it may take a few months to begin to see real results from your budget.

Once they saw where their money was going, Chris and Amy were able to cut $500 out of their budget and put their money where they thought it would be better served without radically changing their lifestyle. They wanted to avoid borrowing from their credit cards, begin to pay them off, and start to save some money. These things were more important than another date or the convenience of shopping down the street. A budget does nothing more than assist you in prioritizing your finances.

Mary had a different problem. A stay-at-home mom, Mary found it difficult to get through to the end of the month because her husband was paid only once a month on the first. By the 25th, she was always out of money and had no credit cards to borrow from.

Mary decided to be fairly strict with herself and her family after reviewing her record. Now, on payday, she writes all the checks for fixed expenses and utilities, and then subtracts from her balance the amounts for automatic withdrawals, such as the mortgage payment and student loans. She transfers money into the savings account for long-term savings and for unscheduled expenses like car repairs and emergency funds.

Then she takes the remaining amount and divides it by four to use as a weekly allowance for groceries, gas, and incidentals. She withdraws that amount in cash from the bank on Monday and pays only cash for purchases. At the beginning of the next week, she takes her allowance again. Mary's method of budgeting demonstrates that a budget can be as flexible and creative as you want it to be.

Budgets and Your Computer

As we said, you can create a budget by hand or with the help of a computer. If you have a computer, you can take advantage of some of the great budget programs that are available.

Both Quicken and Microsoft Money (to name just two programs) make it easy to draw up a budget and monitor compliance. Quicken, for example, comes with a set of categories that handle most of the basics. You can edit the list to create categories that make better sense for your particular household. If you're away from home, you can even track expenses at the Quicken Web site and then download the transactions to your computer later. Also with Quicken (we use this program as an example because it is the market leader), you can produce monthly spending reports in categories you select.

The drawback to electronic budgeting is that entering and categorizing all of your income and outflow can be quite a tedious chore. You can reduce the tedium to some degree by judicious selection of categories. If you are only worried about tracking your spending for recreation and leisure, then you could create categories that cover those types of expenses and let everything else accumulate under "miscellaneous revenue" or "miscellaneous expense."

The problem with that approach is that you forego the opportunity to spot problems in other spending areas that you may not even be aware of. A better solution is to track expenses using electronic banking. That way, you can download your payments and deposits directly from the bank, rather than having to enter them by hand.

> **Two Cents**
>
> One drawback of monitoring your spending by computer is that it encourages overzealous attention to detail. Once you determine which categories of spending can and should be cut (or expanded), concentrate on those categories and worry less about other aspects of your spending.

The Least You Need to Know

- Budgets are a tool to help you.
- Creating a record of your expenditures will help you see where you spend your money.
- Creating a budget will allow you to prioritize your finances.
- Computer programs make budgeting fairly easy.

Chapter 8

How and Where to Cut Back

In This Chapter

- ◆ Attitudes
- ◆ Food
- ◆ Kids
- ◆ Work
- ◆ Travel
- ◆ Pleasure
- ◆ Love

You need to live below your means if you are going to get out of debt. That is a fact. It's like losing weight. Unless you consume less and do things differently, nothing will change. Permanently ridding yourself of debt, like permanently ridding yourself of extra weight, requires a change in habits.

In this chapter, you will find many good ideas that will enable you to trim your budget without too much sacrifice, ideas that you can adopt for the long term. Pick and choose the ones that work for you and implement them into your overall debt reduction plan.

A Good Attitude

Most likely, you are going into this cost-cutting process with a sour attitude. Money is tight, cutting back is not fun, and admitting you made mistakes is not easy. Yet, as with anything else in life, if you attempt to get out of debt with a negative attitude or while carrying around bad feelings, the chances of success are diminished.

In many ways, getting out of debt and living below your means can be enjoyable instead of miserable. Cutting back will require that you change some habits, but if you keep in mind that your old habits are probably what got you into trouble in the first place, replacing them with new ones can be a fun adventure.

It's all a matter of having the right attitude. Spencer's grandmother had an apropos saying in this regard. Always a witty and active woman, Gram was eventually forced by age and ill health to live in a senior community. One day, Spencer went to see her.

He asked how she was doing. She was silent for a second, looked at Spencer with a twinkle in her eye, and said: "I'm in good shape—for the shape I'm in!" That is the type of attitude we are suggesting.

We know it is not easy; if cutting back were in your blood, then this book would not be in your hand. However, we cannot emphasize enough that you have to do some things differently if you are to get out of debt. Starting with a positive attitude makes the process easier.

> **Two Cents**
>
> Getting out of debt is a precursor to getting rich (if that is your desire). Many of the skills that you use to get out of the money pit are the same ones you need to get ahead in life. So do not be too sad. Cutting costs is good training.

Food for Less

Let's see how a positive attitude can affect the bottom line. Aside from mortgage payments, food costs for a family are probably the largest item in the family budget. Depending upon the size of your family, food costs can be bigger than car payments.

It is not difficult to reduce the cost of food. Bulk and discount stores are easy to find. What is difficult is getting out of the habit of paying for convenience. Although it may be much easier to buy tonight's dinner at the corner store down the street, planning ahead and buying at a less expensive supermarket can save you a lot of money every month.

> **Money Talks**
>
> A survey conducted by the American International College discovered that 80 percent of those surveyed said that they would pay an additional 20 percent on a $200 purchase like a gas grill if they didn't have to assemble it themselves.

A key concept to reducing your food bill could be called "shop and stock." Buy food when it is cheaper and stock it away until you need it. You can dramatically reduce your food costs by doing so and still eat what you like. Shop for food at a less convenient and less expensive market. Buy in bulk. Buy on sale.

We especially recommend buying on sale. When you shop, look for items that you regularly use that are on sale, even if you don't need them. Freeze them or put them in the back of your cupboard. Shop and stock. If you get really good at this, you need never pay full price for anything again, because everything in the market eventually goes on sale. If a favorite item goes on sale, buy it, even if you don't need it at that moment (feels like old times, no?). Although it might seem odd to buy things you don't immediately need, the savings are realized in the future when you do not have to buy that chicken that was on sale two weeks previously.

Susan started shopping this way and saved an average of $40 a week feeding her family of five. She then earmarked that extra $160 a month to pay down her credit cards and paid off one of them within a year. Who knew that creamed corn on sale could do battle with the mighty MasterCard and win?

There are plenty more ways to save on food costs:

◆ **Buy markdowns.** Day-old bread and pastries are usually half-price.

◆ **Use coupons.** Coupons can save you a lot of money, but they can also be a hassle. If you find coupons for a thing you use consistently, they can save you lots of money.

◆ **Buy in bulk.** As a general rule, the more you buy of an item, the less each individual portion costs. Bulk purchases of rice, beans, flour, chicken, cheese, and vegetables can all be divvied up into smaller portions and frozen or stored in plastic containers. If you think that you don't have enough room or people to buy in bulk, buddy up with a friend or relative and shop together. Just be sure to avoid thinking that you really need 48 granola bars!

> **CAUTION**
>
> **Over Your Limit**
>
> Prepared frozen meals and snacks are among the most expensive items you can buy at the market. According to the Roper organization, sales of prepackaged frozen meals increased by 35 percent in the 1990s. You will save a lot of money by avoiding these frozen foods.

◆ **Buy generic.** Mark was a struggling director forced to live on almost nothing because of his choice of professions. He learned to buy some generic foods and sundries to save money. Now, although he directs television shows and makes a bundle, he still buys generic because he sees no difference in quality.

If you eliminate the need for convenience, you can still eat the same foods you always have at a fraction of the cost.

Is It Possible to Save Money If You Have Kids?

Yes, you can have the joy of raising children without going broke. No, it will not be easy, especially given their proclivity for saying, "I want one of those!" Larry's father often told Larry, "My name is not Get Me, Buy Me."

We discussed kids and money in detail in Chapter 6 but a few things need to be reiterated here. Although we live in a very materialistic society, it is incumbent upon all of us to teach our children well. They will feel the tug of peer pressure, the "need" to have $100 Air Jordans. If you can teach them money literacy early, you will have gone a long way toward saving them years of financial and emotional grief.

Kids learn best by example. If they see you buying new shoes every month, they will want new shoes. If you get the newest computer every six months, they will want the new Nintendo. If they see you being smart with a dollar, they just might learn that, too.

Two Cents

If you buy your next big-ticket item with cash instead of charging it or financing it, you can save about 15 percent on the cost of the item. If you buy it used, you could save over 50 percent.

There are scores of ways to have fun with your kids, teach them positive values, and still save money. What is your favorite Halloween costume of all time? It is probably safe to say that it was not some prefab, store-bought costume, but rather a homemade, creative masterpiece. Keep that in mind as you strive to give your kids the best without teaching them the worst.

Art projects are a fine example. Children love to make art, to express themselves with pictures when words may be hard to find. Crayons are great for the little ones, and most newspapers sell newspaper end-rolls (just the paper, not the print) for a song just to get rid of it. Add some scissors, glitter, string, markers, beads, and buttons, and you have an afternoon of relative peace and quiet. Maria has a special "gallery" (a wall) where she hangs the best pieces of the week. Why not keep all the packaging you throw away every week? Anything can be a part of a work of art.

Other great, inexpensive activities include …

- ◆ **Cooking and baking.** By incorporating children into your kitchen activities, you kill two birds with one stone. They play (for free), and you get some work done.

◆ **Music.** Teaching children to love music is a reward unto itself. Whether it be listening to Mozart on CD, playing the flute, or drumming that wooden spoon, music can be a compelling, wonderful, affordable activity.

◆ **Reading.** If children learn early enough, they can't stop. That you can check out endless books for free from the library makes reading that much better. Books can also be purchased cheaply at yard sales, book fairs, and church bazaars. Have children write their own books. Read to your children every day.

◆ **Computer.** If you have a home computer, the possibilities are endless. CDs make learning fun and can often be found in the bargain bin at the computer store for a few dollars. The Internet is a vast resource of fun and learning. America Online, for instance, has an entire area for kids only. Install an inexpensive blocking program, and let them go explore the world.

◆ **Sports.** Sports can usually be played for the cost of a football, basketball, or Frisbee.

◆ **Games.** They need not be expensive. Puppets can be made out of lunch bags. Use old clothes for dress-up. Puzzles are pretty cheap.

◆ **Money.** Help them start a business. The kids can solicit neighbors for a summer pet-sitting or pet-washing service. They can wash cars or sell lemonade. They can baby-sit.

It Takes Money to Make Money

Work-related expenses can devour a budget. Utilize these ideas and save a bundle:

Bring a sack lunch. Let's say that you and your spouse could save a conservative $5 a day each by brown-bagging it three days a week. At the end of a year, you would have saved over $1,500.

Buy clothes on sale or even used. A new silk tie may cost $40. On sale, it is $30. Used, it is $5. The same holds true for a suit or dress. Of course, you must look sharp to get ahead at work; no one is saying that you should dress like Cosmo Kramer. We are saying that you can dress your best for less.

Over Your Limit

In 1997, the average American household spent 39 percent of its food budget on meals outside the home.

Save on dry cleaning. People can spend over $1,000 a year on dry cleaning. If you shop around a bit, it is probable that you can find a convenient dry cleaner that will do the same work for one third less. Having that jacket cleaned every other time instead of every time you wear it can also save money. Better yet, check the tags before you buy to avoid purchasing items that are "dry clean only."

Two Cents

Each of these savings alone may be miniscule, but when you add them together, they can make a big dent in your expenditures. When you use that money to pay off credit card debt and corresponding high interest rates, you are really beginning to change your situation.

Use mass transit. Remember, convenience costs. If saving money is going to become a priority, then something will have to give, probably convenience. Driving to work may be quicker, but gas and parking are expensive, and a bus is a lot cheaper.

Save on coffee breaks. Snacks from home can replace that daily $3 bagel and juice, although giving up your latte may just be too much to ask.

We are not telling you that you must become a miserly saint. As Maude said in the movie *Harold and Maude*, "You can't be good all of the time; it spoils the fun!" Pick and choose what works for you.

Traveling on a Budget

Traveling, too, need not be outrageously expensive. If you are willing to spend a little more time getting to your destination, you can save a lot more money.

The Only Way to Fly

Plane flights now can be quite inexpensive. By filling planes that are not full and putting people on flights with layovers, Priceline.com does indeed allow you to name an inexpensive price for plane flights (as well as hotel rooms). No-frills carriers like Southwest and United Express are pretty cheap, and ticket brokers sell discounted airline flights.

If you are really adventurous, you can become an air courier. Large companies ship packages every day around the world, and they require someone to accompany the package. That person is you, the air courier. As a courier, you can fly to Europe, Asia, South America, almost anywhere, and do so at a heavy discount. Whereas a flight from New York to Oslo might cost $2,000 roundtrip, on a courier flight it might be $395. Sometimes, in a pinch, it can be free. Pick up a book on air courier travel, and you are off. The downside is that you usually don't get to choose how long you can stay abroad, and bringing the kids along is impossible.

Other ways to save on airfare include:

◆ Travel during off-peak times of year.

◆ Travel Monday through Thursday instead of over a weekend. Cultural events in most cities are practically free during the week.

◆ Fly standby.

◆ Give up your seat on an overbooked flight and get a free voucher. Tim books a flight every year for December 23 from Denver to New York (making sure the ticket is exchangeable) without ever planning to go. He goes to the plane that day, happily gives up his over-booked seat, gets a free flight anywhere in the country for being so reasonable, and uses his exchangeable ticket on a flight he will use later in the year.

◆ If necessary, use compassion fares. Airlines offer discounted bereavement fares if you can show proof of death and explain your relationship to the deceased.

Check It Out

Discount travel brokers are called **bucket shops.** If you look in the travel section of the Sunday *Los Angeles Times* or *The New York Times*, you will see scores of ads for various bucket shops offering amazing deals.

Traveling Cheaply

Once you get to your destination, you can save even more money. Go to the local Chamber of Commerce and get a tourist kit; inside will be discounts and lots of great offers. Traveling by bus or subway saves money, and if you will be there for a while, consider getting a bus pass.

Lodging can be very expensive or very cheap. If you are going to travel overseas, you can exchange homes with a family in the country you are going to. You can rent an apartment instead of staying in a hotel. You can stay in a discount motel instead of a hotel. You can stay in a college dorm instead of a motel. You can camp.

Be sure to use any discounts available to you. Seniors are offered discounts on car rentals, airline tickets, lodging, admissions, mass transit, and restaurants. Other groups that are often offered similar discounts are members of the military, students, auto club members, and union members.

Young, Broke, and in Love

David and Leslie took one of their most memorable trips ever when they were young and had no choice but to be creative. They took a train from Los Angeles to Tijuana and hopped a plane to Mexico City, because flying within the country was much cheaper than flying internationally.

Once in Mexico, they grabbed an overnight train to the pyramids (saving on a hotel room). They then took a 24-hour bus ride to Cancun (saving another night of hotel expenses). In Cancun, they stayed at the youth hostel for $4 a night. They hitched south (which is not safe nowadays) and found a room on the beach for $10 a night. There they got engaged with a $25 silver ring David had bought earlier in the trip. They just celebrated their 15th anniversary, and although they don't travel like that anymore, they miss it a lot.

Pleasure on the Cheap

Eating out need not be so expensive either. Your newspaper is full of coupons for inexpensive meals for adults and families alike. If you eat out often, dining clubs offer two-for-one deals, and discount coupon books sold by civic organizations pay for themselves in meals many times over, if they are used. Other ways to eat cheaply include …

> **Two Cents**
>
> Movie theatres don't make their real money at the box office; the concession stand is what you need to be wary of. If you are so inclined, bring your own candy and soda in a purse, and you will save 10 dollars. Malcolm pops his own popcorn before going to the movies and sneaks it in, in his backpack. (We told you this could be fun.)

- Utilizing "early bird specials."
- Eating a la carte instead of ordering a full meal.
- Sharing your food.
- Not ordering a drink.
- Going out for lunch instead of dinner.
- Just going out for dessert.

Movies are usually half-price for a matinee. If you are patient, that new Mel Gibson movie will turn up at the discount theatres in a few weeks. If these ideas don't appeal to you, stay home and make it a Blockbuster night.

We are so used to spending money for entertainment that it comes as a shock to realize just how much there is to do for almost nothing:

- Go on a bike ride.
- Go to a museum.

- Take a drive in the country.

- Garden.

- Attend a free lecture at a university.

- Go to the library.

- Play a free sport—tennis, baseball, basketball.

- Make art.

- Go to a street fair.

- Go camping.

Money Can't Buy You Love

Going on a date can also be inexpensive if you use your imagination. (When Tom was a child, he thought his mom was telling him to use his "magic nation.") A picnic in the park or at the beach is quite romantic and a bargain to boot. A walk around the city, stopping for coffee, and browsing in galleries are equally fanciful and similarly inexpensive.

The possibilities for fun, economical dates are endless, if you use your own "magic nation." Use these ideas to get you started:

- Find a dark cafe and spend the night chatting and drinking.

- Test drive a dream car.

- Explore a new neighborhood.

- Take a walk in the woods.

- Fly a kite.

How about this idea: Act as though you and your spouse are going on a getaway for the weekend. Find someone to take the kids, pack your favorite clothes, plan a special Saturday afternoon and Sunday brunch, and stay home. Do it all and have a blast, just do it from home. Dress up, light the candles, feed each other food, trade massages, and go wild. You may end up doing things you have never done, seeing parts of your city you have never been to, and saving a small fortune in the process.

The Least You Need to Know

- Having the right attitude is essential.

- When it comes to food, you pay for convenience.

- Kids can be as happy playing as they can be spending.

- Traveling on the cheap can be a great adventure.

- Romance need not be expensive.

Chapter 9

Call Your Creditor and Say "Hi" (The Plan)

In This Chapter

- The theory
- The power of commitment
- The repayment plan
- Calculating the plan
- Calling all creditors
- Keeping good records

In the last chapter, you began to take a look at your monthly budget and possibly make some changes. Even if you didn't, it remains a fact that the only way you are going to get rid of those debts that hinder you and stress you out, short of bankruptcy, is to earmark some money every month to repay them.

The best way to do this is to formulate a repayment plan. Before you even say that you can't, that it's impossible, that there is no room at the inn, let us say that we will not ask you to make impossible sacrifices in order to get out of debt. This book and this plan are about getting out of debt within the context of making your life work.

Get Out of Debt, Now

Your creditors are probably not too happy with you right now. Although some people start on the path toward financial solvency still current on all of their bills, most people do not. Their utilities may be close to being turned off, and their credit cards are so maxed out that they can no longer even use the cards to continue to accrue interest, finance charges, and penalties.

Check It Out

When a creditor finally decides that it can no longer collect the debt from you, it will **charge off** the debt. This does not mean you don't owe the money anymore. It just means that your creditor probably sold the debt to a collection agency at a steep discount and will get a tax break for the loss.

Two Cents

"Whether you think you can, or that you can't, you are usually right."

—Henry Ford

Late payments like these create even more debt, which in turn may cause more fear and avoidance. Avoidance can then cause more late payments, creating even more debt. Debt begets more debt. Maybe you'll go on a binge-shopping spree to feel better. In this hellish cycle, debts grow and grow and grow. You can put an end to this cycle by putting together a practical repayment plan.

Of course, we realize that some debt is unmanageable and that such debt is bigger than a repayment plan. If that is the case, bankruptcy is probably a better option. We understand that and even endorse that option. After all, one of the authors of this book is a bankruptcy attorney. The repayment plan being presented here is for those of you who plan to get out of debt without declaring bankruptcy. Bankruptcy is discussed in Part 4.

Commitment

To make this repayment plan work, give it your full commitment. Commit totally to repaying everything and everyone to whom you owe money. Of course, it will take time and won't be simple, but that is no excuse for not starting.

A 31-year-old man once asked his wise father whether he should go back and finish his college degree. The man was worried that it would take three years and that he would be 34 years old when he finally finished college. His father looked at his son and asked him, "How old will you be in three years if you don't go?" How old will you be in three years if you don't commit to repaying your debts? You'll be three years older and several more dollars in the hole.

Making a commitment to pay everyone back is very significant. If you do it, you will feel better about yourself. It will give you the confidence to call up your creditors and work out a repayment plan. Fear will begin to evaporate and will be replaced by strength. A commitment to keep your word, have integrity, and live up to your responsibilities fosters self-esteem. It is good for the soul.

Commitment is a very powerful thing. Buckminster Fuller (1895–1983) is best known for inventing the geodesic dome, but he was also a prolific author, mathematician, cartographer, speaker, scientist, and inventor. At one point, he had the longest entry ever in the history of Who's Who.

What many people don't know about Bucky is that he was a complete failure for much of his life. He was kicked out of Harvard, twice (once for blowing his entire semester's allowance on an evening with showgirls), had several businesses fail, and was grieving for a daughter he lost to a childhood illness. An unhappy, unknown failure at 30, Buckminster Fuller decided to kill himself.

As he walked to Lake Michigan in the dead of winter, intent on throwing himself in, Fuller realized that his mistake had been selfishness; if he fully committed himself to helping the greatest number of people he could, he could be a success. He vowed on his deceased daughter's memory to do just that. It was only after making this commitment that he turned his life around and became a lovable genius some dubbed "the da Vinci of the twentieth century."

W. H. Murray wrote the following in *The Scottish Himalayan Expedition*:

> Until one is committed, there is hesitancy, the chance to draw back, always ineffectiveness. Concerning all acts of initiative and creation, there is one elementary truth the ignorance of which kills countless ideas and splendid plans: that the moment one definitely commits oneself, then providence moves too. All sorts of things occur to help one that would never otherwise have occurred. A whole stream of events issues from the decision, raising in one's favor all manner of unforeseen incidents, meetings and material assistance which no man could have dreamed would have come his way. Whatever you can do or dream you can, begin it. Boldness has genius, power, and magic in it. Begin it now.

You don't need to change the world; you just need to make a commitment to yourself and for yourself that you are going to repay all your debts.

The Plan

Again, this plan to pay off your debt will not be at the expense of the rest of your life—in fact, it cannot be done that way. If you set up a plan that involves renouncing all you enjoy, you will not stick to the plan. Because you will not have been spending any money, and when you do break your budget plan, you may well binge, putting yourself worse in debt than before you started. You will continue to eat, live, entertain, go to school, have lunch out, and so on. You will just be adding one more category to your expenses: debt repayment.

> ### Money Talks
>
> About 70 percent of students at four-year colleges have at least one credit card, and revolving debt on those cards averages more than $2,000.

Your payments may not be that much at the beginning; whatever you can afford is what you should pay. This is going to be a plan that works, one you can live with. Although it might be a modest beginning, creating such a plan is a significant moment in your financial life. It is the moment when you stop going into debt and start getting out.

Calculating the Plan

Get out a sheet of paper and write down every single creditor you owe money to on the left-hand side. Next to each name, list how much you owe them. Let's use Ryan as an example. Here are his outstanding debts:

Calculating Your Debt (Example)

Creditor	Amount Owed
Armata Visa	$5,000
Breunig Bank MasterCard	$1,000
Discover Card	$2,000
Dr. Bombay	$1,000
Mom	$2,500
Total:	$11,500

You then need to figure out what percentage each debt is of the entire amount. It's not that hard to do. First, add up your total debt. In Ryan's case, it is $11,500. To figure out each creditor's share of the whole debt, divide each creditor's amount by the entire debt. For example, the Armata Visa bill ($5,000) divided by the entire amount ($11,500) equals .43, or 43 percent. That bill is 43 percent of Ryan's total indebtedness.

The next thing to do is to add that figure onto your list, next to each creditor's name and the amount owed. In Ryan's case, the list would look like this:

Calculating Your Debt Percentages (Example)

Creditor	Amount Owed	Percentage
Armata Visa	$5,000	43%
Breunig Bank MasterCard	$1,000	9%
Discover Card	$2,000	17%
Dr. Bombay	$1,000	9%
Mom	$2,500	22%
Total:	$11,500	100%

This list tells you how much each creditor is going to get each and every month, depending upon how much you can afford to pay. How much can you afford to pay? If you have a budget, you know. If not, you still intuitively know how much you can afford to repay every month—$25, $50, or $200, whatever works.

Let's go back to Ryan and see how this process works. His budget will allow him to dedicate only $100 each month toward these bills. (We are not saying not to pay your bills if you can afford to pay them. This tool is for those bills that you have fallen behind on and/or feel overwhelmed by.) Each creditor will get its percentage of that $100 :

Debt Payment Calculations (Example)

Creditor	Amount Owed	Percentage	Repayment
Armata Visa	$5,000	43%	$43
Breunig Bank MasterCard	$1,000	9%	$9
Discover Card	$2,000	17%	$17
Dr. Bombay	$1,000	9%	$9
Mom	$2,500	22%	$22
Total:			$100

To figure out how much each creditor gets, multiply its percentage by the amount you can afford to pay (we promise there will be no more math after this!). Because Ryan can afford $100 a month and his mom gets 22 percent, he needs to multiply her percentage, .22, by $100: .22 × 100 = $22. If Ryan could afford $200 a month, Dr. Bombay would get 9 percent multiplied by 200: $18.

Ryan, like you, would then need to pay these amounts each and every month to his creditors. As it stands, Ryan will devote $100 to getting out of debt, with each creditor getting a percentage according to how much Ryan owes them.

This is where your commitment comes in. You must set aside that amount, whatever it is, every month and earmark it toward these debts. Each creditor will have to share whatever it is you can afford. The only way to get out of debt is to get out of debt. It is not easy. That is why you must be committed.

For various reasons, your plan may not exactly reflect how much you owe each creditor. One debt may have such high interest that it must be paid more, or another creditor may be bothering you so much that you just want to get rid of it as fast as possible. These adjustments are fine; the important thing is to create a plan that works, that you can live with, and that you are committed to.

Over Your Limit

If budgeting has failed for you in the past, it may be because you failed to plug the cash leaks. Although keeping track of rent and car payments is easy enough, your ATM card may be the dreaded culprit. It's easy to take out $20 or $40, forget to account for it, and wonder where $200 went at the end of the month.

For example, you may decide that the best course of action is to get rid of the credit card with the highest interest rate first and then worry about the others. We have no problem with that—in fact, it's smart. The important thing is to create a plan that you believe in and that works. Pick a plan, any plan. Once you do, the important thing is that you will be getting out of debt instead of going into debt.

Remember Me?

At this point, you may be thinking that Dr. Bombay won't take $9 a month. Maybe not, but maybe he will. Actually, some of your creditors might be very happy to hear your voice. Especially if you have been avoiding them and reneging on your responsibility to pay what you owe them. A phone call with a repayment plan, even a small repayment plan, can be seen as better than nothing.

Explain to each creditor on your list what you are doing. Tell the creditors …

♦ You are sorry for allowing this debt to get out of hand. If you express regret, you may find that the creditor will be far more willing to work with you.

♦ You have every intention of paying them back in full.

♦ Paying them back will, however, take some time. You owe a lot of people money, not just them.

- You have a plan of action to pay everyone back, and in it you will be treating each creditor equally. The creditor to whom you owe the most money will be paid the most. It is a fair plan.

- You understand that they want more money each month than you are proposing, but at this time, you are doing your best. In time, as the debts shrink, you hope to be able to pay more.

- You would like their cooperation. If they could stop adding interest, they would get paid sooner, and your job would be easier.

Two Cents _____

Creditors are people, too, and those customer service representatives have more authority than they let on. Customer relations experts say that customers who treat the person on the phone with respect have a far greater chance of getting what they want.

Sam had ignored his Gottshalk's Department Store bill for five months and owed them $1,100 when he finally created a plan that called for him to pay them $75 a month. Once he got up the nerve to call customer service, Sam explained his situation, apologized, and proposed his plan. Gottshalk's agreed to cut his interest rate from 11.9 percent to 7.9 percent.

This last part is the trickiest. Creditors don't have to agree to anything, certainly not a cessation or reduction of interest. But if you are honest with them and if they see that you are endeavoring to do the right thing, they just might agree. After all, the last thing they want to see is a default.

If they tell you they will not accept $9 a month, that they will sue, or will write off the debt and sell it to a collection agency, listen politely, and send them the money anyway. The odds are that they will cash the check, however unhappily.

Over Your Limit _____

Studies have shown that creditors are less likely to sue over debts under $1,000 and more likely to sue for debts over $5,000.

Credit card companies might not be so generous. They are usually very difficult to deal with and do not often negotiate. Yet, as with other creditors, an honest attempt on your part to settle your bill can go a long way. Do your best to get them to lower interest and finance charges, pay what you can afford to pay, and begin to make some headway. (Make sure to read Chapter 12 and Chapter 13.

There are downsides to this sort of plan. By consistently paying less than you owe there is a possibility that your creditors may report you as paying late every month. Or they may cancel your credit altogether. If this is of concern to you, you may want to pay those creditors whose credit you still want more and the others less, at least until they are paid off.

Keeping Good Records

As you go about restructuring your debt and paying off your bills, you need to keep good records. Good records will help you stay organized and ensure that you know what you are talking about when you deal with a creditor.

Buy a three-ring notebook that you can devote to your debt reduction plan. One section will be the list of creditors and your proposed repayment percentages that you created. Another section will keep track of communications between you and each creditor. The final section will tally your balances and amounts paid.

Keeping Track of Creditors

Designate a separate sheet of paper in your notebook for each creditor with its name and phone number at the top. Especially early in your debt reduction plan, you may be talking with your creditors a lot. As you do, you want to be able to keep track of what is said and agreed to, as shown in the following example.

Tracking Creditors (Example)

Dr. Bombay, 879-7972

Date	Content of discussion
9/27	Spoke with Darla in accounts receivable. Offered to pay $9 a month. She says she doubts it, but will speak with the doctor.
10/13	Called Darla again, left message to call back.
10/15	Darla called, says the doctor agreed, but wasn't happy. I told her I would send my first payment on the first of next month.

Have a separate sheet for each of your creditors. If a dispute ever arises, this information will give you plenty of ammunition. Even if a dispute does not arise, memories are short, and it helps to have the name of your contact person and what was last said. Although you can try and get these agreements in writing, many creditors refuse to do that. It never hurts to ask, though.

Keep a Tally of Your Payments

The final part of your notebook is a running tally of what you have paid, when you paid it, and what you still owe. Again, each creditor should have its own subsection. You may even want to put your monthly bills in their proper place in the notebook. You can even put each check in this section as it clears your account.

You can monitor payments and outstanding debt in various ways:

◆ You can do it by hand by subtracting your payment each month from your previous month's balance.

◆ You can use a spreadsheet. Spreadsheets are part of many computer systems; Microsoft Works, which is found on many PCs, has one built in.

◆ You can buy a computer program, such as Quicken, to help you. These programs have some cool charts and graphs that will let you see your debt shrinking in 3-D.

If you adopt this program and see it through, you should begin to see some dramatic results in a short period of time. Just as debt seems to have an almost mystical way of growing in the blink of an eye, so too does it have a way of shrinking when you begin to take action. As time goes by, and as your debts reduce, you will be able to devote even more money toward your debt-reduction plan, making it shrink all the faster. Before you know it, you will be out of debt.

> **Two Cents**
>
> Customer service representatives type the content of every conversation they have with a customer into their computer. This way, the next representative who deals with that customer knows what was said in the last conversation. If you ever make a deal over the phone, make sure the representative inputs it into the computer.

The Least You Need to Know

◆ You must make a commitment to repay every one of your debts.

◆ You need to create a repayment plan that you can live with.

◆ Each creditor should get its percentage of your debt repaid every month.

◆ Your creditors may be more willing to work with you than you realize.

◆ Keeping good records is essential.

Part  3
When Cutting Back Is Not Enough

This chapter is for special situations. We look at several types of debt; dealing with each can require special knowledge. From income tax to student loans to credit card debt, there are pitfalls that trap thousands of Americans every year. These are common problems, and they do have solutions.

If one of these chapters applies to you, please read it carefully. We've packed a lot of information into a few pages.

Chapter 10

Cleaning Up Your Credit

In This Chapter

- ◆ Understanding your credit report
- ◆ How the Fair Credit Reporting Act helps you
- ◆ Changing your credit report
- ◆ Credit repair scams

We don't have to tell you that you have a credit history; you are only too well aware of that. The good news is that your history can be changed. For instance, there may be mistakes on your credit report that negatively affect you—mistakes that can be removed from the report.

Even better is that sometimes, just sometimes, *accurate* negative items on your credit report can be removed as well. But before we let you in on this exciting little (or big) secret, let's first take a look at credit reports and credit scoring in general. Understanding how they work will help you understand how they can be changed.

Understanding Your Credit Report

Credit reports can be very confusing documents. Full of arcane language and indecipherable numbers, they seem almost intentionally designed to be perplexing, and maybe they are. Fear not, we are here to unravel their mystery.

Credit reports detail the following information:

- Which bills you pay on time

- Which bills you don't

- Credit for which you have applied

- Credit granted to you

- Credit denied you

- Every credit card you have had for the past seven years

- Bank loans repaid, or not

- Late payments

- Foreclosures

- *Judgment liens*

- Bankruptcies

- Criminal convictions

Check It Out

A **judgment lien** occurs after someone has sued you and won the lawsuit. Thereafter, that person can file a lien against your real estate, including your home. The lien has to be paid before you can ever sell the property. That lien is called a judgment lien.

For every account listed in your credit report, the following is itemized:

- The date the account was opened and closed

- The amount due

- The interest rate

- The monthly payment

- Date of the last payment

- Your high balance and the balance owed

- The payment history

Items on your credit report stay there for seven years, except for bankruptcies, which stay on for 10 years. Lenders (banks, credit cards, and so on) use this information to determine your credit-worthiness. If you have a history of late payments, getting credit is harder, and when you do get it, it is more expensive—meaning that you have to pay a higher interest rate.

Getting a Copy of Your Credit Report

There are three major credit reporting agencies (CRAs) in the United States:

Experian (formerly TRW)
P.O. Box 596
Pittsburgh, PA 15230
Toll Free (1-888-EXPERIAN)
www.Experian.com

Equifax
P.O. Box 740241
Atlanta, GA 30374
Toll Free (1-800-685-1111)
www.Equifax .com

Trans Union
Consumer Relations
1561 E. Orangethorpe Ave.
Fullerton, CA 92831
Toll Free (1-800-916-8800)
www.TransUnion.com

Two Cents

Do you qualify for a free credit report? Thanks to the Fair Credit Reporting Act (FCRA) you qualify for a free report if you …

◆ Are unemployed and intend to apply for em-ployment within 60 days.

◆ Are receiving public welfare assistance.

◆ Believe their consumer file contains inaccurate information about you due to fraud.

◆ Have been denied credit or insurance within the past 60 days.

Business credit reports can be obtained through Dun & Bradstreet:

Dun & Bradstreet
Business Information Reports
99 Church Street
New York, NY 10007
Toll Free (1-800-TRY-1DNB)
www.dnb.com

Because each agency may have different information about you—some accurate, and maybe some not—get a copy of all three companies' reports.

Credit reports usually cost about $10 each. You can write to each credit reporting agency and request a copy of your report; it will take a few weeks to get one back. Another, quicker, option is to hire a local credit reporting company to pull all three reports for you for a flat fee.

You can find local companies that sell credit reports by looking under "Credit Reports" in the Yellow Pages. One such company is Evergreen Credit Reporting, online at www.creditreporting.com or 1-888-762-4001.

Reading Your Credit Report

The following sample credit report helps demystify what you are looking at once you get yours.

A sample credit report.

(Equifax)

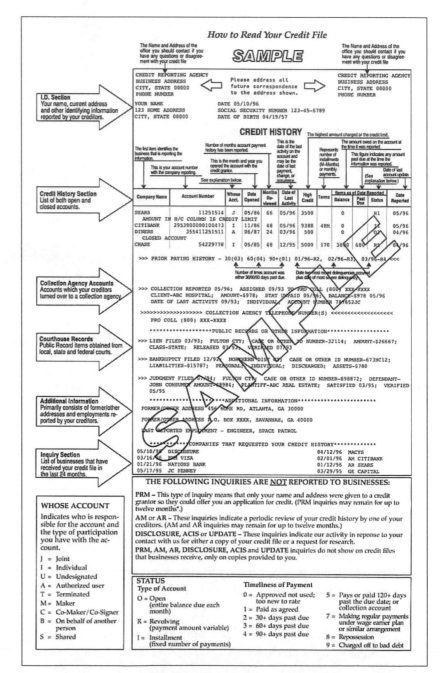

Your FICO Score

In addition to your credit report, creditors look at something called a *FICO score* to determine your credit-worthiness.

FICO credit scores range from 300 to 850, the higher the better. The average score is around 750.

Your FICO score is based upon many factors. Here is how FICO says the scores are derived:

◆ **Payment history (35%).** Late bills, collections, and bankruptcies can really hurt this part of your score. Also, recent problems are weighted worse than older problems.

◆ **Outstanding debt (30%).** Your debt-to-income ratio is critical. If you owe a lot, your FICO score goes down. This is one reason why, ironically enough, filing bankruptcy can sometimes help your credit score—you wipe out all of your debt.

◆ **Length of your credit history (15%).** It is good to have accounts that have been open for some time. However, and conversely, it may harm you to keep open accounts that you do not use.

◆ **Recent inquiries on your report (10%).** For some reason, the more credit inquiries you have, the worse your score.

◆ **Types of credit in use (10%).** Loans from finance companies reflect negatively on your credit, as do too many credit cards. Finance companies are outfits like Household Finance Corporation (HFC).

Check It Out

FICO scores are credit ratings based on your credit history. They are determined by a little-known California company called Fair, Isaac, & Company, hence FICO.

Two Cents

You can order your FICO score online from Equifax.com or from scorepower.com.

Although some credit reports list your FICO score, not all do. So in addition to getting your credit report, you may also need to order your FICO score; the two go hand-in-hand because your FICO score is a reflection of your credit-worthiness and is based upon your credit report. Again, the cost is around $10.

Armed with your credit report and your FICO score, you should be able to determine why you were turned down for that new credit card. It could be that you have multiple late payments, several *charge-offs*, too much debt, or a tax lien or two. Combined, these things show up on your credit report and lower your FICO score.

Is there anything you can do about it? You bet!

Check It Out _____

After a creditor has tried unsuccessfully to collect a debt, it will eventually conclude that the debt is uncollectable. When that happens, they **charge off** the debt, essentially admitting it will remain outstanding. Collection agencies buy charge-offs at steep discounts and try and collect on them.

Your Friend: The Fair Credit Reporting Act

The Fair Credit Reporting Act (FCRA) is a law intended to promote accuracy and fairness in the files of the credit bureaus. All too often, what is on people's credit reports is wrong. It may be obsolete, false, or inaccurate. The FCRA is your tool for making sure that your credit report is true and correct.

What is even more interesting is that it is sometimes possible to have accurate information taken off of your credit report *if* it cannot be verified. This is key: The FCRA gives consumers the right to challenge *anything* on their credit report. Most often inaccurate information is challenged, but that does not mean you cannot challenge accurate information.

Challenging Your Credit Report

Essentially, there are three types of challenges you can make.

1. **You can challenge inaccurate information.** Let's say that your Experian credit report states that your 1998 Toyota was repossessed. The only problem is, you have never owned a 1998 Toyota. You can write to Experian and explain the problem.

   Under the FCRA, Experian (or any CRA) has 30 days to verify the accuracy of the item after you dispute it. If it cannot verify the accuracy of the item, then by law *they must remove it from your credit report and it cannot reappear* unless it is later verified, which is quite rare.

2. **You can dispute obsolete items.** Let's say that the credit report states that in 1990, your Honda was repossessed. Even if that is true, the rule is that items can only be on your credit report for seven years. Anything older than that is obsolete and must be removed.

3. **You can dispute accurate items that cannot be verified.** Again, there is no law stating that you cannot challenge accurate items on your credit report. What the law says is that any challenge you make against any particular item must be verified by the CRA within 30 days or the item must be removed.

> **Over Your Limit**
>
> While most of your credit history, both good and bad alike, can only remain on your credit report for seven years, bankruptcies can stay on there for 10 years.

Do you see what a powerful tool the FRCA is? The burden is not on you, but on the credit reporting agency to prove that what they say is true about you actually is true. They are the ones who have to do the work and verify.

These rules exist because credit reports are rife with inaccuracies. When you consider that roughly 2 billion pieces of information are updated in consumer credit files *each month*, you can see why mistakes are made. It is estimated that at least 50 percent of all credit reports have inaccurate information. Because of this, the FCRA mandates that the CRA must verify the accuracy of any disputed item.

The Process

Follow these steps to challenge any item in your credit report.

1. **Get copies of all three of your credit reports.**

2. **Analyze the reports.** First, note anything that is more than seven years old. This includes ...

   ◆ Lawsuits, collection accounts, tax liens, criminal records (they may be reported indefinitely), late payments, or any other adverse information older than seven years.

   ◆ Bankruptcies older than 10 years from the date of the discharge.

   ◆ Credit inquiries older than two years.

It is equally important to look for incorrect information, because "incorrect" information can be such things as:

♦ Incomplete or inaccurate name, address, phone number, or Social Security number.

♦ Accounts that are not yours.

♦ Incomplete account numbers.

♦ Accounts that are yours that have inaccurate information, such as late payments that were not late.

♦ Open accounts listed as closed or vice versa.

♦ Bankruptcies that are not identified by their chapter number.

♦ Liens that are not yours.

Thus, for example, let's say that you had a credit card that was charged off, ending with the numbers 1234. Let's further assume that on your credit report they accurately listed the account and you as the account holder, but the account number was transposed and ends in 1243 on the report.

You have every right to challenge that entry. It is inaccurate. You need not tell the CRA what the correct account number is, merely say that the account ending in 1243 is not yours. They will not be able to verify it and it will come off of your credit report.

3. **Challenge the problems.** Write a letter to the CRAs explaining specifically what you are challenging and why. In fact, we say that you should challenge everything. We've included a sample letter to give you an idea of what to say when challenging your report.

   The important thing is to dispute the accuracy of whatever negative listing that appears on your report. You need not lie. Simply state that you dispute its accuracy if you have no other challenge, as in the challenge to the charge-off on the Capital One account in the sample letter. See if they can prove it's true.

4. **Send the letter via registered or certified mail.** You need proof that you sent the letter and when you sent it so that you can prove when the 30-day clock started to tick. Keep a copy of each such letter for your records.

5. **Wait.** They have 30 days to prove the accuracy of each disputed listing. If they can't do so in that time, then the item must come off your report.

Steve Strauss
SSN XXX-XX-XXXX
100 West Main Street
Hometown, CA 90000
DOB: 1/1/00

To whom it may concern:

I just received a copy of my credit report and saw several inaccurate items:

1. Citibank VISA Acct: xxxxx-xxxxx-xxxx-xxx:

You state that this account was paid 30 days late. I have never been late on this account.

2. Capital One MC Acct: xxxxx-xxxxx-xxxx-xxx:

You state that this account was charged off. I dispute the accuracy of this claim.

3. Joe's Hardware: I never had an account with this merchant.

In addition, you list three accounts that are more than seven years. Pursuant to the FCRA, all credit older than seven years must be removed from my report:

Sears Acct: xxxx-xxxx-xxxx-xxxx

Chase Visa Acct: xxxx-xxxx-xxxx-xxxx

Macy's Acct: xxxx-xxxx

Enclosed is a photocopy of my driver's license as proof of identity.

Very truly yours,

Steven D. Strauss

Remember that the key thing here is that if the CRA cannot verify information on your credit report, they must remove it. How might that work? Say that the credit agency that listed your charge-off has since gone out of business and so the CRA cannot verify the negative report that was filed on you five years ago. No verification equals a deleted entry. If they don't delete it, then you can do one of two things. First, you can sue them for violation of the FCRA. Second, you can report them to the Federal Trade Commission and your state attorney general.

In the end, even if you don't get the results you want, there is nothing stopping you from challenging the results again and again, making the CRA jump through all of these hoops again.

Money Talks

Some credit bureaus refuse to investigate or delete disputed "inquiries" (when a company—like an auto financer for example—pulls your credit report to analyze your creditworthiness). Instead, they tell people that inquiries are simply a "statement of fact." That's incorrect, and a costly mistake on their part.

The FCRA mandates that any and all disputed items must be investigated. If a CRA refuses to investigate an inquiry or other item, they are breaking the law. Pursuant to the FCRA, you can sue them for $1,000 for each failure to investigate.

If, after all of this, there are still items on your report that you don't agree with or otherwise have an explanation for, then the FCRA also gives you the right to add up to 100 words on your credit report giving your side of the facts about that debt. The CRA must give a copy of your statement to anyone who requests your report.

Two Cents

In the future, if you want to maintain a good credit rating, then ...

- ◆ Pay all bills on time.
- ◆ Pay down your credit cards and leave plenty of room on several cards.
- ◆ Keep some accounts open for a long time.
- ◆ Avoid finance companies.
- ◆ If you had a problem with a creditor some time ago, but have since resolved it, ask them to write a letter to the different CRAs, requesting that the item be removed from your report.

When Worlds Collide

If you are having a problem with a creditor and suspect that it is acting in violation of the FCRA, then you have every right to report the creditor to the proper authorities.

Your state attorney general's office would be the first place to go. Beyond that, it depends upon the creditor. The following table lists the appropriate agencies to contact.

Where to Send Your Complaint

For Questions or Problems Concerning	Contact
CRAs, general creditors, and others not listed below	Federal Trade Commission Consumer Response Center—FCRA Washington, D.C. 20580 202-326-3761
National banks or foreign banks (where the word "National" or "N.A." appear in or after bank's name)	Office of the Comptroller of the Currency Compliance Management Washington, D.C. 20219 1-800-613-6743
Federal Reserve System member banks	Federal Reserve Board Division of Consumer & Community Affairs Washington, D.C. 20551 202-452-3693
State chartered banks that are not part of the Federal Reserve System	FDIC Compliance & Consumer Affairs Washington, D.C. 20429 1-800-934-FDIC
Savings and Loans	Office of Thrift Supervision Consumer Programs Washington, D.C. 20552 1-800-842-6929
Credit Unions	National Credit Union Administration 1775 Duke Street Alexandria, VA 22314 703-518-6360
Air, surface, or rail common carriers	Department of Transportation Office of Financial Management Washington, D.C. 20590 202-366-1306

Beware of "Credit-Fixing" Scams

Challenging your credit report is legal, but creating a brand-new report is not. Despite that fact, a new breed of scam artists claims to be able to create "a brand-new credit file in 30 days." Do not be misled by these statements. These firms are trying to turn credit-challenged consumers into lawbreakers.

Firms such as these sell instructions telling consumers how they can substitute federally issued, nine-digit employee identification numbers or taxpayer identification numbers for their Social Security numbers and then illegally use the new numbers to build new credit profiles. Ads for these scams frequently claim that the practice, known as *file segregation*, is legal. However, using a false identification number to apply for credit is a felony. We repeat: *This is a crime.*

Money Talks

Imagine that you had a computer program that automatically spat out a letter that challenged every item on all three of your credit reports every month. How long do you think it might take to clear up much of your credit report?

If you said a year, you would be just about right, and yes, such a computer system exists, it works, and it's legal. One of your authors (Steve) has seen it in action. While there are many credit repair scams out there (see below), it turns out that there are also some agencies that actually can clean up your credit. So do your homework. (If you would like to know more, feel free to contact Steve at sstrauss@mrallbiz.com.)

Also be wary of illegal scams that involve using a different first or last name to apply for a driver's license or state ID card. People are then taught to change their Social Security number by substituting the first three numbers (or state code) with those of another state. This, too, is fraudulent.

Although it is understandable that you may want a new credit file, exercise extreme caution when you hear such claims. If it sounds too good to be true, it is.

The Least You Need to Know

◆ You need to know how to read a credit report before you can challenge one.

◆ The Fair Credit Reporting Act is your friend—use it.

◆ Changing your credit report is indeed possible.

◆ Beware of credit repair scams.

11

Refinancing Your Home

In This Chapter

- ◆ Knowing when to refinance
- ◆ A risky proposition
- ◆ Types of refinancing
- ◆ Counting the cost
- ◆ Helpful hints

Sometimes, no matter how much fat you trim from your budget, you still don't have enough money to get out of debt. At that point, other measures are needed. Good. We hope you see that there are many different ways to get out of debt and that the best method of all is a combination of different ideas that work for you.

For instance, your plan may include some new money values, a tighter budget, and some negotiated settlements with creditors (see Chapter 13). Or it could be that changing some bad habits and working things out with the IRS suits your situation. Another tool to add to your debt-reduction arsenal is a refinanced home loan. A fine option, it must be used cautiously.

When Refinancing Makes Sense

There are basically five situations in which refinancing seems attractive.

1. **You can lower your interest rate for "no cost."** If you have a fixed-rate loan and can refinance at "no cost" into a similar term loan at a lower rate, you should refinance.

2. **Your adjustable-rate mortgage is about to go up.** If you have an *ARM* that is about to increase, you may want to refinance with a *fixed-rate loan.*

3. **You have an ARM, and your nerves can't take it any more.** ARMs are scary because your rate can go up at almost any time. If you want some more certainty and budget control, a fixed-rate refinance is the way to go.

4. **You have a balloon payment loan.** A large lump-sum payment can wreak havoc on your finances. Trading it in for a more conventional loan makes sense.

Check It Out _____

Know your lingo: An **adjustable-rate mortgage** (ARM) is a loan that goes up and down in conjunction with interest rates in general. A **fixed-rate loan** is a loan that has a set interest rate for the duration of the loan, no matter what interest rates in general are doing. A **balloon-payment loan** is a loan with a large lump-sum payment due at the end of the loan.

5. **You need cash.** The fifth situation in which refinancing seems attractive is when you need some extra cash and you want to refinance the house in order to pull out some money. This proposition is inherently dangerous, and we do not recommend it. However, if you have plenty of equity in the house and are in a severe debt crisis, refinancing may be an advisable approach to solving your problem. Read on.

The first four situations make sense because you will likely be saving money, but the last option is inherently dangerous. Let's look at each situation a bit more closely and show you why you may want to refinance.

"The Lowest Rates We've Seen in Years!"

There are three main factors to look at when determining the costs and benefits of refinancing.

1. What will be the difference between the present rate and the new rate? An old rule of thumb was that if you could lower your interest rate by 2 percent, refinancing was worth it. Anything less than that would have been eaten up in costs and fees. Today, there are many more loan options, so the old rules do not apply. If you can lower your interest rate, you are well on your way to making a good decision.

2. What are the total costs associated with the refinance transaction? The costs of refinancing have decreased greatly in the past several years. With no-point loan options, for example, borrowers can save thousands of dollars up front. Your mortgage lender or broker should give you a specific breakdown of all closing costs so that you will be able to calculate your savings exactly.

3. How comfortable are you with possible payment changes over the life of your mortgage loan? If you are not saving money, there is no point in refinancing.

Risky Business

Refinanced home loans can take many forms: a refinanced first mortgage, a second mortgage, and even a third mortgage. Refinancing to lower your interest rate or to get a loan that you are more comfortable with makes sense to us. Refinancing to pull equity out of your house (so-called equity loans) should be considered with caution.

It is understandable why you would want to use your home equity to help you get out of debt. Home equity has replaced the savings account for many Americans. Instead of dipping into their savings when times get tough, they take out a home equity loan.

To understand why this option looks better than it is, you must first understand the difference between secured and unsecured debts. A secured debt is one that is tied to some sort of collateral. For example, a bank would be happy to loan you the $25,000 you need to buy a new car, as long as it holds title to the car. If you do not pay the bank back, it will repossess the car. The car, which is the collateral, secures the loan.

With an unsecured debt, there is no collateral protecting the creditor. A credit card is an example of an unsecured loan. When you get a new Visa card, the card issuer does not ask you to pledge any property as collateral to secure the debt you will incur using the card. You simply promise to pay back the debt. That debt is unsecured. The majority of debts people have, such as credit cards, medical bills, and department store bills, are unsecured debts.

CAUTION

Over Your Limit

Don't get greedy. Once you decide to refinance your house, you may be tempted to wait for rates to get to their "lowest." Rates go up and down every day, and waiting a day too long to refinance a loan has burned many a homeowner. Are you going to hit the bottom? Probably not. Are you going to save money? Yes. If you want to gamble, go to Las Vegas. It's a heck of a lot more fun.

Money Talks

Ted Turner owns the most real estate in America—approximately 1,700,000 acres. He owns land in New Mexico, Montana, Nebraska, Florida, Georgia, and South Carolina. Among his holdings are 1.15 million acres in New Mexico, amounting to 1.5 percent of the state. Included in his holdings in New Mexico, according to *Forbes* magazine, is the 578,000-acre Vermejo Park Ranch, purchased for $80 million. The oil rights to the land sold for an estimated $81 million over several years (and he keeps the land).

A home equity consolidation loan can be very risky because you are trading unsecured debt for secured debt. When you stop paying an unsecured debt, all a creditor can do is write demand letters, make a lot of phone calls, and possibly sue you. Although this activity may prove to be annoying, it certainly is not devastating.

Over Your Limit

Many equity lenders say that they can loan you up to 125 percent of the equity in your house, that it is easy to apply, and that you can be approved in a matter of days. Why are they so anxious to loan you money? Because they know they cannot lose. You will repay the loan either voluntarily or involuntarily through the sale of your home.

Two Cents

One advantage of refinancing your house to pay off your credit cards is that you will probably be able to take a home mortgage deduction on your income tax for the interest paid on the mortgage (each case is different). You cannot deduct interest paid on credit cards.

But failure to pay back a secured debt can be devastating. When you stop paying a secured debt, not only do you get the same letters and threats, but, far worse, you also lose the collateral that secures the debt. If you fail to stay current with that second mortgage you took out last year to pay off your credit cards, your lender can foreclose and sell your home out from underneath you. That is far worse than getting sued by a credit card company.

This is exactly what happened to Sandy. She was having a very difficult time repaying the $40,000 she owed on her eight different credit cards. Sandy decided to take out a second mortgage on her house at 8 percent interest, which was substantially less than the interest rate on her credit cards, and pay off all of her debts.

Unfortunately, two years later, she lost her job, was unable to continue to pay both mortgages, and lost her home in a foreclosure sale. Had Sandy not swapped her credit card debt for a second mortgage on her house, she would not have lost her home.

Had she not taken out the second mortgage to pay off her debts, Sandy probably would have had about $50,000 in credit card debt when she lost her job. At that point, she could have stopped paying the credit cards and earmarked any money she did make to pay her existing mortgage. Although she undoubtedly would have received many nasty phone calls from her credit card companies, an unsecured creditor cannot foreclose on a house like a secured lender can. Sandy would have kept her home.

If you are refinancing to pull money out of your house, you'd better be very careful. You need to be pretty darn sure that you will be able to pay the new secured debt. On the other hand, if you are refinancing in order to reduce your interest rate and thereby make your monthly budget work better, go right ahead; we're with you.

Types of Loans

It used to be that a lender would not lend more than 80 percent of the value of a property. Say Maria owned a $100,000 home that had a $70,000 first mortgage. In the old days, Maria would have been able to qualify to borrow only $10,000 (80 percent of 100,000 is 80,000, minus 70,000 is 10,000). It is a much different world today.

A New World Order

Over the past few years, the highly competitive nature of home equity lending has caused lenders to offer an increased number of programs to consumers. In addition to the usual rate competition, lenders continued to increase the maximum amount they would loan on a property. Programs have leaped from 80 percent to 90 percent to 100 percent, and lately they have topped out at a whopping 125 percent.

What that means is that today, Maria could not only borrow the entire amount of the equity in her property ($30,000), but she could borrow up to 125 percent of the value of her home. Unbelievable as it may sound, Maria could obtain a loan for $55,000 in addition to the existing first mortgage. Borrowing this much is a risky proposition if she cannot afford the monthly mortgage payments.

> **Money Talks**
>
> Lenders look at a borrower's credit score when determining whether to give the loan. The lower the score is, the higher the interest rates are. Components of a credit score include good credit, the ability to handle debt, and adequate, documented monthly cash flow.

Not only are loans more flexible, but credit standards have also been relaxed to a certain extent. Now borrowers who do not meet normal credit requirements will not be rejected automatically, but they probably will be offered a different loan at a higher rate.

Equity Lines of Credit

The typical home equity credit line is different than an equity loan. An equity loan is a lump-sum loan secured by the house. An equity *line of credit* is a revolving line of credit. A borrower is approved for a specific amount of credit, which will become the maximum amount that can be borrowed under the plan. Lenders usually require the line to be at least $5,000, but total credit lines can range up to $500,000.

> **Check It Out**
>
> A **line of credit** is an open account at a bank that the borrower can use at any time. He can take out as much or as little money as necessary.

Once the home equity line is in place, a borrower can borrow up to the credit limit at any time. Many plans require a minimum draw against the line of between $250 and $500. The borrower is usually required to repay at least the minimum interest due each month for the first 10 years. The interest rate on home equity lines is variable, is usually based on the prime rate, and is capped at a maximum that ranges from 15 to 20 percent.

Qualifying for a New Loan

How does a mortgage lender decide to approve or deny an application? Basically, there are three fundamental areas that a mortgage underwriter looks at when making his decisions. Those areas are commonly referred to as the three Cs of refinancing underwriting. They are credit, character, and collateral.

> **Money Talks**
>
> In a recent survey, the largest real estate lender in the country was Lehman Brothers out of New York, lending $10 billion in a single year. Lehman Brothers was followed closely by San Francisco-based Nomura Capital with $9.4 billion loaned; Wells Fargo Bank came in third with 9 billion dollars in loans.

- ◆ **Credit.** The first C, credit, refers to qualifying for the mortgage payment based on your monthly income. The monthly housing expense (principal and interest, plus one-twelfth of the annual taxes and insurance) cannot exceed a certain percentage of your income, usually 28 percent, although lenders offering mortgages at 125 percent of the value of the property are more lenient.

◆ **Character.** This area has to do with how faithful applicants are in making their credit payments on time. It is the most crucial indicator, because if someone has paid credit cards, car payments, and a previous mortgage on time, he will be more likely to pay his new mortgage on time as well.

◆ **Collateral.** Collateral refers to the home being refinanced. An appraisal may be done to ensure that the house is worth the amount being loaned. An independent appraiser uses recent sales of comparable homes in the area to determine whether your price is similar.

How Much Will This Cost?

Interest rates for home loans are based on a number of factors. The most important factor is the total loan-to-value that the loan or equity line will create. The higher the equity line (80 percent, 90 percent, 100 percent, and 125 percent), the more the loan will cost.

The total loan size also determines the interest rate for many lenders. A $7,500 home equity loan may carry a rate of 9.75 percent, but a $100,000 loan may be charged only 8.5 percent. Some programs also carry introductory teaser rates for the first three or six months, often at 6 percent or less.

With an equity line of credit, an important factor is whether the borrower will be taking out funds when the credit line is established and whether the borrower is transferring or consolidating other debt balances. One New York lender, for example, offers a home equity rate at the prime rate for the life of the loan if a borrower is transferring at least $40,000 from another home equity line. Usually, this lender charges the prime rate plus 1 percent for the same loan.

The last factor affecting rates is based on whether the borrower or the lender will pay closing costs. Some lenders give borrowers the option of a lower rate if they pay closing costs, which include appraisal, attorney, recording, and other fees that, usually, are under $1,000.

Over Your Limit

Don't say you were not warned. One leading lender even has this caveat on its Web page: "Simply because lenders are lending furiously to anyone who will borrow, consumers should be extremely wary of not getting in over their heads with home equity debt. Home equity loans of any type should never be used for day-to-day expenses."

Other lenders tie closing costs to the total loan amount. If the lender knows the borrower will take out $25,000, for example, then the lender will not mind paying the closing costs because it will make back the costs with interest payments within a few months.

You should pay the closing costs if doing so will mean a lower rate of interest. Throughout this book, we have emphasized the need for long-term thinking. People primarily go into debt as a result of short-term thinking. Refinancing a home loan is a perfect example of this.

A debtor thinks short-term, "I need the money, so paying closing costs is a bad idea." A saver thinks long-term, "I want a lower interest rate more than I need an extra $1,000 right now, so paying closing costs is not so painful." The saver knows that paying 7 percent instead of 8 percent on a $40,000 loan over 30 years, even if it means paying $1,000 in closing costs, would save him a lot of money over the life of the loan. Debtors never prosper.

Winning at Refinancing

When looking to refinance your house, you need to know about a few things that can help you in this process. The first thing is to determine whether you would prefer to deal with a *lender* or a *broker*.

Check It Out

A **lender** is the company that makes the loan to you (Citibank gives you a Citibank loan, for example). You can deal directly with a lender or you can deal with a **broker**. For a fee, a broker will shop you around to different lenders, trying to find you the best deal.

Over Your Limit

Brokers may not issue a rate lock-in agreement themselves. They may only transmit a lender's lock-in offer to an applicant.

Lender or Broker?

One of the advantages of applying for a loan with a lender is that you will deal directly with the entity (person or company) that will make the decision on whether to approve your loan application. This direct contact offers less opportunity for miscommunication to occur during the application process. Brokers, in contrast, are unable to make credit decisions or issue mortgage commitments.

Nevertheless, you may find that a broker can provide you with more choices of loan products than any direct lender. If you have bad credit, brokers may be better because they can shop difficult applications to a variety of direct lenders.

Although there are no fixed rules to determine whether you should choose a direct lender or broker, you should know, when submitting your application, which type of mortgage origination organization you've selected.

Lock It In

It is also important to find out whether you are getting a *lock-in agreement*. A lock-in agreement is a lender's agreement to make a loan at a particular rate, with or without certain points, provided that the loan is closed by a specified date.

A lock-in agreement can hurt you or it can help you. When interest rates are rising, a lock-in agreement protects your lower rate while the loan is being processed, but in an environment where interest rates are falling, a lock-in may prevent you from obtaining the lowest possible mortgage rate.

A decision on whether a lock-in may be advisable will depend on whether you think interest rates will rise, fall, or remain steady during the time it will take to process your application. You'll also need to consider that some lenders may require a fee for such a lock-in agreement, which can often be as high as one *point*.

Beware of short lock-in periods. Ask about the average time it takes to process an application, and do not accept a lock-in period that fails to provide a reasonable cushion of time for you to receive a decision. Do not accept an oral lock-in agreement. Always ask for the lock-in agreement in writing so that it will be enforceable.

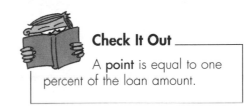

Check It Out

A **point** is equal to one percent of the loan amount.

Keep in mind that lenders do not need to comply with the terms of the lock-in agreement if the information they request is not provided promptly. If, after a lock-in is made, an applicant fails to comply with all of the conditions contained in a loan commitment, or if any information given in the application proves to be significantly inaccurate, a lock-in agreement will be invalid.

Be sure to meet all of your obligations. Be sure that your application contains detailed and accurate information. Lenders may find errors while processing your application and inaccuracies will needlessly delay the process. Provide all the additional information requested by a lender and retain documentation. If you are unclear about what a lender needs, request a clarification. Do not make assumptions.

Final Thoughts

When applying for a new mortgage, you can help your loan officer by supplying as much information as possible at the time of application. Information such as W-2 forms for the last two years, a recent paycheck stub, and your last two monthly checking and savings account statements will help move your mortgage application through the processing system smoothly and quickly.

From the beginning of the process, be honest about any credit problems you have had in the past. Doing so gives the loan officer the opportunity to confront any negative credit history head-on. Most credit problems can be easily explained.

The Least You Need to Know

♦ Refinancing makes the most sense when it means you will lower your monthly mortgage payments.

♦ Exchanging unsecured debt for secured debt must be done judiciously.

♦ Many types of loans are available today.

♦ Be a saver, not a debtor. Think long-term.

Chapter 12

Taming the Credit Card Goliath

In This Chapter

- ◆ Avoid the credit card trap
- ◆ Get better terms
- ◆ Double your grace period
- ◆ Challenge mistakes
- ◆ Use credit cards correctly

Credit card debt is probably the most common debt issue that people face today. It's a terrible cycle. The cards are easy to use, but before you know it, the interest rate makes them difficult to pay off. In this chapter, we will show you some tactics that you can use to drastically reduce both your overall credit card indebtedness and your interest rates.

Credit Quicksand

Throughout this book we have consistently warned you against falling for the credit card trap. You know what that is. Charging, taking cash advances, getting stuck with a huge bill, paying a big interest payment every month, and thereby ensuring that the balance is never paid off. It's a trap because you are caught in a predicament that is difficult to get out of.

There are two ways to fall for the credit card trap. The first is to not understand or care about what you agreed to when you took out the card and thus get socked with needless fees. The second is to fall for the minimum payment ploy.

Read the Fine Print

It's amazing how many people don't know the terms of their credit card agreements. All they know is that it is difficult to pay off the cards. Because one way to pay them off is to make more money, here's an idea: Do like the credit card companies do. Issue a credit card, make unrealistic promises that you can break, charge interest rates that would make a loan shark blanche, issue fees for the slightest infraction, sit back, and wait for the dough to roll in. That situation is in fact what many people have agreed to.

Credit card companies have a lot of ways to make money. The smart consumer will be wary of them:

> **Over Your Limit**
>
> If you applied for a credit card in your name alone, the responsibility to pay for charges on that card is yours. Even if you had another card issued to a spouse later on, if that person's name is not on the application contract, that debt is yours alone. Conversely, if you co-signed for someone but never used the card, you are equally responsible for the debt on that card.

- **Exorbitant interest rates.** The Federal Reserve lends money to banks at around 5 percent interest. Banks loan money for mortgages at around 6 percent and to commercial customers at around 8 percent. The average credit card interest rate is 17 percent.

- **Diminishing grace periods.** The grace period is the time you have to pay the money back without paying interest. It is usually between 10 and 30 days, although some cards have eliminated it altogether.

- **Cash advance thievery.** To get a cash advance on a credit card, you usually pay a transaction fee of around 3 percent per advance, and there is no grace period. Interest is charged from the moment the money lands in your hands.

♦ **Disingenuous offers.** Credit card issuers will offer a card "as low as 8.9 percent" and then send you one at 15.9 percent. Or they send you the card at the advertised rate, but don't clearly mention that the rate will triple in three months.

♦ **Fees, fees, and more fees.** Late fees of $42 on a card with a $50 balance seem to be legal only in the world of credit cards.

You fall into their trap if you fail to see or just don't care about what they are doing to you. All of these tricks can be avoided if you are educated and know what you are doing. After you read this book, you will be!

The Worst Trap of All

The amount of interest you pay each month is based upon the interest rate you have agreed to pay and your remaining balance. Most card issuers have a minimum payment, which is 2 percent of the balance or $15, whichever is greater (if only $15 were greater!).

Many people get their bill, look at the minimum amount due, and pay that amount. *This is the absolutely biggest mistake you can make with credit cards.* Minimum payments can stretch your payments on, ad nauseum, and guarantee that you will pay for what you bought many times over.

Say that you have a card with a $7,000 balance and an interest rate of 17 percent. How long do you think it will take you to pay off that balance paying a minimum payment of 2 percent? Three years? Five years?

Let's do some simple math. A monthly interest payment of 17 percent (your interest rate) on $7,000 is $104. Adding that to your balance means that you will have a new balance in month two of $7,104. Your minimum payment is 2 percent of that amount, which is $142. So if you just paid the minimum, your balance the next month would start at $6,962. Thus, by paying the minimum payment of $142, you knocked a whopping $38 off of your original balance.

If you followed this minimum-payment course of action, it would take (get ready for this) over 40 years to pay off the entire card! Don't worry; it gets worse. You would also end up paying almost $14,000 on your $7,000 balance. And you wonder why you are in debt?

CAUTION

Over Your Limit

The Consumer Federation of America reports that 60 percent of all households now carry credit card debt. The average debt is $7,000, and those families pay $1,000 a year in interest alone.

There Has to Be a Better Way

As you can see, the cost of paying the minimum payment on your credit cards is high indeed. To reduce your credit card debt, then, you must begin to pay more than the minimum amount on your cards.

The results of doing so can be impressive. In the preceding $7,000 example, the 2 percent minimum payment amount goes down every month as the principle decreases. However, if you keep paying the original minimum payment of $142 instead of the new, lower minimum, you will decrease the time it takes to reduce your credit card debt from 40 years to just about 5 years.

The key then to the first way to reduce credit card debt is to pay more than the minimum payment due, as much more as you can afford. Use the information in the chapters on budgeting to help you figure out how much you can pay. If you could increase the payment from $142 to $242, that $7,000 debt would be repaid in just less than three years. (Unless you fall for the seduction of getting more cards once your balance starts to decrease!) Another way to accomplish the same goal is to make 13 payments a year instead of 12.

If you are able to cut back on some other expenses and pay more on your credit card debt, you can get out of debt before you know it. Although paying more than the minimum is just one way to free yourself from the credit card trap, it is probably the most important.

The Balance Transfer Dance

One of the easiest, and best, methods of lowering both your monthly credit cards payments as well as your overall credit card indebtedness is to transfer the balance on your cards with a high interest rate to a card or cards with a much lower rate. The interest rate on your credit card is the biggest factor in how much you will have to repay.

The Cost of High Interest Rates

It is important to understand just how insidious these incredibly high interest rates are to your economic health. Let's say that you have five cards on which you owe about $2,000 each and that have an average interest rate of 16.9 percent. Between interest payments and fees, your total yearly cost for these cards would be about $2,400. This amount is not what you charged, your principal; it is just what you would be charged to borrow $10,000 from your credit cards.

If your interest rate were, say, 8.9 percent, your annual cost would be about $1,400; you would be saving roughly $1,000. If you had a card with something like a 5.9 percent rate, your annual savings would be about $1,300. Multiply this amount by each of your cards, and you will begin to see some real savings.

Negotiate Like a Pro

Where can you find cards with low interest rates? We suggest that you begin with the cards that you already have. Call your existing card issuers and ask for a lower rate:

- Tell them that you are a loyal, existing customer and that you therefore deserve a lower interest rate.

- Find out what your existing card issuer offers as an introductory rate and go up from there: "You offer new customers 5.9 percent; I am paying 17.9 percent, and I have been with you for six years. I think 7.9 percent is a good idea if you want to keep my business."

- Explain that if they agree to a lower rate and increase your credit limit, you will transfer your other balances onto their cards. This negotiation then becomes a win-win situation; you get a lower interest rate, and the credit card issuers get to make more money off of the higher balance.

- Finally, tell them that if they cannot agree to a new, lower interest rate, another card has offered you an incredible introductory rate and that you will be transferring your balance from this card to the new card.

Asking for more than you want is a basic tenet of any good negotiator, so ask for a rate lower than what you hope to get. If you want to get all of your debts onto one card with a 7.9 percent interest rate, ask for 5.9 percent to begin with. If this tactic does not work, then we suggest that you find a new card with a lower interest rate that really wants your business.

Two Cents

One thing creditors look negatively upon when reviewing a credit report is *potential* credit, that is, accounts that are open. Close all accounts that you are not using and don't plan to use.

Introductory Rates Are Best

Locate a card that you do not yet have that offers a low introductory rate. When you get the new card (need we say), do not charge with it. Transfer your high balances onto it and use its introductory rate to your advantage.

Check It Out

A **teaser rate** is an introductory interest rate offered by a credit card issuer to get your business. Some teaser rates are indeed very good, but you must be sure to check the terms and conditions. If the rate sounds too good to be true, it just may be.

Over Your Limit

Before applying for a new card, check to see whether there will be any charges for balance transfers. If so, find another card. You should also double-check the limit on the card and be sure not to transfer more than that amount onto the card. It is also important to understand what the annual fees will be.

What you have to be especially conscious of is how long the rate is good for; this fact is often buried in the fine print. Sometimes these *teaser rates* can last up to a year; other cards may only offer them for three months. Make sure that when the card comes in the mail, the rate you will be paying is the one you agreed to.

Azriela was offered a card once with a great rate and a $4,000 limit. She accepted the offer, got the card, and transferred $4,000 from a different card with a higher rate onto this new card. She was shocked when the transfer check bounced. It turned out that the new card charged a $4 transfer fee, so she was over her limit by $4. The card issuer assessed her a $25 bounced-check fee to boot!

About a month before the introductory rate is set to expire, call up the company and see whether they will extend it another six months. Many will. If not, plenty more cards out there offer introductory rates that you can use. A few phone calls and a couple of simple forms to fill out can save you thousands of dollars a year.

Fees, Fi, Foe, Fum

If you do what we tell you to in this chapter, the big, bad giant of a credit card company can be tamed. One way credit card issuers get away with murder is with their beloved fees. Card issuers make a lot of money off of late fees, over-the-limit fees, and the like. Let's say that you are late one time or that your husband used the card without telling you, thereby putting you over your limit. Can you do anything about it? Absolutely.

Pick up the phone and complain. The discussion will be much like the one when you requested a lower interest rate. Tell the credit card issuer …

◆ You are a loyal customer and have been for some time.

◆ The fee is outrageous, and you won't pay it.

◆ You will transfer your balance elsewhere and cancel your account if it does not reverse the charge.

Especially if you have no consistent history of being charged fees, this tactic should work when you need it.

A Real Grace Period

Understanding what the *grace period* is and how it works can help you stay out of debt. Remember that a grace period is only available on cards with a zero balance. Using a card with a zero balance and timing your purchase correctly can mean that you will never have to pay interest again on any major purchase; in effect, the credit card company will be loaning you money interest-free if you play the game correctly.

Say that you want to buy a new washer and dryer. You are billed on the first of the month, and your payment is due on the 25th. That means that you have 25 days to repay the debt without getting charged interest. It is quite possible, however, to effectively double that interest-free time.

If you buy the washer and dryer on the second of the month, you won't even receive a bill until the first of the following month. You then won't be charged interest until the 25th of that month. Thus, just by timing your purchase correctly, you can avoid all interest payments for the washer and dryer and still have almost two months to pay it off (or transfer the balance to another card if absolutely necessary).

> **Over Your Limit**
>
> The **grace period** is the amount of time from the billing date to the due date that is interest-free. Most cards only give you a grace period if you do not carry forward a balance.

When Disputes Arise

Credit card billing errors do occur, but they can easily be resolved if you know the law. In 1975, Congress passed the Fair Credit Billing Act (FCBA) to help consumers challenge disputes over credit card bills.

Pursuant to the FCBA, if you ever see a mistake on your credit card statement, you need to write the company a letter explaining the problem within 60 days after your receipt of the bill. They then have 30 days to respond to you and begin to investigate the matter. As they investigate, they cannot harm your credit rating or take any action against you.

In your letter, provide the following information:

◆ Name

◆ Address

◆ Account number

◆ Reason for the dispute and why you think there is a mistake

Two Cents

If a creditor fails to follow the FCBA procedure, you can sue it in small claims court and win up to $1,000.

The creditor must then investigate the matter. If an error is found, the FCBA mandates that the creditor write to you, explain the corrections it will make to your account, and remove all finance charges and late fees. Similarly, if they conclude there was no mistake, you must be told this in writing, too, and be given an explanation.

Bankruptcy

A final way to get out of credit card debt is to file Chapter 7 bankruptcy. Chapter 7 completely wipes out unsecured debts such as credit cards. You could owe $100,000 on your credit cards and have that entire amount wiped clean. Almost all consumers who have filed Chapter 7 in the past few years have done so to get rid of excess credit card debt.

But be forewarned: Credit card issuers have been spending a lot of money recently lobbying Congress to make credit card debt virtually impossible to wipe out in bankruptcy. Although it was still possible to do so when this book was published, the laws could easily change.

In 1998, Congress passed a bill radically restructuring bankruptcy laws, but it was never signed by President Clinton and thus never became law. There were allegations that the law was an attempt by credit card companies to prevent consumers like you from declaring bankruptcy.

The Smart Way to Use Credit Cards

You can do several things to make sure that you do not fall for the "buy now, pay later" ruse again. The most important is to begin to use credit cards properly, to use them as the financially literate do.

These suggested proper uses of credit cards won't get you further into debt:

- **Pay the bill in full every month.** This is the first rule for a reason. Every time you allow your balance to carry forward to another month, you are giving your credit card issuers more of your hard-earned money. If you can't afford to pay for the charge, then you shouldn't be charging it.

- **Borrow when it costs you nothing.** As we said earlier, charging something at the right time of the month allows you to go almost two months without paying any interest.

- **Budget for an emergency.** As we discussed in earlier chapters, you should have some money set aside for a rainy day. Some of that money ($3,000 is a good amount) should be earmarked for credit card emergencies. Credit cards come in most handy in a crisis. If you need a tow truck or have to go on a sudden trip, charging it makes a lot of sense. Just remember to use your emergency stash to pay off the card when the bill comes and then replenish your emergency fund.

- **Budget for pleasure.** Credit cards are a necessity when you travel for fun. Use them all you want, but be sure that you won't be breaking the first rule by doing so.

- **Toss solicitations in the trash.** Throw away, unopened, all credit card offers you are receiving in the mail. You don't need more credit.

- **Cut up cards you are no longer using and cancel the accounts.**

Credit cards are great. They are easy to use and allow you the opportunity to buy and do things you would otherwise normally not be able to. In fact, they are too easy to use. That is how you fell into the trap in the first place, and it is a difficult trap to get out of. It will take time and effort on your part.

CAUTION

Over Your Limit

The Consumer Federation of America reports that credit card solicitations have doubled in the past five years.

The Least You Need to Know

- Don't make getting out of the credit card trap harder by continuing to do what you have always done.

- Get better terms, either from your existing cards or from a new one.

- When all else fails, complain.

- The FCBA allows you to dispute possible mistakes on your bill.

Chapter 3

Talking to the Lion: Dealing with Creditors

In This Chapter

- ◆ Cutting a deal
- ◆ Understanding your legal rights
- ◆ Getting creditors to leave you alone
- ◆ Cleaning up your credit report
- ◆ Avoiding scams

What we want to do in this chapter is show you some tactics you can utilize when it is just not possible to pay the full amount you owe. At that point, your creditors will be harassing and threatening you. Here, we show you how to force creditors to leave you alone and how to negotiate a reduced payoff. Fear not. Relief is in sight. Creditors can be tamed, if you know what to do.

Dealing with the Original Creditor

The first thing to ask yourself is whether you are dealing with the original creditor or a collection agency. As a general rule, original creditors are not nearly as difficult to deal with as collection agencies.

Who you are dealing with usually depends on how late you are with your bill. After a debt is more than say, six months old, the original creditor will probably sell it at a discount or give a percentage of any recovery to a collection agency.

The Payment Plan

Your chances of settling your problem reasonably and with a modicum of dignity are best when you deal with the original creditor. The department store or doctor will usually try to work with you to settle your outstanding debt. The plan usually means that you make regular monthly payments for an amount you can afford. If you do make a concerted effort to pay your bill, even at something like $25 a month, the original creditor will usually accept the payment, albeit begrudgingly. It is when you stop paying altogether that creditors become upset.

We Can Work It Out

When you cannot pay your bills in full, another option is to negotiate with your creditors and see whether any of them would be willing to accept less than full payment. Here is how to do it: Write a letter explaining to your creditor that you would like to settle your account in full, but that you are unable to do so. Your letter should go on to offer a settlement for an amount less than you owe.

Why would a creditor accept such a proposal? Because, you explain, if it does not, you will have no choice but to declare bankruptcy, in which case, it will get nothing. Fifty cents on the dollar starts to look like a pretty good deal.

Although you can try to get your creditor to accept monthly payments for the reduced sum, we think you will have a much better chance of success in your negotiations if you can offer to pay the reduced sum in full.

It is important to realize that if this letter does not work, or you otherwise ignore your creditors, you will end up with a very negative credit report, not to mention the fact that you will lose peace of mind and future credit. If you can settle these debts before things get out of hand, you are better off.

> **Money Talks**
>
> Unsecured debts such as credit cards, doctor and legal bills, and bounced checks are completely wiped out in a Chapter 7 bankruptcy. The creditors holding these debts get paid nothing. Bankruptcy is discussed in detail in Part 4.

XYZ Creditor
2734 Marty Way
Sacramento, CA

Re: Account No. 2727

Dear Customer Service:

As I have told you over the phone, I am unable to pay my debt to you any longer. I am writing today to see whether you would be interested in settling my account. I have learned that I could completely erase all of my debts by filing Chapter 7. I would like to avoid that if at all possible. Therefore, I make the following offer:

1. In consideration for immediate payment of $ _____ (the "Settlement Amount"), which is 20 percent of the outstanding balance I owe your company I, _____ ("Debtor"), and your company, _____ ("Creditor"), agree to fully, completely, and forever compromise and settle this debt. *(Start your offer low, at 20 percent or so, so that you can negotiate a bit higher if necessary later on.)*

2. Creditor agrees to accept the Settlement Amount as payment in full for all possible obligations Debtor may have with Creditor. *(Once your creditor accepts this offer, or something similar, this "Settlement Amount" is all you will owe.)* Creditor further agrees to cease all collection activities regarding this debt, to cease all legal proceedings against Debtor, and to fully release and hold harmless Debtor from any further obligations arising from this debt. *(These points are negotiable. What you really care about is settling your debt for an amount substantially less than you owe.)*

3. Within five days of receipt of a signed copy of this letter, Debtor will forward to Creditor the Settlement Amount via cashier's check or money order. This settlement will only take effect after both parties have signed this letter and the Creditor has received the Settlement Amount. *(If you fail to pay, the settlement will be of no effect.)*

Considering the fact that I could pay you back nothing by declaring bankruptcy, I think that this settlement offer constitutes a quick and equitable solution to this problem for both parties. If you agree to the terms of this settlement, please have the appropriate person sign below, return this letter back to me, and I will immediately forward the Settlement Amount to you. Thank you for your consideration in this matter.

Very truly yours,

Dated _____ (Your name)

AGREED AND ACCEPTED

Dated _____ (Your creditor)

Pay No Attention to That Man Behind the Curtain

If you are unable to pay your doctor bill, for example, at some point the doctor will sell your debt to a collection agency. Most original creditors would rather sell the debt at a steep discount than continue to try and pry money from you if you don't have it.

An important thing to realize about collection agencies is that their bark is usually far worse than their bite. Yes, they can threaten you, seemingly harass you (which is illegal, as you'll find out later in this chapter), and cause you to stop answering your phone. But that is about it.

Empty Threats

There is much collection agencies cannot do. Can they garnish your wages? No. They may threaten to if you do not pay that bill, but the truth is that they cannot do it. There are only three instances when a creditor can *garnish* your wages:

♦ If you owe on a student loan, special rules allow that creditor to garnish your wages.

♦ If you owe child support, your monthly payment can be garnished from your paycheck.

♦ Any other creditor can garnish your wages only when it has sued you, won the suit, and received permission from the court to garnish. You will know if this is happening to you.

If none of these situations applies to you, you should understand that when a creditor threatens to garnish your wages, he is blowing smoke.

Can collection agencies have you thrown in jail? No. Debtor's prison was outlawed in this country long ago. Can they threaten you? Sure. But so what? Most of their threats are hollow. They tell you that if five post-dated checks are not received by the next day, a suit will be filed. Or they might say that if $500 is not in hand by Friday, your bank accounts will be seized. Baloney.

> **Check It Out**
>
> A **wage garnishment** or **wage assignment** occurs when the court, sheriff, or district attorney has instructed your employer to withhold part of your wages to satisfy a debt. A percentage of your check will be withheld until the debt is paid in full.

The truth is, most of their threats are empty, and there is no deadline. They make it all up. If the deadline passes, nothing happens. The threat and deadline are nothing more than tactics they use to try and get some money out of you. Do not fall for their threats.

Will the collection agency sue you? Probably not. Lawsuits for consumer debts happen in a surprisingly small number of cases. Depending upon the size of your debt, it is normally too expensive for the original creditor or the collection agency to file suit. And even if it did win a judgment, what is the likelihood that it will ever collect on it? These lawsuits are usually just not cost-effective. That is why collection agencies prefer to make threats: They're cheaper.

Turn the Tides

Knowing that a lawsuit is unlikely, you can turn the tables and demand that the debate be held on your terms. The key thing to remember when dealing with a collection agency is that, believe it or not, you have all the power. You control the checkbook. If you decide not to pay, the collection agency doesn't get paid. If you tell the agencies to leave you alone, they have to leave you alone. Most collection agencies are nothing more than bluffing bullies.

Know Your Rights

Collection agency harassment got so bad that it took congressional action to rein it in. The Fair Debt Collections Practices Act (FDCPA) is a *federal law* that regulates what creditors may and may not do when trying to collect a debt.

The essence of the FDCPA is that debt collectors must behave in a reasonable manner and are forbidden from harassing you. Impermissible actions may include …

- **Calling at the wrong place or the wrong time.** A bill collector cannot call before 8:00 A.M. or after 9:00 P.M. If you so desire, the collector cannot call you at work.

- **Making inappropriate threats.** The collection agency representative cannot use foul language or threaten you with violence, seizure of assets, or imprisonment.

- **Using other forms of harassment.** The debt collector cannot misrepresent who he is or what he is calling about, cannot repeatedly call you, and is forbidden from publishing your name and the nature of the debt.

Knowing what is acceptable creditor behavior can pay tremendous dividends. If an annoying creditor persists in calling you at work, tell him to stop. If he threatens to have your car sold to pay the debt, tell him such threats are illegal. Make sure that when you speak with an annoying creditor, you use the words "Pursuant to the Fair Debt Collections Practices Act, you cannot …." This phrase lets him know that you know what you are talking about.

If a collection agency continues to violate the law after being told to stop, you have two options:

1. **Contact the proper authorities.** The Federal Trade Commission polices the FDCPA. Contact the office closest to you and explain the nature of the problem. State authorities, such as your Attorney General, State's Attorney, or Department of Consumer Affairs, also may investigate a serious violation of the law.

2. **Sue.** The FDCPA permits lawsuits for violations of the act. If proven, the violator could be liable for any out-of-pocket expenses you incurred as a result of the violation, penalties of up to $1,000, and possible attorneys' fees and costs. Such a suit would normally be brought in your local small claims court.

Two Cents

The address for the Federal Trade Commission division that deals with creditor harassment is FTC, Debt Collection, Washington, D.C. 20580.

Stopping All Creditor Harassment

Maybe the best part of the FDCPA is that it allows you to force the creditor to stop all phone calls. If you have ever been subject to a pit-bull creditor who would not leave you alone, you do not have to be told what a relief this is.

To stop the harassing phone calls, write the creditor a "cease and desist" letter. This letter tells the creditor that he is to stop all further communication with you regarding this debt. Once received, the creditor must leave you alone. Although a creditor retains the right to sue you, he cannot write or call anymore.

Two Cents

The FDCPA also prevents a creditor from talking to your boss or co-workers about your debt.

The following is what your letter should look like:

Knowing what your rights are and being able to force a collection agency to stop harassing you with one of these letters should make your life much easier and less stressful.

ABC Collections
1800 Mariposa Lane
Fullerton, CA

Re: Acct. 2727

Dear ABC Collections:

Pursuant to the Fair Debt Collections Practices Act, 15 U.S.C. 1592 et. seq. *(this is the specific law you are using; make sure it is in your letter just like it is written here),* you are hereby notified to cease and desist all further communication with me, and anyone associated with me, regarding the above-referenced debt. Failure to abide by this law will result in a complaint being filed against you with the Federal Trade Commission and the Attorney General of my state. I also reserve the right to file suit against you for any future violations of the law.

Very truly yours,

Dated_____ (Your name)

Do Nothing

A final option is to merely take no action at all. If you ignore your creditors' threats, they may make a lot of annoying phone calls and threaten to sue you, but, as we have said, if the debt is not too large, they usually eventually forget about you. If you live month-to-month and have few assets, you are what lawyers call an "empty pocket" or "judgment proof." No creditor would waste money suing you because the likelihood of ever getting any money back is remote.

In most cases, your creditor will probably write off your debt as uncollectable and get a tax break for it. After seven years, the bad debt will fall off your credit report.

CAUTION
Over Your Limit

If you are ever sued for a debt you did not pay, the suit will likely occur in small claims court. Though each state is different, the maximum a creditor can collect in small claims court is usually $5,000. You cannot have a lawyer defend you in small claims court.

The Least You Need to Know

◆ Credit collectors love to make empty threats.

◆ You have the right to be left alone.

◆ You may be able to negotiate a lower payment if you can come up with a lump-sum settlement.

◆ If you are judgment-proof, doing nothing may be a fine solution to creditor problems.

Student Loan Strategies

In This Chapter

- ◆ Understanding student loans
- ◆ A plan of attack
- ◆ The idealistic option
- ◆ Postponing payments
- ◆ Dealing with default

Student loans are one of the largest forms of debts people take on. One sometimes wonders whether those carefree days of college were worth debts that can escalate into six figures. We suppose they were, but sometimes …

How Student Loans Work

If you have student loans, the first thing you need to do is find out what sort of loans you took out and what repayment plans you agreed to. Once you know that, you can begin to deal with them. But until you take the paper bag off of your head, and see what you owe to whom in what amounts and when it's due, you're never going to pay them off.

The most common student loans are the following federally guaranteed loans:

♦ **PLUS Loans:** "PLUS" stands for Parent Loan for Undergraduate Students. These loans are available to parents of undergraduate students who are dependents. Parents must normally begin repayment of PLUS loans within 60 days after the final loan disbursement.

♦ **Perkins Loans:** Perkins loans are federal loans with a low interest rate. Eligible students may borrow up to $4,000 a year for undergraduate study and up to $6,000 a year for graduate study. You do not have to repay a Perkins loan until nine months after you leave school, and often much later (discussed later in this chapter).

♦ **Stafford loans:** Stafford loans are low-interest federal loans available to students attending school at least half-time. You do not have to begin repaying a Stafford loan until six mouths after you leave school.

Repayment Options

You can repay your student loans in a variety of ways. However, unless you make special arrangements (discussed later in this section), you will be expected to follow a *standard repayment* plan. Under standard repayment, principal and interest payments are due each month throughout the loan repayment term, which usually begins six months after graduation. The following table shows how much you will end up repaying under some fairly typical scenarios:

Typical Repayment Schedule

Amount Borrowed	Interest	Length	Monthly Repayment	Total Paid
$10,000	8%	10 years	$121.33	$14,559.16
$10,000	8%	20 years	$83.64	$20,075.98
$25,000	8%	10 years	$303.32	$36,398.21
$25,000	8%	20 years	$209.11	$50,186.41
$50,000	8%	10 years	$606.64	$72,796.43
$50,000	8%	20 years	$418.22	$100,372.82

Notice that by stretching your $50,000 loan repayment terms from 10 to 20 years, you end up paying another $27,000 in interest! Obviously, the sooner you begin to pay back your loans, the less you will end up owing.

Graduated repayment plans are designed to have lower payments at the beginning of the repayment period—when you are first out of school and can afford less—and then "graduate" into higher payments as the loan matures.

Income-sensitive repayments are based upon the borrower's gross monthly income.

Two Cents _____

Can't find your loan information? The National Student Clearing-house has an online loan locator: www.studentclearinghouse.org/ secure_area/loan_locator.asp, or call 1-800-4-FED-AID.

Finally, *extended repayment* allows borrowers to get payment relief through a lengthened repayment term, sometimes as long as 25 years. This plan is available to most borrowers and is explained in more detail later in this chapter.

The thing to do now is to pull that student loan file out of the cabinet and begin to make some phone calls. Find out what type of loans you have, who owns them now (because they are bought and sold like so much cattle), and ask for a copy of your current statement.

In all likelihood, some or all of your loans are handled by Sallie Mae. Also known as the Student Loan Marketing Association, Sallie Mae is the largest student loan provider in the country. Even if you took the loans out from a different institution, it is highly probable that Sallie Mae now owns them.

In any case, once you know what you owe to whom, you can move forward and make changes to your repayment schedule, if needed.

Money Talks
I got a call from the company that holds my student loan, Sallie Mae. Sallie Mae sounds like a naïve and barefoot hillbilly girl, but, in fact, they are a ruthless and aggressive conglomeration of bullies located in a tall brick building somewhere in Kansas. I picture it to be the tallest building in that state and I have decided they hire their employees straight out of prison. They scare me.   —David Sedaris, *Barrel Fever*

Formulating a Plan

Maybe you have been afraid to figure out how bad your student loan situation is because you hoped it might go away if you didn't look at it. Alternatively, maybe you know only too well how much you owe, but see no way out. Either way, hopefully it is some consolation to know that most ex-students find themselves in similar situations. It should be even more consolation to know that there is an answer.

Let's get this clear up front: You will have to repay your student loans, either with money or through labor. The only way to get out of them, and it is a remote hope at best, is by filing Chapter 7 bankruptcy and then convincing the court that it would cause you an undue hardship to repay them. It is a very difficult thing to accomplish.

For the rest of us, the question then becomes: What sort of repayment plan works best? Let's begin with the one that will cost you no actual money, but, rather, time and effort.

Money Talks

In 1998, Congress changed bankruptcy laws regarding student loans. Prior to that, student loans that were over seven years old were eligible to be discharged through bankruptcy. Now student loans can only be discharged if you can prove that you cannot maintain even a minimal standard of living if forced to repay the loan. Sometimes courts will reduce the total amount owed, but getting rid of the debt altogether has become very difficult.

Service with a Smile

The government will pay off all or part of your student loans for you if you agree to serve your country in a needed capacity. This is called student loan "forgiveness," and it's a nice option for people in certain fields or who want to help out those in need.

The following programs include student loan forgiveness as a benefit:

♦ **Americorps/VISTA:** If you agree to volunteer for a year of Americorps or VISTA (Volunteers in Service to America) you can defer your loans, get a stipend of $7,400 for the year, and end up with a final payment of $4,725 that can be applied to student loans.

If you would like to teach or otherwise help people in low income areas, Americorp/VISTA may be for you. For more information, go to www.Americorps.org or call 1-800-942-2677.

♦ **Peace Corp:** Again, you can defer your student loans until after you leave this overseas volunteer program, and what is even better is that you may even get some of your loans substantially reduced (up to 75 percent!) Visit www.Peacecorp.gov or call 1-800-424-8580 for more details.

♦ **Military Service:** By joining the Army Reserves or National Guard, you can receive up to $10,000 to pay off your loans. If you agree to be stationed in areas of hostility, even more money is available.

◆ **Teaching:** If you agree to teach special education, or in a school that services low-income families, or in an area where there is a designated shortage of teachers, you may qualify for loan forgiveness. Check with the United States Department of Education for details: 1-800-USA-LEARN.

◆ **Social Services:** If you can help the disabled, people in low-income communities, or if you are a nurse, medical technician, or a law enforcement official, loan forgiveness may be available. Contact the United States Department of Education for details: 1-800-USA-LEARN.

◆ **Public Interest Law:** There are many legal positions available that offer loan forgiveness to law students who take public interest or non-profit positions. Contact the National Association for Public Interest Law at www.napil.org, or by calling 202-466-3686.

◆ **National Health Service Corps:** NHSC has a program that offers an annual salary and some loan forgiveness in exchange for serving in needy areas. Contact NHSC on the Web at http://nhsc.bhpr.hrsa.gov// or call 916-654-2102 for more information.

◆ **Occupational and physical therapists:** Some hospitals and other health care organizations may help pay off some of your loans if you agree to work there. Ask your employer or prospective employer about this option.

Money Talks

Teachers serving in a low-income or subject matter shortage area may be able to cancel or defer some student loans. Specifically …

◆ If you have a Perkins loan, you may be eligible for loan cancellation for teaching at a low-income school or in specialized subject areas.

◆ If you have a Stafford Loan and have taught for five years in a low-income school, you may be eligible to have some of the loan cancelled.

◆ If you have a Paul Douglas Teacher Scholarship, you may be eligible for reduced obligations. Once called the Perkins Scholarship Program, and then the Congressional Teacher Scholarship Program, and now the Paul Douglas Teacher Scholarship Program, the program is intended to encourage students to become teachers in elementary or secondary school.

Although it might sound like a great deal—getting your loans repaid in exchange for work—remember that these are not easy jobs; if they were, the government and employers wouldn't offer to pay your student loans in exchange for taking one.

Double Your Payments

What if you can't take one of these jobs but you want to get rid of this student loan debt as quickly as possible, and can afford to? Your best bet, as with any loan, is to begin to pay as much as possible in order to reduce interest payments and shrink your principal.

Consider: If you have $30,000 in student loans and a repayment schedule of 10 years, it will cost you about $360 a month to pay them back at 8.25 percent. But if you can afford to pay back $500 a month, that loan will be paid off in six years.

> **Two Cents**
>
> In 1998, Congress created a new student loan ombudsman to help borrowers deal with problems relating to lenders, guarantors, and the Department of Education. To reach the Ombudsman, visit http://sfahelp.ed.gov/ombudsman/index.html, or call 1-877-557-2575.

Note, too, that over 10 years, the total loan repayment will be $44,154.81. You will be paying $14,154.81 in interest. If you pay the loan off in six years, your total repayment will only be $38,135.95, of which, only $8,135.95 will be interest. You will save $6,018.86 by paying the loan off early.

So one way to get rid of your loans quickly is to pay as much as possible as soon as possible. If that's not an option, then keep reading.

When in Doubt, Delay!

Sometimes the only thing that works is to delay the inevitable. Yes, you will have to pay off those loans, but maybe now is not the time to start. If you need a break from beginning or enduring those payments, you have a variety of options available for delaying repayment.

Deferment

Deferment allows borrowers to delay loan repayment for specified periods of time. Different loans have different deferment programs, but generally speaking, these are the types most often offered:

- **Economic Hardship:** This might apply if, for example, your total monthly federal education debt equals 20 percent or more of your monthly gross income. This might happen if, for example, you get injured and are unable to work for a year.

- **Fellowships:** If you are involved in a post-graduate educational fellowship program, you probably qualify.

◆ **Internship:** This applies if the internship is required by a state-licensing agency to be certified for professional practice. Maximum length of deferment: 24 months.

◆ **Military:** You qualify for 36 months of deferment if you are engaged full-time in the Army, Navy, Air Force, Marines, Coast Guard, National Guard, or the Reserves.

◆ **National Oceanic and Atmospheric Administration Corps:** You qualify if you are on active duty, full time. Maximum deferment: 36 months.

◆ **Parental Leave:** You can get six months' deferment if you are taking care of a newborn (or newly-adopted) child and are unemployed and not attending school.

◆ **Peace Corps, VISTA, and Americorps:** You can get a 36-month deferment for participating in one of these activities full time.

◆ **Public Health Service:** If you are an officer in the U.S. Public Health Service, you qualify for 36 months of deferment.

◆ **Rehabilitations Training:** You qualify for an unlimited deferment if you are disabled and as long as you are engaged in an approved, licensed, rehabilitation training program.

◆ **Student:** As long as you are enrolled at least half-time, you qualify for an ongoing deferment.

◆ **Tax-Exempt Volunteer:** If you volunteer full-time in a tax-exempt organization and the U.S. Department of Education has determined it to be comparable to the service of a Peace Corps volunteer, you are eligible for 36 months of deferment.

◆ **Temporarily Totally Disabled:** If you are temporarily totally disabled, or are caring for a spouse who is, you qualify for 36 months of deferment.

◆ **Unemployment/Underemployment:** If you are seeking full-time employment you may get up to 36 months' worth of deferment.

◆ **Working Mother:** A mom with preschool-aged children who earns no more than one dollar more than the minimum wage may qualify for deferments for 12 months.

CAUTION

Over Your Limit

The average American undergraduate leaves school owing roughly $17,000 in student loans. The average graduate student owes about $60,000.

Forbearances

A forbearance is for borrowers who have a temporary financial problem. It can be used to reduce or stop payments for specified periods, up to one year. Basically, there are three types of forbearances:

◆ **Mandatory forbearance.** If you are not in default, and you meet any of the following conditions, you qualify:

    a. You are in a medical or dental internship or residency program and have exhausted your deferment eligibility or do not qualify for a deferment.

    b. You are involved in Americorps.

    c. You are in a qualifying program administered by the Department of Defense.

◆ **Debt Burden Forbearance.** Your federal student loan payments equal or exceed 20 percent of your gross monthly income.

◆ **Lender Forbearance.** Many private lenders have their own forbearance programs for those times when you need some extra help.

Consolidation

Consolidation is what it sounds like. It is a chance to group together various different loans into one nice, neat loan with one nice, neat monthly payment. Consolidation is great for people who have a hard time scraping together enough money every month to make their payments, because the monthly consolidated loan repayment amount is significantly less than what you would pay for each loan separately. How can this be? The consolidated loan servicer extends the time for repayment, thereby reducing the monthly payment amount. So, for example, if you have three loans and you pay $250 on each ($750 total), a consolidation loan may cut that monthly payment amount to $375 or even less, but will also extend repayment terms for another 15 years beyond what they already were. Of course, this means that by consolidating, you will eventually pay more interest on your loans.

Consolidating doesn't make sense if you have just a few years left on your loans. Also, you can only consolidate once. However, if you haven't consolidated yet, have more than a few years left to pay, and need to reduce your monthly payment, then there are a variety of benefits to consolidating your loans, including the following:

◆ Reduced monthly payments

◆ One lender and one payment

- Various repayment options

- No minimum or maximum loan amounts

- Varied deferment options

Two Cents _____

To find out more about loan consolidation, contact your lender, or one of the following agencies:

- Sallie Mae
  Salliemae.com
  1-800-524-9100

- Federal Direct Consolidation Loan Info Center
  http://loanconsolidation.ed.gov
  1-800-557-7392.

Avoiding Default

Defaulting on a student loan can cause you much grief:

- Your loans will likely be turned over to a collection agency, and you will have to pay additional fees.

- It will severely damage your credit.

- You may be subject to a lawsuit.

- You can have your wages garnished.

- State and federal income tax refunds may be withheld.

- You will be ineligible for any further federal financial aid until you repay the loan in full or make arrangements to repay it.

- You will be ineligible for further deferments or forbearances.

So it is imperative that you work hard to avoid default. Rather than defaulting on your loans, it is far better to use any of the tactics listed previously in this chapter. Beware the default monster—he can ruin your credit and make loans that you need later in life (to buy a home for example) much more difficult to obtain.

Already in Default

What if you have already defaulted? Take a deep breath, there is an answer for that, too.

Here is what you do: Contact the current owner of the loan(s) and ask to get on a minimal repayment schedule. Even as little as $50 a month may be acceptable (after all, it is far better for them to get something than nothing).

Then, after making 12 payments on time, you will be considered out of default and the various deferment and forbearance options available to you above are again back in play.

Money Talks

The government has some great ideas about student loans generally and its various loan programs specifically:

Request the booklets entitled *Direct Student Loan Consolidation* and *Paying For College* from the U.S. General Services Administration:

U.S. General Services Administration
Consumer Information Center
S. James Consumer Information Center—6C
P.O. Box 100
Pueblo, CO 81002

Write to the Federal Trade Commission and ask for the booklet entitled *Knee Deep In Debt:*

Federal Trade Commission
Public Reference Branch
Room 130, 6th Street and Pennsylvania Ave.
NW Washington, D.C. 20580

The good news is that you have a lot of options when it comes to your student loan, even if you are already in default. All you need to do is either go online or make some phone calls to see which option is best for you.

The Least You Need to Know

- Understanding what sort of student loans you have will enable you to make intelligent decisions.
- If you can afford to take a job in a needy area, you may get your loans forgiven.
- The longer you wait to pay your student loans back, the more it will cost you.
- Postponing payments is possible through deferment and forbearances.
- Avoid default at all costs.

Chapter 15

IRS Folks Are People, Too

In This Chapter

- ◆ How the IRS really works
- ◆ Filing returns
- ◆ Payment plans
- ◆ Audits
- ◆ Audit appeals

Taxes are a special breed of debt problems. All of the techniques and tools that have been offered so far in this book are inapplicable to tax problems because the IRS is, as you probably know all too well, an animal unto itself. In order to get out of your current tax situation, you must adhere to the IRS's special rules and regulations.

You can have a variety of problems where taxes are concerned. Simpler issues, such as filing returns, creating a payment plan, and dealing with an audit, are discussed in this chapter. More difficult issues such as levies, liens, and settlements are explained in the next chapter.

Know Thy Foe

The IRS, a branch of the United States Treasury Department, has three different computer centers throughout the country, and the organization itself is divided into 10 regional service centers, 63 district offices, and scores of subdivisions. These service centers process over 200 million returns annually and collect more than $1,000,000,000,000 (that's trillion!) annually.

> **Money Talks**
>
> The IRS estimates that 18 percent of all taxpayers cheat on their taxes in any given year. A recent independent survey put the number at 22 percent. Do not cheat on your taxes: Tax fraud is a crime.

A slow-moving, huge bureaucracy, the IRS often acts arrogant and may seem ineffectual. The sooner you embrace this reality and learn to play the tax game according to IRS rules, the better off you will be.

The good news is twofold. First, the IRS, in its attempts to become more user-friendly, is often open to a reasonable resolution to your tax problem. Secondly, the IRS offers many programs you may not know about that can help you resolve your situation, sometimes for less than you owe.

IRS Employees Are People, Too

IRS employees are people like you. They have careers and families. They want to stay employed and advance in their careers. They like to work with people who are reasonable and dislike working with people who are not reasonable.

Your first piece of advice, then, is to treat any IRS employee with whom you deal with understanding and respect (even if she may not deserve it). She has a job to do, and her job requires her to follow certain rules. If she does not follow these internal regulations, she will get demoted or fired.

You may have very good reasons to hate the IRS, but if you come in with guns ablazing, not understanding the rules you are playing by, you will likely shoot yourself in the foot. Even though your IRS contact may agree with you, she may not be able to say yes to you and your proposed resolution (and then again, she may). After you read and digest this chapter and the information in the next chapter, you will be far better equipped in your IRS negotiations because you will know what the IRS can and cannot do.

The IRS Is Inefficient

The IRS gets millions of letters and phone calls every year. The people you deal with there fit the very definition of bureaucrats. In other words, IRS employees tend to work slowly and methodically in order to compensate for their lack of self-motivation. They are not self-starters.

Compounding the human factor is the computer factor. IRS computers are notoriously inefficient. The organization has many different systems, and the person you have on the phone, for example, may not have access to your records on his or her system.

These two factors combined mean that you have to be patient when dealing with the IRS. Resolving your individual problem may be your highest priority, but it certainly isn't theirs.

Initially, one of the best things you can do when contacting the IRS is to find out whether it has any forms that deal with your situation. There is an IRS form for practically everything, and IRS employees know what to do when a certain form comes in the door: what section to forward it to, which *revenue officer* handles it, and so on. But employees may have no idea where to forward an angry letter, for example.

Check It Out _____

A **revenue officer** is an IRS employee who specifically deals with collecting taxes and resolving taxpayer problems. This person may also be called a revenue agent.

The First Commandment: Thou Shalt File Thy Taxes

The first thing to understand about taxes is that even if you don't have the money to pay them, your return should be filed on time. Not filing on time, even if you do not have the money to pay the amount due, is just plain dumb. The penalty for not filing your tax return on time is 5 percent per month, whereas the penalty for not paying your taxes on time is only half of 1 percent per month. File on time, even if you can't pay a penny. Just send in the forms without out a check.

For example, assume that Marty owes the IRS $10,000. If he files on time and doesn't send a check, he will owe the IRS another $50 a month (half of 1 percent). If he does not file at all, he will owe the IRS an additional $500 a month (5 percent of $10,000).

Two Cents _____

If you have a computer and an Internet connection, you can download almost any IRS form from its website. You can reach the IRS by going to www.irs. ustreas.gov.

Filing for an Extension of Time

If you cannot file your taxes by April 15, you will need to ask for an extension of time with which to file. Every year more than 5 million taxpayers file Form 4868, asking the IRS for an extension. Understand that this form is asking for an extension of time to file your tax return, not an extension to pay any taxes due.

As long as you send the form to the IRS by April 15, Form 4868 is an automatic extension, giving you until August 15 to file your tax return. Anyone can ask for an extension, thus there is no excuse for waiting to send in your return.

If you need even more time to prepare your return beyond August 15, file Form 2688 before August 15. Form 2688 is an application for an additional extension of time to file your return. This one is not an automatic extension; the IRS will give you an additional two months to file only if you have a good reason for the delay. Therefore, the latest possible time you can file in any given year is October 15.

Failing to File

Failure to file your taxes is a crime, although it is unlikely that you will get arrested for it (unless your non-filing is chronically egregious). Our society has decided that people who smoke dope are more of a threat than tax cheats, so the likelihood of facing jail time for unfiled returns is remote. There are simply not enough jail cells for both drug criminals and tax cheats.

The IRS has several methods of finding out whether you have filed a return. The most common are the following:

> **Over Your Limit**
>
> The IRS has six years from the due date (April 15 of the next year) of the unfiled return to file criminal charges for failing to file a tax return.

- **W-2s.** These wage statements are filed by employers. If an employer declares in a W-2 that he paid you $2,500 last year, and the IRS computer fails to find a return by you stating the same thing, you are caught.

- **1099s.** These are income statements. If your bank reports that you earned 100 dollars in interest on your account last year, and those nasty IRS computers find no corresponding return, you're caught.

Besides the possibility of criminal prosecution, whenever you fail to file, the IRS also has the right to file a return, called an *SFR*, on your behalf. You can bet that it won't file the same friendly return that would have been filed by your own accountant.

Because an SFR return will inevitably cost you far more in taxes, interest, and penalties than a return you file on your own, it is in your best interest to have an SFR return overruled. Overruling an SFR is surprisingly easy. All you need do is file an original return yourself for the year in question, sign and date it, and write on the top in red ink "SFR PROTEST RETURN."

The IRS will then process and accept your new return. Because your SFR protest return will probably calculate taxes lower than what the IRS said you owe, penalties and interest will also be reduced. Very few of these returns are ever audited or dismissed.

Check It Out
When the IRS files a return on your behalf, it is called a **Substitute for Return**, or **SFR**.

Two Cents
Half of all taxpayers file their taxes before April 1. You should, too.

If You Do Not Have Records

If you do not have records for the year(s) in question, you can request that the IRS give you its copy of your records, and it has to comply with your request for free. The catch? You must use form 4506 (we warned you) to make this request. The IRS will then send you copies of old W-2s and 1099s, but don't expect to get them right away.

You can also get a copy of your IRS account by asking for a transcript of your individual master file (IMF) or your business master file (BMF). The file may be indecipherable when you get it, but if you call your local taxpayer service representative at the IRS office, he or she will explain it to you.

Over Your Limit
The average non-filer has not filed taxes for four years and owes around $50,000 in taxes.

Payment Plans

When you file your return, you may not be able to afford to pay the taxes due. When this is the case, the best course of action is to pay as much as possible and request a monthly payment plan for the balance. Of course, you have to fill out the proper form. A form 9465 Request for Installment will do the trick. The 9465 allows you to request payments for up to 36 months and permits you to declare how much you think you can pay each month. Be sure to attach the request form to your tax return. The IRS is supposed to get back to you within a month, ruling on your request.

The Dreaded 500 Notices

One limit on the 9465 Request for Installment form is that it is best used only for taxes up to $10,000. If you owe more, or do not file a 9465, you will begin to get a series of notices from the IRS:

♦ Form 501: Reminder of Unpaid Tax

♦ Form 503: Urgent–Payment Required (you may get several of these)

♦ Form 504: Final Notice

Two Cents

The best way to slow down the IRS once you begin to get 500-series notices is to write back every time you get one and request more time to pay. The most you can ask for is 60 days at a time, but that can buy you almost a year to pay your taxes during the course of a 500 letters series.

Being ignored makes the IRS cranky. Do not ignore the 504 letter (Final Notice)! Ten days after the 504 letter is sent, the IRS can begin to seize your property. Although Uncle Sam is not likely to seize your assets at this point, it legally has the right to do so. At a minimum, you must call the IRS once you have received a final notice. If you continue to avoid your tax obligations during the 500 notice letters era, a more likely result will be that your file will be sent to the morass called the Automated Collection System (ACS).

ACS

The ACS is the largest collection division of the IRS. Most taxpayers are involved with the ACS due to either unpaid taxes or unfiled returns. Once the ACS has contacted you (usually by letter), procrastinate no longer. You must get in touch with an ACS employee and work out a suitable payment plan.

Two Cents

You can obtain any IRS form you need by stopping by your local IRS office. The office will have a public-access room where every possible form is available for free. If you have access to the Internet, you can download IRS forms by going to www.irs.ustreas.gov/prod/forms_pubs/index.html.

What the ACS employee will want to know is how much you can afford to pay back every month. At this point, it should not surprise you to learn that IRS rules allow only a certain dollar amount for expenses, based upon local and national standards. If you spend more, too bad. For example, the IRS does not permit credit card payments as an "allowable expense." You can find these guidelines on Form IRM 5323, of course.

Getting in touch with the ACS is another hassle altogether. When you call, you can easily be on hold for an hour before speaking with an ACS employee. Before calling, be sure to have the following ready:

1. All returns for the years in question.

2. Completed forms 433-A and B. These forms lists income and expenses. Form 433-A is for individuals; B is for businesses.

3. Your reason for calling (for example, to create a payment plan or to get a wage garnishment released).

If you do not have your ducks all lined up before calling, you are wasting your time. The last page of form 433A lists income and expenses. This information is what the ACS employee will want to know. Do not try and work outside the 433A form; the employee's computer will not let him work outside that format.

What you want to do is create an acceptable repayment plan, one that you can live with. To do so, you will need to be charming, understanding, and flexible. ACS employees are people. Some days they seem more willing to make a deal than other days. Presenting yourself as likeable and reasonable helps you get the job done.

If your tax bill is less than $10,000, the revenue officer can agree to a payment plan. Agreements for tax bills larger than that must be approved by a manager. You will then get a copy of the agreement in the mail.

Installment agreements will be revoked for any of the following reasons:

♦ Missing a payment.

♦ Failure to file a tax return.

♦ Failure to pay taxes that come due after the IA was entered into.

♦ A change for the better or worse in your financial situation.

After all taxes due have been paid through the IA, any tax liens that were filed for the years in question should be released.

Check It Out

IRS payment agreements are called **installment agreements,** or **IAs** for short.

The Taxman Cometh

It causes consternation among even the strongest amongst us. It evokes fear and loathing in Los Angeles (city of the fearless). It has the ability to make even the bravest of us quake in our boots. A Pauly Shore movie, you say? No, my friend, it is the dreaded tax audit.

The time limit given to the IRS to audit a taxpayer is three years from the original filing of the taxes. If you underestimated your income by more than 25 percent, the limit is six years. If you are suspected of fraud, there is no *statute of limitations*.

Check It Out

The time the IRS has to audit you is called the **statute of limitations**. If it does not audit you within that amount of time, it cannot legally ever do so. (There is a statute of limitations for every crime; the length of time during which you can still be prosecuted varies depending on the severity of the crime.)

Two Cents

The taxpayers' bill of rights forbids the IRS from evaluating an auditor's performance based upon the revenue generated by the audits.

Money Talks

Although your chance of being audited in any given year is only about 1 percent, the chance of being audited sometime in your life is more like 45 percent. The more money you make, the greater your chances are, and if you are self-employed, your chances are even greater still.

You may be targeted for an audit for several reasons:

1. **Your expenses seem high for your level of income.**

2. **You are singled out through computer analysis.** IRS computers analyzing supersecret audit factors generate 80 percent of all audits.

3. **You are in a special class of employee.** Attorneys, auto dealers, telemarketers, and many other professions are under special IRS scrutiny.

4. **You lost a previous audit battle.** The IRS figures, why not mess with you again if it worked before?

5. **You were randomly selected.** Who says you are unlucky? We do!

Types of Audits

Most audits are conducted at IRS field offices. You are informed of an office audit by a letter that often requests that you bring along certain documents. The IRS is probably looking for one or more of the following:

- Under-reported income
- Excessive expenses
- Improper exemptions
- Improper deductions

Auditors are overworked and, despite what you might think, will probably not pour over every aspect of the return in question. Far more likely is an audit that covers a few main areas of concern and lasts no more than a few hours.

Less likely are *field audits* conducted at your place of business. Field audits are more common for small business owners and are much more likely to result in additional money being owed. You are therefore advised to hire a tax professional to assist you with your field audit.

The field auditor will be interested in the following:

- Verification of business expenses.

- Unreported income, especially if you have a cash business.

- Bank deposits. An auditor can easily tell if you underreported your income by checking to see how much money you deposited in the bank that year.

CAUTION

Over Your Limit

Besides banks, the auditor can get records from employers, ex-spouses, friends, government agencies, motor vehicle departments, and public records.

Preparing for an Audit

When you get the dreaded audit notice, take a deep breath. The experience will probably not be as bad as you fear. Although you will probably owe additional taxes as a result of your audit (most audits end that way), you can minimize the amount you will owe by making a good impression. You do so by being informed, organized, and confident.

The first thing to do is to go over your return for the year in question. You need to understand how and why you listed things as you did. You must be able to answer the auditor's questions intelligently.

You also need to locate all records for the year in question. Get receipts, cancelled checks, books, records, logs, and calendars. Make a set for you and a set for the auditor. Not only will this save time, it will also make you look professional.

It is equally important to act appropriately at your audit. Be neither a meek mouse nor a loud lion. Stay cool. It is akin to a job interview; you want to act your best. Be polite, respectful, and confident and speak clearly. In the process, heed these warnings, too:

- **Do not say too much.** Offering too little information is always better than offering too much.

- **Do not be too helpful.** You should not volunteer to answer questions not asked and should not do things not requested.

- **Do not be a jerk.** The revenue officer is only doing his job. You don't have to like it to respect it.

After the audit is over, you will receive form 4549, an Audit Examination Report. (Did you expect anything less?) This form will show any adjustments your examiner has made to the tax return in question. Taxes, interest, and penalties will be explained.

Two Cents

Do not be intimidated by the prospect of an appeal. The average appeal usually results in a net reduction of taxes, penalties, and interest by about 50 percent, and you need not hire a lawyer to help you.

If you agree (or simply want to get this over with), you will need to sign the form and return it along with a form 870 (yes, another form). You can then either pay the amount due or request a payment plan.

If you disagree with the proposed assessment, you can try to informally work out an agreeable solution with the auditor or his manager, or you can do nothing. If you do nothing, you will then get a letter telling you that you have 30 days to appeal the audit results.

It Is Appealing

If you refuse to sign the Audit Examination Report, you will be sent a letter explaining how to protest the report. After that, you will be given the chance to explain why you think the auditor's conclusions and requests for additional taxes were incorrect. Be concise and accurate, and make sure your reasons are justified with records and receipts.

You will then have to wait, and wait some more. Your appeals hearing may not occur for another year, or it may happen in a few months. While you are waiting, your tax bill will continue to accrue interest. In the meantime, you can get a copy of the auditor's notes and files from your audit. This information will help you immensely in your appeal. To get this information, send a Freedom of Information Request (FOIA) to the FOIA officer at your local IRS.

Your appeals hearing will be surprisingly simple. It will not occur before a judge; instead, you will go to your local IRS office and meet with an IRS employee, your appeals officer. What you need to do is then present a simple, straightforward case. Do not be overly emotional. Explain why the auditor was wrong and why you are right.

There may then be a negotiation between you and the appeals officer. He wants to get your case over with and will be far more willing to settle if you seem reasonable and have presented a decent argument—that is, a reasonable justification for a certain deduction, for example. The appeals officer may, for instance, be willing to drop all penalties. If, by the end of your hearing, you still have not settled the matter, your next option is either to fight on by taking the case to tax court or attempt a settlement using one of the tools discussed in the next chapter.

The Least You Need to Know

- Do not expect your interaction with the IRS to be quick or easy.
- When dealing with the IRS, do as the IRS does; use the proper forms and speak the proper lingo.
- The biggest mistake you can make with the IRS is failing to file your tax returns.
- If you cannot pay all taxes due, a payment plan is a fine option.
- Audits are a game that can be won.

Chapter 16

Beat the IRS!

In This Chapter

- ◆ Getting penalties reduced
- ◆ Eliminating liens and levies
- ◆ Appealing collection
- ◆ Settling for pennies on the dollar
- ◆ Wiping out taxes in bankruptcy
- ◆ Telling it to the judge

Stung by criticism that it is an unresponsive, often predatory organization, the IRS has attempted to mollify both the public and Congress by creating more rapid and responsive resolution programs (remember, of course, that everything is relative). Now, more than ever before, there are programs designed to expedite solutions to IRS problems. In this chapter you will find a variety of programs and options that will allow you to resolve your IRS problem.

The Penalty Box

In case you had not noticed, the IRS loves penalties. Penalties are assessed for just about everything. Mail your taxes in a minute too late, and you are penalized. Incorrectly add your taxes due, and you are penalized. Have black hair, and you are penalized. (We exaggerate only slightly.) Luckily, it is possible to have penalties discarded, even if you have black hair.

The IRS looks to "reasonable cause" when determining whether a penalty should be *abated*. Penalties can therefore be abated for almost any valid reason. Indeed, the IRS has abated penalties for the following reasons:

> **Check It Out**
> When the IRS decides to reduce or eliminate a penalty, this is called **penalty abatement** or having the penalty **abated**.

- The war in Afghanistan
- Alcoholism
- Poor business decisions
- Forgetting to file
- Dishonest bookkeepers

As you can see, almost anything is an acceptable reason. What the IRS is looking for is something beyond your control.

For example, take the case of Ron and Rosemary. The same year Ron sold his business, Rosemary began to lose her sight and therefore lost her lucrative job as a real estate agent. When taxes were due on the business sale the next year, Ron and Rosemary were unable to pay. Three years later, they wrote a letter to the IRS explaining that Rosemary's health was worse and was the original cause of their penalties. The IRS abated their entire $3,280 in penalties.

In order to have your penalties abated, you need to write a letter to the IRS requesting that the penalty be abated (shockingly, no form is available) and send the letter to your local IRS service center. Do not send the letter to the taxpayer services department! Your letter must provide a justifiable reason why you did whatever you did that caused the penalty. It must also request a complete abatement of all penalties.

> **Money Talks**
>
> In a 2002 abatement case, a nursing home was assesed $300,000 in back taxes and penalties. The nursing home was convinced the IRS was wrong and so hired a tax lawyer. The lawyer appealed the assessment, arguing that, although some tax was due, it was not due to mismanagement but rather "reasonable cause." The Appeals Division of the IRS agreed and reduced the taxes and penalties by $245,000.

The person who gets your letter is a human being. If you explain the cause of your problems and explain that there were real reasons and circumstances beyond your control that forced you to do the things that caused you to incur penalties, you stand a fairly good chance of getting at least some of the penalties reduced. If you have had no previous problems with the IRS, your chances are even better.

Penalty abatement letters usually take some time to get a response, especially because no form is involved. If you have not heard back from the IRS within 60 days, send another letter. You may have to contact the problems resolution department to get an answer to your request. Do you need an attorney for all of this? Having one may help, but it is not necessary.

Ridding Yourself of Liens and Levies

The IRS has many methods of enforcing its tax claim against you. Two of the most common are tax liens and tax levies. You can get rid of these, but, as always, it is not simple.

Lien on Me

A tax lien is like a mortgage. It is a document filed at your local county recorder's office securing the debt you owe to the IRS, filed once the IRS determines that you owe money (usually a few months after not paying). When you sell your real estate, the tax lien must be satisfied before you ever get your money and the title is transferred to the new owner.

Because tax liens make your property harder to refinance and possibly even more difficult to sell, it behooves you to get rid of these liens. Here's how:

- ◆ **Wait.** The statute of limitations for collecting taxes through a tax lien is 10 years. That means that if the IRS filed a tax lien against you in 1991 and you neither sold your house, refinanced, nor paid the tax, the IRS had to have removed its lien by 2001.

- ◆ **Have the lien subordinated.** You can always borrow money against your property's equity to pay off the lien, except that no lender will loan money to you if you have a tax lien. It's a classic catch-22. What you can do is get the IRS to subordinate its lien to the new lender. Subordination means that the IRS allows the new lender to take primary position for funds upon any future sale and the IRS agrees to take second position. If a lender can get the first position, it will then agree to lend the money. However, the only way that the IRS will agree to this is if it gets some of the money owed it upon the closing of the refinance.

Over Your Limit _____

Do not think that the IRS will not file a tax lien against you. It files more than one million tax liens every year.

Two Cents _____

In 2001, 40 million tax returns were filed electronically (approximately 30 percent of all returns filed). The IRS is hoping to get that up to 80 percent by 2007.

♦ **Have the lien removed from some of your real estate.** A tax lien attaches to all of your real estate. The problem is, again, selling property is difficult with a lien attached to it. The IRS may agree to release a lien against one of your properties and keep the lien to others. The catch? The IRS must get some of the proceeds from the sale.

♦ **Settle.** The last option is to get the IRS to settle its claim with you for less than you owe and release its liens in exchange for payment in full of the agreed-upon lesser amount. This is the best option. Called an offer in compromise, this possibility is discussed in detail later in this chapter.

Before the Levy Breaks

A _levy_ is a seizure of your property, other than your wages (which is a garnishment). With a levy, the IRS physically takes away your property. It then has the right to sell it within 45 days of the seizure.

The first thing to understand about levies is that the IRS cannot levy certain property:

Clothing

Furniture up to a value of $1,650 total

Tools of the trade up to $1,100

Unemployment, disability, public assistance, and Workers' Compensation benefits

Certain pensions

Child support payments

Wages (only a portion may be seized)

The two things to be concerned about when dealing with levies are avoiding them in the first place and releasing them once they have occurred. There are many techniques that you can use to avoid a levy, and most involve hiding your assets. We are not recommending you do this, but you do need to know what your options are and what other people do in similar circumstances. We advise that you speak with a tax attorney before doing any of these things to make sure that you are acting properly and not breaking the law:

◆ **Transfer your bank accounts.** Some people have found that if the IRS does not know where their money is, it cannot be seized. It is an especially good idea to transfer your accounts to a main branch outside your city.

◆ **Give your property away.** Transfer title to a relative or friend. If you sell property, be sure to sell it for face value to avoid the appearance of impropriety.

◆ **Lease a car.** If you lease instead of buy, you are not the legal owner of the auto. Similarly, rent a home instead of buying one.

Money Talks

The Mustang Ranch, the infamous house-of-ill-repute in Nevada, owed the IRS more than $13 million in back taxes. The IRS seized the property, accepted a bid, and sold the ranch to a supposedly new owner for $1.5 million. It turned out that the new owner was merely the old owner hiding behind a new corporation. He is now hiding out of the country as the IRS still chases him.

When your property has been seized, getting it back is difficult. You will need to do one of the following:

◆ Submit an offer in compromise (covered later in this chapter).

◆ Propose an installment agreement (see Chapter 15).

◆ Offer an alternative solution, such as the sale of some real estate.

Appealing a Collection Action

Sometimes, no matter how hard you try to work out a solution to your IRS problem, you and the revenue officer cannot agree on the proper outcome. This disagreement may occur for a variety of reasons. Maybe your revenue officer is being too much of a stickler or has learned to dislike you. Maybe he does not have the authority to release the lien or wage garnishment. Whatever the reason, the IRS has recently instituted a new program that allows taxpayers to appeal collection actions and get the lien released, the levy withdrawn, and the sale cancelled.

Over Your Limit

The federal Privacy Act of 1976 makes tax returns confidential. However, the truth is that the IRS routinely shares its files with other federal and state agencies.

Note that this program has nothing to do with reducing your taxes. That issue is dealt with later in this chapter. This program is only for stopping a collection action. You can conduct a collection appeal against tax liens, notices of levy, actual levies, and property seizures.

The collection appeal is filed with form 9423, and instructions for how to proceed are available in IRS publication 1660. The form is simple, and the publication explains all the steps in the appeals process. Send the 9423 form to the manager of the IRS division that you are dealing with. Request the manager's name and address the appeal to him directly.

Do not be discouraged by what will happen next. The manager will agree with his employee. Fortunately, when that happens, the manager is required to forward the appeal to the appeals division of the IRS.

Your collection appeal will be assigned to an appeals officer for immediate review. Surprisingly, regulations require the appeals officer to reach a decision within five days. This requirement works to your advantage. Five days is faster than a speeding bullet to the IRS.

Because your appeals officer will not know who is right and who is wrong in this expedited case, he will probably want to resolve the matter to everyone's benefit. Appeals officers are negotiators by trade and like to get win-win results. If you propose a fair solution to your problem in your appeal, you will likely get a fair result from the appeals officer.

Let's Make a Deal

The offer in compromise (OIC) is our favorite tax tool. It is a program that allows taxpayers the chance to get rid of their tax problem for less than they owe, often pennies on the dollar. Almost all other tax programs, except penalty abatement, require a payment in full of some sort or another. As such, the OIC is a unique opportunity.

Two Cents

The average settlement for accepted offers in compromise is 14 cents on the dollar.

You must fulfill a couple of prerequisites to qualify for the OIC program. The first is that you must be current on all filings and paying requirements. This means that if you have any unfiled returns, you must file them before you can submit an OIC. If you have estimated quarterly payments due, you must pay them. If you are a tax protester, you will be denied an OIC.

Although many of the things outlined in this chapter can be done on your own, it might be a good idea to hire a tax professional (either a tax lawyer or an accountant) to help shepherd your OIC through the IRS maze. You stand to gain a lot by doing this correctly.

Beyond these housekeeping formalities, an OIC is not for everyone. You have to meet two requirements before the IRS will accept your OIC. First, you must offer more than the net value of all your assets. Second, you must offer more than the IRS could expect to receive through an installment agreement.

> **Money Talks**
>
> In the early '90s, the acceptance rate by the IRS of all offers in compromise was about 4 percent. By the end of the decade, the number had risen to 50 percent.

The Value of Your Assets

Your offer to settle your tax bill must be more than what the IRS would receive if it seized and sold all your assets. Thus, the first part of your OIC will be an asset evaluation.

When valuing your assets for this purpose, be sure to use the lowest possible, albeit ostensibly reasonable, price. What is the quick sale value of your house? That is the number to use. What would your furniture be worth at a garage sale? That is the value to use. Use the low blue book value on your car and be sure to deduct for anything that might lower the sale price, such as high miles. Understand, too, that the IRS cannot levy certain household items (listed earlier in this chapter), so these items need not be part of your analysis.

> **Check It Out**
>
> The **equity** you have in an item is the total value of that property less what you owe. If your car is worth $6,000 and you owe $4,000 on it, then your equity is $2,000. The IRS is only concerned with how much equity you have in an item.

Say that Spencer owes the IRS $40,000. Assume further that his house is worth $100,000 and his mortgage is $90,000. His car is worth $2,500, and his personal effects have a yard sale value of $1,000.

The first half of Spencer's OIC would look like this table:

OIC Calculation (Example)	
Home equity:	$10,000
Auto:	$2,500
Furniture (exempt):	$0
Total:	$12,500

Spencer has to offer the IRS an amount comparable to what the IRS would realize if it seized and sold all his nonexempt assets. That would be his home *equity* and his car, so his offer, at a minimum, must be for at least $12,500.

How Much Can You Afford to Pay?

The second part of the OIC analysis is this: How much could you pay the IRS if you paid it back in a monthly installment agreement for five years? You must add that amount to your previous figure.

In Spencer's case, he takes home about $2,000 a month, and his expenses are just about the same. Maybe he has $50 a month left over. He needs to add that amount ($50 multiplied by 60 months equals $3,000) to his previous $12,500 figure. Thus, Spencer's entire OIC offer would look like the following table:

OIC Ability to Pay (Example)	
Equity in all assets:	$12,500
Ability to pay:	$3,000
Total:	$15,500

Two Cents

Only about 2 percent of all taxpayers are ever investigated for tax fraud. Even then, only about 10 percent of those individuals are ever fined or criminally charged with tax fraud. Tax fraud is evading taxes intentionally and with an "evil purpose."

Thus, Spencer has to offer an IOU of $15,500 to the IRS in his OIC. This amount is what the IRS would receive if it took everything it could from Spencer and forced him into a repayment plan. Although this amount certainly is a lot of money, remember that Spencer owes the IRS $40,000. Settling for $15,500 is less than 50 cents on the dollar.

Preparing the OIC

Preparing an OIC is a fairly straightforward affair. You will need to fill out form 433-A if you are an individual, and forms 433-A and B if you are self-employed. You will also need to file form 656, Offer in Compromise.

You should also type up an analysis of your offer: why you say your home is worth what you said, why your car is valued so low (high miles, needs work)—that kind of thing. Finally, submit a down payment with your offer. It does not hurt and can only help to make the right impression.

Expect this process to be fairly lengthy. The IRS has a special OIC unit, but do not expect an answer for a few months. The IRS may want additional documents, and it may take up to nine months for your offer to work through the different levels of bureaucracy and settle the tax bill for an amount everyone can live with.

After the OIC has been agreed to, it will need to be paid within about 60 days. Sometimes your payment can be divided into two payments, but not often. It would be better to get a loan for the agreed-upon amount than to let this opportunity to settle your tax debt slip away.

The Bankruptcy Option

Part 4 discusses bankruptcy in detail, but what you need to understand at this point is that taxes can sometimes be wiped out (discharged) in a Chapter 7 bankruptcy. Taxes are dischargeable if the following conditions are met:

1. A tax return for the year in question was filed on time, or if not, it was filed at least two years before the bankruptcy.
2. The tax debt is over three years old.
3. The tax was assessed more than 240 days before the bankruptcy is filed.
4. The debtor is not a tax protestor.

For example, Matan and Tamar filed their taxes on time in 1994, but they never paid the bill. They now owe the IRS $8,000 and have never had a new assessment. They could file Chapter 7 bankruptcy and completely wipe out this debt without paying the IRS a penny.

Check It Out

A **tax protester** is a person who intentionally fails to file and/or pay taxes under the mistaken belief that federal tax law is illegal.

You should know, however, that this option does not get rid of tax liens. Although you won't technically owe the IRS money any more, if the IRS has filed a lien against your home, that lien remains valid after the bankruptcy is over and will have to be satisfied upon any sale of the property. You will not owe the money anymore, but your house will. Who said the law is logical? Not us!

Tax Court

Assuming none of these solutions has worked for you—that you lost your audit and your appeal, that an OIC won't work, and that you do not want to file bankruptcy—then your final option is to take the IRS to tax court. There are several advantages to this option:

1. **Your chances of success are excellent.** The IRS knows you are serious now. Half of all cases taken to tax court settle for less than the amount allegedly due.

2. **You do not have to hire a lawyer.**

3. **It gives you time.** At least another year will go by before any settlement occurs and taxes again come due.

The only downside is that interest and penalties will continue to accrue while you await your trial.

If you owe less than $10,000 for any one year ($40,000 for four years would therefore work, too), then yours is a small case and will be heard in that tax court. Cases for taxes in excess of $10,000 require the assistance of a tax attorney and are too complicated to discuss in any detail here.

Small case tax courts are much like any other small claims court. They are the kind of thing you see on *Judge Judy* or *The People's Court*. The key to winning a small claims case is the two P's: preparation and proof.

♦ **Preparation.** You know your case inside and out. You understand why you think you are right and why the IRS is wrong (your home office should be an allowable deduction, for example). Preparation also means having everything ready when you go to court. You have all documents organized and legible, and you have extra copies for everyone. You have your witnesses ready to go the day of the trial. You are on time and have an outline of your case. Preparation means acting like a professional.

♦ **Proof.** You must be able to prove your argument. If you go in with no documents, no witnesses, and no way to prove that what you are saying is true, you will lose. If it comes down to your word against the word of a revenue officer, the judge will believe the revenue officer.

Like any trial, your case will begin with opening statements, go on to your presentation of your case, your testimony, evidence and witnesses, cross-examination, and the IRS's case, and then will conclude with closing arguments. The judge will rule on your case within a few months. You are not allowed a jury trial in tax court.

In order to begin a tax court case, you will need to go down to your local IRS service center and ask for all the proper forms. You will need a petition, a designation of place of trial, your deficiency notice, and any other forms that the clerk may require. You will have to pay a fee (under $100). You will then get back in the mail a confirmation letter, a case number, and a trial date. Good luck.

Two Cents

If you are going to represent yourself in tax court, you must act accordingly. Dress professionally. Speak only to the judge or the witness on the stand. Do not smoke or chew gum. Do not get overly emotional or combative. Never interrupt a judge.

The Least You Need to Know

◆ Penalties can be abated.

◆ Liens and levies can be removed.

◆ Appealing your collection action has a good probability of success.

◆ An offer in compromise may be your best tax friend.

◆ Under the right circumstances, bankruptcy is a viable option, as is tax court.

Handling Business Debts

In This Chapter

- ◆ Creatively cutting costs
- ◆ Expanding out of the problem
- ◆ Borrowing your way out
- ◆ Keeping business and personal debts separate
- ◆ Going out of business

If you own your own small business, money and debt may be a constant issue. For many small businesses, money tends to come in the door in waves. When surf's up, all is well, but when things die down, you may feel stuck in the middle of an ocean with no land in sight. When you have serious business debts, you have a few basic alternatives. You can cut back, expand, or go out of business.

Reduce Your Overhead

First, you can cut your overhead and scale back. These are the same concepts we have discussed throughout this book, and they make sense in this situation, too. Sometimes you have to scale back a little; sometimes you have to scale back a lot. There are several ways to make sure that you are running a lean ship:

◆ **Control labor costs.** Labor is probably your highest business expense. Whole books are written on such management issues; all we suggest here is that you be sure that you are not overstaffed. Ask yourself whether you could further reduce labor costs by making an employee an independent contractor, thereby taking insurance, benefits, and tax withholding out of the labor equation. Use voice mail instead of having a receptionist. Be creative.

◆ **Reduce overhead.** Cut entertainment and other perks, compare insurance costs, and cut back on travel expenses.

◆ **Reward efficiency.** Make it profitable for employees to point out potential cost savings that you may have overlooked by giving them a bonus for any cost-saving ideas of theirs that you implement.

CAUTION

Over Your Limit

The IRS has rules for determining whether someone is really an independent contractor or merely an employee in contractor's clothing. The main things it looks at are the amount of independence the person has (contractors have more, employees have less), where the work is done (contractors may work out of their home), and the number of employers the person has (contractors tend to have more than one). If the IRS disagrees with your analysis, you may get stuck paying taxes on the individual.

However, although we do recommend running a tight ship, we do not recommend running a ship so tight it cannot sail. Scaling back your business, if done incorrectly and with too much zeal, can mean scaling back your primary source of income. Do not get rid of employees you will need again later. That is going too far.

We would never recommend that you work fewer hours (and thereby make less money) to get out of personal debt, and we do not recommend scaling back your business to the point of making less money as a way to get out of business debt. We understand that there are times that a radical scaling back of the business is necessary. That is fine and should definitely be explored. The important thing to remember is that you need to make more money right now, not less; although tightening the belt is good, doing so to the point of cutting off all circulation is bad.

Begin with the Right Attitude

Your second option is to make more money. Instead of constricting your business, consider expanding it instead to solve your cash crunch.

In order to expand your way out of your problem, you are going to have to return to your roots and think like you did when you first started your enterprise. When you began your business, you were undoubtedly creative when it came to initial financing. Maybe you used your life's savings to start your business. Maybe you financed it with credit cards. Maybe you took out an SBA loan. A family member could have helped. Possibly you used a variety of sources to get started.

The important thing to remember, and the mindset you have to get back to, is that nothing stopped you. Those who start their own businesses are passionate, driven people. It is trite, but true: You would not take no for an answer. Otherwise, you never would have been successful enough to worry about business debts in the first place.

If you have lost that mentality, you must regain it. (If you cannot regain it, then you must seriously consider shutting down the business or scaling it back to a part-time operation.) Humans are creatures of habit. What you must do is break some bad habits and try something new. How do we know that? Because if what you have been doing was working, you would not be reading this.

Take, for example, Omar. He and his wife immigrated to the United States from Poland with nothing more than $50 in their pockets. A craftsman by trade, Omar began a small construction company, doing all the work himself initially. Within 10 years, he was grossing more than a million a year. Then his accountant embezzled $400,000.

Omar's business went bankrupt, and he had to start all over again. The problem was, he had no working capital. In construction, the bills come due as the job proceeds, but payment is not made until the project is completed. A lack of operating capital severely restricted his ability to run, let alone expand, his business.

Omar could not get a loan. Finally, after a year, he asked his bank for a line of credit. He was denied. He then took his banker out to lunch and asked again, and again he was denied. At the end of the lunch, he told his banker that he was going to be

> **Money Talks**
>
> Billionaire Richard Branson, the founder and CEO of the Virgin Group (Virgin Records, Mega-stores, Virgin-Atlantic Airways, Virgin Cola) has said that whenever he was faced with a cash crisis as he grew his business, he would always try to expand out of it rather than constrict his business. He is not so unlike you. He began with a single record shop.

 **Two Cents**

Friends and family finance 25 percent of all new business startups.

writing checks against his account that he would not be able to cover for a few weeks and that the banker better figure out a way to cover them. He did write those checks, sometimes for as much as $11,000 over his balance. The bank covered every one. Omar was then able to rebuild his company, and his relationship with his bank continued to prosper.

The moral? What one person can do, another can do. If Omar can do it, you can, too. Think creatively. Do not take no for an answer.

Time for Some New Sources of Income

Aside from being creative financially when you started, you were probably pretty darn flexible when it came to making money. You were not sure what would work and in all likelihood tried a number of different methods for bringing in customers, clients, and cash. It is time to do that again.

After much trial and error in your business, you finally figured out what worked. In all likelihood, you then did that same thing over and over again. It could have been an ad that worked, a sale that brought in customers, a seminar, a location, or a stall at the Saturday public market.

In essence, you figured out your recipe for success and money. That is why money is called dough. You make your business dough by utilizing a recipe, a moneymaking recipe. Think about it. Isn't that what you did?

All successful businesses do the same. The entertainment industry does it. Hollywood has several recipes for movie-making success. They are called the romantic comedy, the teen-slasher picture, and the action adventure. Producers use these recipes over and over and over again. Stephen King's recipe is to scare the heck out of his audience. Television's favorite recipe is called the sitcom.

Microsoft, too, has a recipe (no, it's not called "protect your crappy product by creating a monopoly"). The recipe is to put out a new edition of Windows every few years. Ben & Jerry's Ice Cream's recipe is to create a great-tasting different flavor every so often and give it a cool name.

One way to expand out of your cash crisis is to create or learn a new recipe, a bigger and better recipe. This does not mean that you have to throw your old recipe away. It does mean that it may be time to learn a new one in addition to the one(s) you already have, as in the following examples:

♦ A lawyer may want to begin to handle probate and divorce cases, in addition to his regular bankruptcy practice.

♦ An antique dealer may want to start selling his wares on eBay in addition to selling from his store.

♦ A writer can start writing newsletters for big corporations in addition to the books she writes.

♦ A housekeeper can try to get some commercial clients in addition to her residential clients.

♦ A locksmith can start up a mobile service in addition to his shop.

Remember: A new recipe means more dough.

Alternate Sources of Income

Here is a revolutionary concept: You may want to get a job or start a second business. Stay with us here. Your probable problem is that you do not have enough income to cover your expenses. Finding a new recipe for your existing business is one way to create income. Another way is to create a second source of income.

The idea here is to create enough additional revenue to cover your overhead. A new income stream means more money for your business. Although we understand that you want to work for yourself, taking a job for a short-term infusion of cash is a way to keep the business afloat. It is not a sell-out if it allows you to keep the dream alive.

By the same token, starting another business is also a way to bring in more money. Azriela is a good example of this strategy. Besides a successful writing career—she writes books and has a nationally syndicated column, three online biweekly newsletters, and an entrepreneurial coaching practice (four recipes)—she is also a professional speaker. She does not rely solely on one occupation to bring in the money. You may want to consider the same thing.

Check It Out

When you expand your business to include more than one enterprise, it is called **diversification**. Diversification is a standard financial tool used to hedge against bad times in any one industry.

A smart stock investor knows not to buy just one stock. That stock may go up, but it may go down. Having more than one stock ensures that when one stock does go down, the likelihood of taking a big financial hit is remote. *Diversification* is a good tool to use to adapt to changing financial situations.

As a savvy entrepreneur, you may want to do the same thing. Think in terms of multiple income sources instead of just one. This way of doing business has multiple advantages.

> **Money Talks**
>
> Apple Computer, Dell Computer, Intuit (makers of Quicken software), and The Learning Annex all began as home-based businesses.

All businesses have cycles. When one of your businesses is slow, it is unlikely that another will be as well. Instead of suffering a cash crisis, you are still able to keep money coming in.

Large businesses do the same thing. Amazon.com began selling books online. Now it sells CDs and gifts, conducts auctions, and has an interest in a pharmacy business.

Give Yourself a Raise

Robyn runs a day-care business out of her home. She loves her kids and loves what she does. She is also always strapped for cash. Does she need a new recipe or another business? No. Robyn's problem has a far simpler solution. Robyn has not raised her prices in 10 years.

Because you are your own boss, you set the prices. When was the last time you raised your prices? Although you should be concerned that you will drive away clients if you do, it is still worth a shot. If your fears are valid, you can always lower your prices again. But if your fears are ungrounded, you will be giving yourself a well-deserved raise.

Azriela coached a professional who was very concerned about "inflicting" higher prices on her clients until she was able to see that it was also for their benefit. The woman was burning out and was unable to give her clients the service they deserved because she was taking on too many clients in order to pay the bills. By raising her prices, she was able to say no to some new clients and better serve her existing ones.

You will never know until you try. People who buy apartment houses for a living are always looking to purchase units where rents are too low for the area because they can raise rents upon completion of the sale. Such units are quite easy to find. If many landlords are charging too little, you certainly could be as well.

Receive Your Receivables

When you allow someone to buy your product "net 30" (that is, payable 30 days after the purchase), you are essentially lending that person money. Permitting these people extra time beyond 30 days to pay for a purchase is a commonplace, yet easily correctable, mistake. Would your bank allow you an extra 60 days to pay your loan? Of course not. Your business should be run the same way.

Always remember that *accounts receivable* (AR) are the lifeblood of your business, representing your business's cash flow and liquidity. Getting your receivables current, therefore, has two advantages:

> ### Check It Out
> Your **accounts receivable** is the total amount you are owed by all customers who have not yet paid you and is a great source of income in hard times.

- ◆ It will bring in immediate cash.

- ◆ It will make your business look better to potential lenders.

Here is how to get those friendly deadbeats to pay up:

- ◆ **Assign someone the task of contacting all AR over 30 days old** (or if you are a sole proprietor, you must prioritize this task for yourself). Get a specific date as to when the debt will be paid and call again on that day if the money is not received. You must remember this: A vow is just a vow. Begin with a friendly reminder but get increasingly aggressive as time goes by. Once an AR is more than 60 days old, you have a real problem.

- ◆ **Add interest.** Institute a new policy of at least 10 percent interest on all AR over 30 days old.

- ◆ **Stop all shipments.** Inform your repeat customers that all outstanding balances must be made current before any new product will be sent out.

- ◆ **Hire a professional.** As a penultimate resort, hire a lawyer or a collection agency to commence collection activities.

- ◆ **Sell the debt.** The money owed to you is a commodity and can be sold like one. Collection agencies buy bad debt every day, for a sharply discounted price. Expect bidding to begin at 50 percent of what you are owed.

Business Loans

It's highly ironic: One way to get your business out of debt is to go into more debt. Sometimes business owners just need a short-term infusion of cash to get things moving again or maybe a long-term note or a line of credit might help.

Then again, a loan may be nothing more than a bandage. Take Stephen, for example. He ran a consignment furniture store and got into the bad habit of not paying some consignors after he was paid. He ended up $10,000 in the hole, so he took out a loan and solved the short-term crisis, but he never changed his ways. He was finally forced out of business a few years later. Make sure that your loan will not fortify bad business practices, but will instead enable you to get through an unusual money crunch.

Several different types of business loans may be right for you:

1. **Accounts receivable financing.** This revolving line of credit is based upon your accounts receivable. Depending upon how much you are owed and the likelihood of repayment, this type of loan can speed cash flow to meet current obligations. As cash needs vary, the borrower is able to increase or reduce the loan amount without renegotiations, and the ability to borrow grows directly with accounts receivable.

    A typical program enables a client to borrow a predetermined percentage of accounts receivable, usually 80 percent. You would then receive periodic advances, upon request, deposited directly into your bank account. Interest is charged only on the amount of funds advanced to you.

2. **Purchase order financing.** Say that you have a purchase order for $50,000 worth of widgets, but you need capital to service the account and get everything shipped. Using this method of financing, a borrower can obtain advances on designated purchase orders that can be repaid directly by the borrower's customer. This method of borrowing can be particularly convenient for large projects or when you only need to borrow money occasionally (only when you receive unusually large orders, for example).

3. **Inventory loans.** These funds are usually short-term and are used to take advantage of attractive purchasing opportunities or to support seasonal increases in inventory.

4. **Fixed asset loans.** These loans are based upon fixed assets (such as machinery you own) and can be used to acquire additional equipment and to improve a company's financial position by increasing working capital, consolidating debt, and reducing monthly payments.

5. **SBA loans.** The federal Small Business Administration guarantees loans made by banks to small businesses. What is great is that these loans are fairly easy to get and have very favorable repayment terms. Because the federal government guarantees these loans, banks like to make them. You can contact the SBA at www.sba.gov or 1-800-U-ASK-SBA.

6. **Personal loans.** Mom and dad or other relatives may lend you money.

Check It Out _____

The SBA also sponsors privately owned small venture capital organizations that lend money to entrepreneurs for start-up capital or to expand a business. These organizations are called **Small Business Investment Companies,** or **SBICs.**

Keeping Business Debts and Personal Debts Separate

You may be tempted to dip into your personal pocket to help out your business. Maybe you want to use your credit cards to finance your business during a rough stretch, or you are being asked to personally guarantee a business loan.

Although we understand the desire to do this, we do not recommend this course of action. Yet we also know that it is commonplace. Indeed, both of your authors have broken this rule and mixed personal and business debt in order to keep their respective businesses going. If you do mix these debts, the important thing is to keep the debt manageable.

Caren made the mixing mistake. She helped found a nonprofit AIDS awareness organization and ran it for six years. Every time fund-raising slowed down, Caren took an advance on her credit cards to keep the organization afloat. After 10 years, it finally folded, and Caren was $40,000 in debt and unemployed. She was forced to file for bankruptcy.

One great way to keep your business and personal money lives separate is to incorporate your business. Although expensive (roughly $2,500 for attorney and state filing fees), incorporation has tremendous financial advantages.

The main one is that once you incorporate, you are personally off the hook insofar as liability goes. A disgruntled customer could sue your corporation, but not you. A creditor

Money Talks
The three main types of corporations are called C corporations (where the corporation pays the tax), S corporations (where the shareholders pay the tax), and Limited Liability Corporations (also known as LLCs, for smaller companies that might otherwise be partnerships).

could legally go after the business, but not you personally. Incorporating protects your personal assets, your home, and your spouse's income from your creditors. To learn more about incorporation, visit bizfilings.com, the largest Internet provider of incorporation services.

Closing Up Shop

Going out of business, although unpleasant, is not the worst thing in the world. If your business debts are so bad that keeping the doors open is too difficult, closing up shop may be more a relief than a failure.

When shutting down a business, remember to do the wrong thing. You may be tempted to do the right thing, namely, borrow from yourself to pay off your business creditors (even though we already told you not to!). For instance, you might be tempted to take out a second mortgage to pay off everyone and close the doors with nothing owed. It would feel good. It would be dumb.

First, you will be unemployed. You do not know where you will be working or how much you will be making. Taking on additional debt at this point is the complete antithesis of everything we have been trying to teach you in this book. There are other ways to solve money problems besides incurring additional debt.

Second, you will be trading unsecured debt for secured debt. If you fail to pay some vendors, there is not a whole lot they can do. They surely cannot repossess your house. But if you pay them by refinancing your house, and then cannot pay the new mortgage, the bank can take your home. Never trade unsecured debt for secured debt.

You may have to go to the court of last resort. Although it is not our favorite solution, bankruptcy is one way to close a business, wipe out the debts (at least legally), and start over. We discuss this option in more detail in Part 4.

The key point to take away from this chapter is this: There are many ways to get out of debt. Use your imagination and figure out what will work for you.

The Least You Need to Know

- Cutting back your business is okay; cutting into it is not.
- Expanding out of the problem is your best solution, if you can figure out a way to do it.
- Getting a loan to get out of debt may be oxymoronic, but it just might work.
- If you do mix business and personal debts, do so with caution.

Chapter 18

Debtors Anonymous

In This Chapter

- ◆ Humble beginnings
- ◆ What to expect
- ◆ A self-test
- ◆ Meetings

This debt stuff is a serious matter under any circumstances. However, for some, it is more serious than for others. For some people, debt issues are so out of control that going into debt is more of an addiction than a predicament.

In that case, the situation requires more than the ideas being presented in this book. It requires a fundamental restructuring of some basic psychological matters and the support of other people in the same boat. You can get that help through a group called Debtors Anonymous (DA).

In essence, DA is a group for people whose indebtedness issues rise to the level of some sort of compulsive behavior that they feel they have no control over, for those whose debt problems are destroying their lives the way alcohol or gambling can destroy lives. If you feel that your debt issues are not that drastic, DA is probably not for you. If, on the other hand, you feel that going into debt is a matter out of your control, you may have just found your answer.

Roots

Debtors Anonymous is a group of like-minded people (they call themselves a "fellow-ship") designed to help others in the group get out of compulsive debting. It is not unlike the other Anonymous groups you may have heard about: Overeaters Anonymous, Narcotics Anonymous, and the granddaddy of them all, Alcoholics Anonymous (AA). Indeed, Debtors Anonymous began as an offshoot of AA. Understanding where AA comes from will better help you understand where DA can take you.

Alcoholics Anonymous

AA itself had its beginnings in 1935 in Akron, Ohio. There, Bill W., a New York stock-broker, and Dr. Bob S., an Akron surgeon, met for the first time. The world was changed for the better as a result.

Both men had been hopeless alcoholics. Bill explained to Bob that he believed that alcoholism was not merely a weakness on the part of the alcoholic but was instead a malady of mind, emotions, and body—that, in fact, alcoholism was a disease. Dr. William D. Silkworth of Towns Hospital in New York, where Bill had often been a patient, taught this revolutionary concept to Bill. Though a physician, Dr. Bob, like the rest of the world, had not thought of alcoholism as a disease. The founding spark of AA had been struck.

> **Money Talks**
>
> Alcoholics Anonymous has helped more than two million people overcome alcoholism and now has chapters in almost every country around the globe. Women make up 35 percent of the total membership.

Both men immediately set to work with alcoholics at Akron's City Hospital. They achieved a quick success with their first patient. Though the name Alcoholics Anonymous had not yet been coined, these three men made up the nucleus of the first AA group.

Debtors Anonymous

Debtors Anonymous began in 1968 when some members from Alcoholics Anonymous held a meeting to discuss their money problems. They first called themselves the "Penny Pinchers" and later "Capital Builders." By 1971, the essence of the DA pro-gram had unfolded in much the same way AA had begun: With an understanding that for these members, the act of debting itself was a disease. The founding members knew that their best solution was to adapt the 12 steps of Alcoholics Anonymous, and so they did.

Debtors Anonymous evolved into a fellowship of men and women who share their experiences, strength, and hope with each other so that they can all recover from compulsive debting. The only requirement for membership is a desire to stop incurring unsecured debt. Today, there are over 500 DA meetings throughout the United States and in 13 other countries throughout the world.

Over Your Limit _____

The average household has 11 credit cards and pays more than $1,000 in interest in a year. According to *Parade Magazine*, 40 percent of these households say they have "great difficulty" making their payments.

Does This Sound Familiar?

Karen B.'s story is a common one (last names are prohibited to ensure privacy and recovery). She says that she was a compulsive spender "as long as I remember." She received her first credit card by age 17 and was $20,000 in debt before she graduated from college. She went to work and was soon another $20,000 in debt, always sure she would be able to pay the cards off "later." By the time she had found DA, she had given up balancing her checkbook.

She began to attend DA meetings. She cut up her credit cards (they were all maxed-out anyway). It was not easy for her, but she kept with the program. She made regular payments on her debts. She recorded all her spending.

Soon she was able to take short vacations (paid for with cash). She got married (paying for the wedding in cash) and later bought a beautiful Victorian house in a nice neighborhood. She says that she would never have dared dream that she could get out of debt and afford to buy a house but for DA.

Two Cents _____

Because of interest (and possibly penalties) most people will spend 112 percent more on a credit card purchase than they would have had they used cash.

How the Program Works

The only requirement for DA membership is a desire to stop using any form of unsecured debt. DA is not allied with any sect, denomination, political group, organization, or institution. It neither endorses nor opposes any cause. Its primary purpose is to help other compulsive debtors to achieve solvency and peace of mind. There are no dues or fees for DA membership. It is a self-supporting organization run on contributions.

The keys to the program are these concepts:

- **Abstinence.** Members practice abstinence by not incurring any more unsecured debt, taking one day at a time.

- **Meetings.** Members attend meetings for solidarity and camaraderie.

- **Record maintenance.** DA members maintain records of their daily income and expenses, as well as the retirement of any portions of their outstanding debts.

- **Anonymity.** Members practice anonymity, which allows them freedom of expression by assuring that what is said at meetings or to other DA members at any time will not be repeated.

- **Telephone.** Members maintain phone contact with one another, especially during difficult steps in their recovery.

- **Pressure-relief groups and pressure-relief meetings.** After they have gained some familiarity with the DA program, members organize *pressure-relief groups* that consist of the member and two other people from the group who have been abstinent for three months. The group meets to review the member's financial situation.

Two Cents

A simple way to cut back is to take stock of what you buy. Do you read that paper you have delivered every day? Do you look at those magazines you buy and those premium cable channels you pay for? Cutting back in areas like these can create an extra $100 a month easily.

- **Spending plans.** The pressure-relief meeting usually results in the formulation of a spending plan (putting needs first) and an action plan (for resolving indebtedness). Making these plans is considered one of the main steps for creating financial solvency.

- **Sponsorship.** A sponsor is an abstinent member of DA more experienced in working the 12 steps. The sponsor aids the member in implementing the action plan and in working the steps.

- **Service.** DA believes that only through service can members give to others what has been so given to each one.

Is DA Right for You?

It may be hard for you to decide whether attending a DA meeting makes sense for you and your situation. Certainly it is not an easy conclusion to come to, however necessary this step may be. Attend a meeting; there is no commitment necessary, and going to a meeting will help you get a feel for the group.

Another way to see whether DA might help you is to take the following quiz that DA has put together. Be brave. Take this test; you have nothing to lose but your indebtedness. Columbus took a chance, and you know what happened to him, don't you? He died. (We jest!)

Over Your Limit

Approximately 60 million Americans are "addicted" to spending or shopping.

Take the following quiz and then tally up your score:

1. Are your debts making your home life unhappy?

2. Does the pressure of your debts distract you from your daily work?

3. Are your debts affecting your reputation?

4. Do your debts cause you to think less of yourself?

5. Have you ever given false information in order to obtain credit?

6. Have you ever made unrealistic promises to your creditors?

7. Does the pressure of your debts make you careless of the welfare of your family?

8. Do you ever fear that your employer, family, or friends will learn the extent of your total indebtedness?

9. When faced with a difficult financial situation, does the prospect of borrowing give you an inordinate feeling of relief?

10. Does the pressure of your debts cause you to have difficulty in sleeping?

11. Has the pressure of your debts ever caused you to consider getting drunk?

12. Have you ever borrowed money without giving adequate consideration to the rate of interest you are required to pay?

13. Do you usually expect a negative response when you are subject to a credit investigation?

14. Have you ever developed a strict regimen for paying off your debts, only to break it under pressure?

15. Do you justify your debts by telling yourself that you are superior to the "other" people, and when you get your "break," you'll be out of debt overnight?

If you answered yes to eight or more of these questions, you have a problem with compulsive debt or are well on your way to having one.

Money Talks

Some signposts on the road to becoming a compulsive debtor are frequent use of the term *borrow* for such everyday things as cigarettes and pencils, associating charging with being a grown-up, inordinate apprehension when applying for credit, an unwarranted embarrassment during a normal discussion of money, and the underlying feeling that you need someone else to help you get out from under your financial problem.

Do not be ashamed if you decide that you need help. Asking for help is the first step toward solvency. You are to be commended for having the courage to ask for help.

The Meeting

If you decide that Debtors Anonymous is right for you, you should know what you are getting into. The core of the program is its meetings. They provide love and support for those going through difficult life changes.

Most meetings start with the chairperson or secretary welcoming everyone and then introducing himself or herself by saying: "Hello. My name is (first name only), and I am a compulsive debtor. Welcome to the (name of group) meeting of Debtors Anonymous." Many groups choose to open their meetings with a prayer, such as the Serenity prayer, or with a few moments of silent meditation.

A reading of the preamble usually follows the prayer or meditation:

> Debtors Anonymous is a fellowship of men and women who share their experience, strength, and hope with each other so that they may solve their common problem and help others to recover from compulsive debting. The only requirement for membership is desire to stop incurring unsecured debt. Our primary purpose is to stay solvent and help other compulsive debtors to achieve solvency.

Some groups pass around copies of the "12 Steps" and "Tools of Debtors Anonymous" for readings by group members. After the readings, groups will ask newcomers and out-of-towners to introduce themselves so that they can be welcomed.

Next, the speaker is introduced and asked to share his or her experience with the group. This sharing usually involves explaining what happened before the speaker came to DA, how the speaker found DA, and what life has been like since coming to DA. The length of the speaker's sharing depends on the meeting's format. At designated speaker meetings, the speaker may have 30 minutes or more; at discussion meetings, he or she may have perhaps 10 or 15 minutes.

When the speaker is finished, the meeting is then open for sharing from the group. Announcements and closing statements conclude the meeting. The chairperson will normally reiterate that the opinions expressed are those of the individuals who gave them and that the things heard were strictly confidential.

Over Your Limit

According to PBS, "Americans charged more than one trillion (1,000,000,000) dollars in purchases with their credit cards" in 2001.

The Magic Number: 12

At the heart of any Anonymous group are the 12 steps. They form the backbone and core of any so-called 12-step group. A caveat: Do not be intimidated by the religious overtones you are about to read. DA is strictly nondenominational. Whatever your views are on religion, you will be accepted in DA. Know this, too: These 12 steps have saved many a life.

The 12 Steps of Debtors Anonymous

1. We admitted we were powerless over debt—that our lives had become unmanageable.

2. We came to believe that a power greater than ourselves could restore us to sanity.

3. We made a decision to turn our will and our lives over to the care of God, as we understood him.

4. We made a searching and fearless moral inventory of ourselves.

5. We admitted to God, to ourselves, and to another human being the exact nature of our wrongs.

6. We were entirely ready to have God remove all these defects of character.

7. We humbly asked him to remove our shortcomings.

8. We made a list of all persons we had harmed and became willing to make amends to them all.

9. We made direct amends to such people wherever possible, except when to do so would injure them or others.

10. We continued to take personal inventory and when we were wrong promptly admitted it.

11. We sought through prayer and meditation to improve our conscious contact with God, as we understood him, praying only for knowledge of his will for us and the power to carry that out.

12. Having had a spiritual awakening as the result of these steps, we tried to carry this message to compulsive debtors and to practice these principles in all our affairs.

These 12 steps are based upon the highly successful Alcoholics Anonymous 12 steps. They are not easy to follow, but you can rest assured that if you follow them, your life will never be the same.

How to Contact Debtors Anonymous

DA has groups throughout the country, indeed, throughout the world. If you would like to attend a meeting, you can contact the national organization, which will tell you about groups in your area.

The Least You Need to Know

- ◆ Like AA, Debtors Anonymous helps people whose problem has become a compulsion.
- ◆ It is a highly organized, yet very flexible group.
- ◆ You are expected to attend meetings regularly.
- ◆ DA has a proven track record of success.
- ◆ The 12 steps are key to any successful recovery from addictive debting.

Part 4

A Last Option: Bankruptcy

Sometimes you need to file bankruptcy to beat debt. Many people feel that bankruptcy is shameful (because it may be an indication of incompetence) or wrong (that people have a moral obligation to pay back all debts, even those charging 17 percent or more). Bankruptcy is an option you should consider. It's legal, and you're allowed to do it. Once you've done it, you cannot be discriminated against on the basis of your bankruptcy filing. And once you've gone through bankruptcy, your debts are gone, subject to some special exceptions explained in detail later in the section. Bankruptcy is complex; if you decide to file bankruptcy, you will probably need a lawyer. This section contains a lot of information about bankruptcy. The decision is yours.

Chapter 19

Bankruptcy Basics

In This Chapter

- Why you may be considering bankruptcy
- A word of caution
- Advantages and disadvantages of bankruptcy
- Chapter overview: types of bankruptcies

Throughout this book, we have endeavored to give you a variety of methods for handling your money problems. If budgeting better doesn't work, then maybe rethinking your relationship with money might. If negotiating has not worked, then possibly Debtors Anonymous is the answer. Then again, maybe none of these strategies is the answer. Maybe it's time for a fresh start. Maybe it's time to consider bankruptcy.

Luckily, we live in a country that believes in second chances (just ask Bill Clinton!). With regard to debt, Congress provides for that second chance in the form of the bankruptcy code. Take a deep breath. Although bankruptcy sounds scary, for many people, it is nothing short of a blessing.

It's Not So Bad

You have valiantly tried to do everything in your power to fix your money problems. You are determined to handle money differently in the future, but nothing you do now can seem to get you out of the huge hole you have put yourself in. There comes a point for some people where they just want to raise the white flag over their money ship, give up, and start over. They do not want to explain their situation to even one more unsympathetic creditor. They do not want to even answer their phone at all. Their ship is sinking.

One of Steve's clients, John, had a successful career as a BMW salesman and made a fine living. Then his wife left him one day, and he grew despondent. A short time later, he was fired. He lived off of his credit cards for a few months, sure that he would be able to get a new job and repay the debt in no time.

His depression was getting worse, so he finally decided to ride his bike across the country as a kick-start for a new life. The night before he was to leave on his adventure of renewal, he tripped over his bike and shattered his leg. John was in the hospital for two weeks and in rehab for three months. By the time he was finally able to get a job and go back to work, he had been unemployed for almost eight months. His credit card debt had gone from a manageable $35,000 to an unmanageable $60,000. What was he to do?

His massive debt was enough to put him over the edge. John never thought he was the type to file for bankruptcy, but he had few options left. No amount of fancy letter writing or negotiating would ever get him off the hook. Eventually, his creditors would sue him and win. This is called getting a judgment against a defendant.

Check It Out

A **judgment** is a court order to pay a certain amount of money. The person who sued (the **plaintiff**) can use a variety of methods to collect on the judgment. He or she can attach wages (a **wage garnishment**), can seize bank accounts (a **levy**), or can file a lien against the debtor's real estate. Judgments are normally valid for 10 years, but most states allow judgments to be renewed for another 10 years.

For many people, the threat of a lawsuit or a wage garnishment is what finally forces them to seriously consider bankruptcy. But far less desperate circumstances can also hasten a bankruptcy. You merely have to be at a place where you feel you need a new financial beginning and see no other viable solution.

The bankruptcy code does not ask why a person is in debt. Losing a job is equal to getting divorced is equal to binge-shopping is equal to illness is equal to poor money skills. You could owe your creditors $10,000 or $100,000—it does not matter. The decision to file for bankruptcy is strictly a personal decision based upon individual circumstances.

In the right circumstances, bankruptcy can be a safe harbor in the financial storm. It is a place that can stop all creditor harassment, allow for a new beginning, and forgive your debts.

Forgiveness, doesn't that have a nice ring to it? Almost all of the law is about the opposite of forgiveness, namely retribution. Lawsuits are all about retribution. The entire criminal justice system is about retribution. The truly amazing thing about bankruptcy laws in this country is that they are founded upon the idea that sometimes, just sometimes, people need a break. Bankruptcy is about forgiving your debts, forgiving your mistakes, and letting you start over, at least financially. Take a deep breath. That last option is not so horrible.

A Caveat

Before we get into an extended discussion about how bankruptcy works, a word of caution is in order. For the past several years, Congress has been heavily lobbied to change the bankruptcy laws. Not surprisingly, it has been the credit card issuers who have done most of the lobbying. As a result, bankruptcy reform has passed both the House and Senate several times since the late '90s.

However, at the end of his term, President Clinton twice vetoed the bill. Then, when George W. Bush became president, the bill passed Congress and again got stalled in conference committee. As of the writing of this second edition, it still had not been passed into law, and whether it ever will remains to be seen. But it might, so you need to know what the proposed changes are.

The reason that there has been such a strong desire to reform bankruptcy laws is that over the past decade, bankruptcy filings have skyrocketed and credit card companies have lost a lot of money in the process. But the reform may be throwing the baby out with the bathwater. The problem with the reform is two-fold: the argument and the proposed solution.

The Argument

Proponents of bankruptcy reform have said that there is a need for reform because there is too much bankruptcy fraud going on today; that people have been using "lax" laws to thwart the system. Anyone reading this book, however, knows that debt is all too real these days. Moreover, several studies conducted by industry groups have concluded that bankruptcy is a necessary safety net and that bankruptcy fraud is very rare.

The Proposed Solution

The new measure, if it ever makes it to law, would change bankruptcy laws in several ways:

◆ **Means testing:** Presently (as you will read about later in this chapter), when you file a Chapter 7 bankruptcy, almost all of your debts are wiped out and you pay nothing back. That is why it is called a "fresh start." Under the proposed legislation, however, if you have at least $100 left over after paying your bills, you will be required to file a Chapter 13 bankruptcy and repay your debts over a three- to five-year period.

◆ **Approved budgets:** Under the bill, only certain expenses would count toward your budget. Expenses for say, cell phones and entertainment, would be unacceptable.

◆ **Credit card priority:** Presently, credit card charges of more than $1,000 on any single card are difficult to discharge in a bankruptcy. Under the new law, *all* credit card expenses for the three months prior to filing bankruptcy would need to be repaid in full.

Consumer groups have said that these changes, and other similar ones, will effectively wipe out the safety net that is bankruptcy law.

Women's groups in particular have been very vocal about what they consider to be the negative effects of the bill. Specifically, because it will be harder to wipe out credit card bills and car loans, these groups feel that divorced women especially will be put in direct competition with powerful companies when trying to get a bankrupt ex-husband to pay alimony and child support. That is, if a husband could previously get out of a bad car loan and large credit card payments by filing a Chapter 7, then paying alimony and child support would theoretically be easier. But if the new bill becomes law that would no longer be true.

What all of this means is that you better be sure what the state of the law is before ever filing bankruptcy. And in any case, as we have advised throughout this book, bankruptcy should be considered a last option. What follows, then, is a discussion of bankruptcy law as it stands today. Hopefully, it will be this way tomorrow, too.

Your Creditors Will Survive

Of course, you would rather pay your debts if you could. But if you are reading this, then maybe you cannot. Although it is certainly understandable that you might feel bad for your creditors, it also might be helpful to know that most of them will be just fine.

Money Talks

Ever wonder why you have been paying 18 percent on many of your credit cards? One reason is that credit card companies know that a certain percentage of their customers will never be able to fully pay all amounts due on the card (either because of default or bankruptcy). Thus they charge everyone a higher interest rate than necessary to offset these losses. You have been subsidizing other people's bankruptcies for years.

Do you think that the people who service your Visa account go home and worry at night about the fact that if you pay the minimum on your card you will owe more next month due to penalties and interest? Of course not. Furthermore, these companies are in the business of making money and have made a fortune off of you already. They will get by just fine without your $119 payment every month. That is one of the costs of capitalism. Do not fret. Your creditors will survive.

Know this, too: Bankruptcy is a legal right that has been a part of civilized societies for thousands of years. You may notice that corporations file for bankruptcy protection all the time. Like you, sometimes they need help. Even the Bible says that creditors should forgive debts every seven years.

So if you are feeling ashamed and despondent over your need to file bankruptcy, get over it. You are in good company. Of course, you should learn your lessons and not get in this pickle again. But both bankruptcy and this country are about second chances. If you need to, take yours.

Is Bankruptcy Right for You?

Right now you are probably feeling very defensive. Creditors are probably calling you at all hours of the day and night. You may be getting threatening letters, possibly even lawsuits and threats of foreclosure. What to do? Bankruptcy to the rescue!

Bankruptcy Benefits

The moment you file your bankruptcy, the bankruptcy court issues an order called an *automatic stay*. This is the first step in your redemption. The stay is a federal court order that puts you back in the driver's seat and puts your creditors on the defensive. (Doesn't that sound nice?) The stay is automatic because it occurs in every bankruptcy case that is filed. It is called a stay because it forces everything to stay put.

The stay immediately puts a halt to all collection activities. It stops lawsuits. It stops wage garnishments. It stops all phone calls and letters. It stops auto repossessions. Your house could be on the block, ready to be sold by your bank at a foreclosure sale tomorrow, and if you file bankruptcy today, the sale will be stopped. No matter what action a collector is about to take against you, you hold the ultimate trump card: bankruptcy and the automatic stay.

Although the stay is a fantastic tool for all debtors, sometimes it can be lifted. If that happens, then the creditor who gets it lifted can proceed with collecting the money you owe. Relief from stay is a rare occurrence. You will know it is happening to you if you get something in the mail called a "relief from stay" motion. If it does happen, the stay is only lifted for that one creditor who filed the motion; it remains in effect for everyone else.

The automatic stay normally remains in effect for the duration of the bankruptcy, usually about four months for a Chapter 7. For most people then, the filing of the case and the issuance of the automatic stay means that they will never have to deal with their creditors again. The stay stops all communication during the bankruptcy, and the conclusion of the case wipes out the debts altogether.

If you think that the automatic stay is a great benefit of filing for bankruptcy, just wait until you hear about the discharge. For people in deep financial debt, it's truly a wonderful thing.

The discharge occurs at the end of your case and states that your debts have been wiped out (discharged) and your liability for those debts has been forgiven (there's that word again). You could owe $60,000 to six different credit cards, and the entire debt will be forgiven at the conclusion of your case.

Suppose you pay $800 a month in credit card bills. The filing of the bankruptcy means that you need never pay that money to your creditors again. The opportunity to get rid of $800 a month in payments produces a lot of disposable income.

The last benefit of bankruptcy is peace of mind. Few things in life cause more marital strife and personal stress than money problems. Bankruptcy, with its chance to start anew, get creditors off your back, wipe out debts, and create disposable income, will help you to get along better with your mate and sleep better at night.

> **Money Talks**
>
> Surprisingly, bankruptcy makes some people more attractive to lenders than they would have been had they not filed bankruptcy. Because home loans are based, at least in part, upon one's debt-to-income ratio, and because Chapter 7 bankruptcy wipes out most debts, a debtor's ratios look better, thereby improving his chances of getting the loan, if he has recently received a discharge.

Although many people think of bankruptcy as a horrible last resort, many people have the exact opposite experience. Take our friend John, whom we mentioned previously, for example. Through bankruptcy, he was able to wipe out all his credit card debt. After that, he got a job at another BMW dealership, and he eventually remarried. Bankruptcy was the tool that gave him the chance to start over, both financially and emotionally.

The Dark Side of Bankruptcy

Of course, filing bankruptcy has its downside, including the following:

- **The effect on your credit report.** Most items remain on your credit report for seven years. A Chapter 7 bankruptcy stays on for 10 years.

- **The effect on future credit.** Filing for bankruptcy does not mean that you will never get credit again. What it does mean is that the credit you do get will be more expensive. For example, although you might be able to get a car loan at 10 percent interest today, that same loan will cost around 20 percent after you file. Although people routinely get home loans about two years after their discharge, they will definitely pay higher interest and have to deal with more points. Credit cards will be secured rather than unsecured for a few years. However—this may shock you—within three years after a bankruptcy, most people have A-1 credit again.

- **Loss of property.** In a few cases, a person may lose some of his property to the bankruptcy trustee. This loss occurs only when the person either files a bankruptcy without the assistance of an attorney, has a bad attorney, or owns too much property. (See Chapter 20 for a detailed discussion about keeping property.)

- **Stigma.** Although there used to be a great stigma attached to filing bankruptcy, that is far less true today. With so many people doing it, and so many notable businesses and celebrities doing it (Burt Reynolds, MC Hammer, and Kim Basinger), for good or ill, there is not much of a social stigma left.

Money Talks

Every bankruptcy case is administered by a bankruptcy trustee. This person is appointed by the United States Department of Justice (the division of the government that oversees bankruptcies). The trustee may or may not be a lawyer. The trustee's job is to review your paperwork and discover whether you have failed to disclose any assets that you own (definitely a no-no). Be honest throughout the process, and all should go well.

You especially want to make sure that you will be able to protect all your assets when you file. Each state has different laws and limits regarding the amount of property a debtor can keep when he files bankruptcy. Some states are generous, and some states are stingy. Speak with a bankruptcy attorney in your state before filing to figure out your property situation.

Although there are certainly some negative aspects to filing bankruptcy, the truth is, for those who are seriously contemplating it, the benefits of bankruptcy usually outweigh the burdens.

Types of Bankruptcies

Once you have decided that bankruptcy is a viable option, the next thing to consider is what type of bankruptcy you will file. There are four types of bankruptcies individuals may consider: Chapter 7, Chapter 11, Chapter 12, and Chapter 13 (these are chapters of the United States Bankruptcy Code).

Two kinds of bankruptcies probably won't apply to you. Chapter 11 is used by large businesses that want to reorganize their debts and is sometimes used by people with at least six zeroes' worth of debt. It is inapplicable to almost all consumer debtors. Chapter 12 is a type of bankruptcy specifically designed to help family farmers. It, too, is fairly rare.

Chapter 7 is the most common bankruptcy used by consumers and is usually the best choice. Like Chapter 11, Chapter 13 is also a type of reorganization, but it is intended for consumer use. In a small number of cases, using Chapter 13 makes sense. Almost all consumers or small businesses will file either a Chapter 7 or a Chapter 13 bankruptcy.

Chapter 7

You want to (and most likely will) file a Chapter 7 bankruptcy. First of all, it is quick; a Chapter 7 normally takes about four months from start to finish. Also, a Chapter 7 bankruptcy costs less than a Chapter 13. (See Chapter 21 for information about costs.) Best of all, it solves the problem; debtors normally pay nothing back to their creditors.

The reason that a Chapter 7 bankruptcy makes sense for most people is that they have a lot of *unsecured debt*, usually credit card debt. Whereas a Chapter 13 forces you to repay some of this money over a period of several years, a Chapter 7 completely wipes out the debt without forcing you to pay another penny once the case is filed.

Chapter 7 is also attractive because most states allow most debtors to keep all of their property. This chance to discharge all debts and keep all property is what makes Chapter 7 so attractive. Combined with its relatively short duration, a Chapter 7 is usually preferable to a Chapter 13.

If you have a lot of unsecured debt, or a mix of secured and unsecured debt, then a Chapter 7 makes sense. If you are about to lose a home or car to a bank, have a lot of nonexempt property, or tax or child support issues, then a Chapter 13 is your best bet.

Check It Out

Unsecured debt is debt that has no collateral attached to it. **Secured debt,** on the other hand, is debt that is tied to collateral, such as a car loan. If you don't repay the loan, the car is repossessed; the car secures the loan. Unsecured debts have no such collateral. Unsecured debts include credit cards and medical bills.

Chapter 13

A Chapter 13 is used only in very specific, limited circumstances. It is most often used to save a house from foreclosure. If you are behind on your mortgage (called *in arrears*), you cannot wipe out that debt in a Chapter 7 bankruptcy. Chapter 7 bankruptcies only wipe out unsecured debt (or secured debt for which you want to give back the collateral). The arrears on your house are secured. If you want to deal with these debts in bankruptcy and still keep your house, the only way is to catch up your payments through a Chapter 13 repayment plan.

A Chapter 13 bankruptcy is basically a repayment plan that lasts from three to five years, depending upon the circumstances. The debtor promises to pay a certain amount of money each month to the Chapter 13 trustee, who, in turn, pays back the debtor's creditors. Typically, secured debtors are repaid 100 percent, and unsecured creditors get pennies on the dollar.

For example, Susan is four months behind on her mortgage, for a total of $3,600. If she wants to keep her house, she could file Chapter 13 and propose to pay that amount back over a three-year period. Her payments would be $100 per month ($3,600 divided by 36 months of repayment). This payment would be on top of her normal ongoing monthly mortgage payments. You can see why fewer people file Chapter 13. Paying this extra payment every month (which can run anywhere from $100 to $1,000 depending upon the circumstances) on top of all other payments is very difficult.

The other time a Chapter 13 is normally used is when a debtor has property that he would lose to the bankruptcy trustee if he were to file Chapter 7. This property is called *nonexempt* assets.

Check It Out

Any property that you would lose in a Chapter 7 bankruptcy is **nonexempt**. Each state has its own rules regarding exempt property.

Each state has a different set of rules, called exemptions, which are used to determine how much property a debtor can keep in a Chapter 7 bankruptcy. Essentially, exemption means protection. If you are able to exempt property, that means you are able to protect it and keep it. Although the exemption rules are generous, they are not limitless. If the value of your property is more than the exemption rules of your state allow and you filed a Chapter 7, the trustee in your case would take and sell whatever property you own that is over the limit.

For example, if you live in California and own a home free and clear worth $100,000, and you filed Chapter 7 for some reason, you would lose your home to the Chapter 7 trustee. Here's why: California limits Chapter 7 debtors to a total of $50,000 in home equity. A paid-off $100,000 home is $50,000 over the limit. The bankruptcy code permits a Chapter 7 trustee to seize and sell any asset over the exemption limit and use the excess money to repay your creditors. (Again, each state has different exemption limits; see Chapter 20.) Chapter 13 is used to avoid that possibility. Chapter 13 lets you keep all your assets, no matter how much over the exemption limit you are.

Finally, a Chapter 13 can be very effective if you have tax debts or child support arrears you need to handle. (Chapter 22 covers Chapter 13 bankruptcies in detail.) Again, most people have a lot of credit card debt and other unsecured debt. If that is your situation, Chapter 7 is surely the best way to go.

The Least You Need to Know

- Bankruptcy is not such a bad option when all else fails.

- You have paid your creditors a lot of money, and they will survive just fine without your money.

- Most people would be better off filing a Chapter 7.

- Chapter 13 is used only in specific circumstances, such as preventing a house foreclosure or handling large tax or child support debts.

20

Chapter 7 Prefiling Considerations

In This Chapter

- ◆ What kind of debts do you have?
- ◆ Wiping out your debts
- ◆ What kind of assets do you own?
- ◆ Protecting your assets

There are many things to consider when contemplating bankruptcy besides your desire to get out of debt. The main thing to understand is that the bankruptcy code sets standards and limits; if you don't meet these requirements, there is no use in filing. Either your case will not go through, some of your debts will not get discharged, or you will lose some assets to the bankruptcy trustee. None of those are desirable outcomes, so you need to understand what is required, what type of debts are discharged, and how to best protect your assets.

All Debts Are Not Created Equal

There are two primary categories of debt: secured and unsecured debts. There are also other types of debt that you may have that don't fall into these broad categories, such as taxes, student loans, child support, and alimony. The important thing to figure out right now is whether a Chapter 7 bankruptcy will get rid of your particular debts.

Secured Debts

Again, a secured debt is one that is attached to some sort of collateral, such as a car loan. A bank will happily lend you money to buy a car as long as the car is used as collateral to secure the loan. If you fail to pay back the loan, the bank will repossess the car and sell it to pay back the loan. The car secures the loan.

There are many other sorts of secured debts:

- ◆ **Mortgages.** Any time you borrow money against your home, a mortgage is created. All mortgages are secured against the house.

- ◆ **Judgment liens.** The holder of a judgment can file a *lien* against the property of the one who owes the judgment. That is called a judgment lien. When the property is sold (usually a house or car), the lien is paid before the defendant receives any money.

Check It Out

A **lien** is a document filed with the county recorder. It attaches to the property and must be paid off before title to the property is transferred to a new owner. Liens usually involve mortgages.

- ◆ **Big-ticket items bought at department stores.** Creditors such as Sears and JC Penney's, as well as most electronics stores, have a security agreement as part of their standard credit applications. That means that many of the expensive items you buy at these places are considered secured merchandise. If you bought a washer and dryer last year at Sears, that is a secured debt. Surprise!

The important thing to understand before filing bankruptcy is that secured debts are not automatically discharged in a bankruptcy. Although your personal liability for the debt will be discharged, the security interest survives the bankruptcy. Stay with us here; this is a very important (albeit very difficult) concept to grasp. We'll try and make it simple.

Check It Out

When you buy an item on credit like a house or a car, the lender has two methods of being repaid. The first is the right to repossess the property and sell it again if you don't pay. The lender can do this because it has a stake in the property, called a **security interest.** The second method of repayment is the right to sue you for the money owed, because of your **personal liability** under the contract.

A secured creditor essentially has two methods of collection if the debt is not repaid. The first is to take back the property securing the debt by repossessing the car or foreclosing on the house. But what if the resale of that property repossessed is not enough to cover the debt? Then the lender can always sue you for the difference. Why? Because of the second method ensuring repayment: your personal liability under the contract.

Jillian was sued for this very reason. She still owed $10,000 on her car when she was laid off from her job. She was unable to continue to make her car payments and thus her lender eventually repossessed her 1997 Honda Accord. The lender sold the car at a wholesale auction for $4,000 and then sued Jillian for the $6,000 balance she owed on her contract.

Had Jillian filed bankruptcy, she could not have been sued. Why? Because bankruptcy wipes out your personal liability for your debts. No liability means there is nothing to sue you over. Debts in bankruptcy are wiped out because the bankruptcy court issues an order stating that your personal liability for all debts has been discharged. Thus, for example, when a credit card debt is discharged, the credit card company can no longer come after you.

That is not true for secured creditors. In a Chapter 7, the security interest survives the bankruptcy even though your personal liability does not. What that means is that after a bankruptcy, a lender holding a security interest can still take the property back, but because your personal liability for the debt has been discharged, it cannot sue you for the difference. In Jillian's case, had she filed bankruptcy, the entire $6,000 balance on her car loan would have been wiped out because she would no longer have had any personal liability for the debt.

Thus, when you file bankruptcy, you have a few different ways to handle secured debts. Two of these options relate to keeping the debt. The third is a way to get rid of the debt.

1. **Reaffirm the debt.** A reaffirmation is an agreement between you and the creditor stating that you want to keep your property, you agree to keep paying for it, and you agree to remain personally liable for the debt. Thus, you and the creditor enter into a new contract by signing the reaffirmation. For example, the company that finances your car may require that you sign a reaffirmation agreement if you want to keep the car. Because the whole idea in bankruptcy is to wipe out your personal liability, take this piece of advice: If possible, avoid reaffirmation agreements.

2. **Redeem the debt.** A *redemption* is also a new contract between you and the creditor. But whereas a reaffirmation is a contract to pay back the debt in monthly installments, a redemption is a contract to pay back the debt in a reduced lump sum. Sears might agree to let you keep that washer and dryer if you agree to pay $250 within 30 days. The best part about a redemption is that no new personal liability is being created. Accordingly, a redemption is better than a reaffirmation.

> **Two Cents**
>
> The surrender option is very powerful. If you own a car in which you are *upside down* (say you owe $10,000, but it is worth $4,000), you can surrender the car to the lender during your bankruptcy, get out of the contract, and owe nothing more on the vehicle. Where else can you unilaterally get out of a bad contract? Answer: nowhere.

3. **Surrender the property.** Reaffirmation and redemption allow you to keep property but force you to keep debts. Because the idea here is to get rid of debts, you might want to consider the surrender option. With a surrender, you simply give the car back to the lender. Because your personal liability will be wiped out with the bankruptcy discharge, and because your giving back the property means the lender already has its collateral back, your responsibility for the debt will be completely wiped out by the discharge. Your personal liability is gone, and the property is returned, so the lender has no more tools to get at you.

The key point, then, when contemplating bankruptcy is that it is only your personal liability, not the security interest, that is discharged in your bankruptcy. If most of your debts are secured ones, Chapter 7 bankruptcy may not solve your problems, although the option to get out of a bad contract still makes it attractive to some people.

Unsecured Debts

Unsecured debts are not associated with any sort of collateral. Most of us have a lot of unsecured debt. The typical example is a credit card. When a credit card company issues you a credit card, it normally does not ask for any sort of collateral and so any debt you incur is considered unsecured debt.

Besides credit cards, the following are other types of unsecured debts:

- ◆ Medical bills
- ◆ Legal bills
- ◆ Utility bills
- ◆ Unsecured lines of credit
- ◆ Bounced checks

The advantageous thing about unsecured debts (where bankruptcy is concerned) is that these debts are completely wiped out by a Chapter 7 discharge. You could owe $75,000 to 10 different credit card companies, $3,000 in medical bills, and another $2,000 in other bills and have all of this debt discharged in your bankruptcy. In a Chapter 7, there is no limit as to how much unsecured debt you can have discharged (which is not true for a Chapter 13).

Two Cents

Bankruptcy is an upside-down world. In real life, lots of unsecured debt is a bad thing, but in bankruptcy it is a fine thing. No matter how much unsecured debt you owe, it will be wiped out. In real life, creditors can harass you if you do not pay, but in bankruptcy, they cannot do a thing. In real life, you want assets that are valuable, but in bankruptcyland, you want your assets to be less valuable, so you can keep them.

If you are having a difficult time figuring out whether a certain debt you have is secured or unsecured, the key question to ask yourself is this: Have you pledged any sort of collateral to secure the debt? If the answer is no, then the debt is unsecured. Most people have a lot of unsecured debts (credit cards mostly) and a couple of secured debts (car and home loans).

If you have a lot of unsecured debts, then filing Chapter 7 will help you a lot. Unsecured debts are the easiest type of debts to get discharged in a bankruptcy.

Special Debts

Other than secured and unsecured debts, you may also owe student loans, past-due child support, or taxes. Should you file bankruptcy if you have these sorts of debts? Are they dischargeable? "Maybe" is the answer to both questions.

The only way to get rid of child support or alimony arrears is to file a Chapter 13 bankruptcy and repay them in full over a period of several years. They cannot be wiped out in a Chapter 7.

Student loans can only be discharged if you can pass the following undue hardship test:

1. The debtor cannot maintain even a minimal standard of living if forced to repay the loan.

2. This state of affairs is likely to exist for a significant portion of the repayment period.

3. The debtor has made good faith efforts to repay the loan.

All three parts of the test must be met to qualify for a hardship discharge. If you are not almost destitute, do not waste your time and money trying to get student loans completely discharged this way. However, you should know that, while it is almost impossible to get them totally eliminated, it might be possible to get them reduced in some states.

Taxes, too, are not easily discharged (surprised?). Although there are too many kinds of taxes for any sort of detailed discussion here, essentially, taxes are dischargeable if the following conditions are met:

CAUTION

Over Your Limit

If you are filing bankruptcy to get rid of student loans, divorce-related arrears, or taxes, exercise extreme caution. These debts are not easily discharged. Read this section carefully.

1. A tax return for the year in question was filed on time, or if not, then it was filed at least two years before the bankruptcy.

2. The tax is over three years old.

3. The tax was assessed more than eight months before the bankruptcy was filed.

4. The debtor did not willfully evade the taxes.

For example, if you filed your 1993 taxes on time, but you still owe and have not received a new assessment recently, you could get those taxes discharged in a Chapter 7. If this situation does not apply to you, it still may be possible to get rid of the debt in a Chapter 13 bankruptcy.

Can You Keep Your Property?

Aside from figuring out whether your debts are dischargeable, the other major consideration before filing bankruptcy is whether you will be able to keep your property. One of the great fears people have about bankruptcy is that they will lose their property. Although understandable, this fear is mostly a misconception.

You could not really get a fresh start if you were to lose your home or your car in your bankruptcy, could you? Accordingly, bankruptcy laws are fairly generous with regard to property. Most (not all, mind you) people are able to keep all of their property throughout their bankruptcy.

Money Talks

Congress has recently been considering changing the bankruptcy laws. Credit card companies have spent millions in the past few years lobbying Congress to tighten bankruptcy laws due to alleged fraud and abuse. Despite the fact that the General Accounting Office has concluded that such fraud and abuse hardly exists, nothing talks in Congress like money. Thus, you should discuss any possible changes in the law with a bankruptcy professional.

Your Bankruptcy Estate

In your bankruptcy paperwork (called your *petition* and *schedules*), you are required, under penalty of perjury and a $500,000 fine and possible jail time, to list all of your assets, both real property and personal property, including household goods and items, cars, real estate, pensions, clothing, and bank accounts.

Before you file, you want to make sure that you will be able to keep all of these assets. Bankruptcy trustees do not make a lot of money per case, so they are on the hunt for unprotected assets that they can seize because they get a percentage of whatever the asset is sold for. Because it is awfully hard to get out of bankruptcy once you have filed, you better be pretty darn sure before you file that you will be able to keep most, if not all, of what you own.

In order to keep everything you own (your estate), it all must be *exempted* in your paperwork. When you exempt a piece of property, you tell the trustee that you plan to keep that property. The process of exempting property consists of nothing more than listing all property you own in your schedules and then listing the corresponding laws that allow you to keep that property.

Although this process may seem simple, it is not, because each state puts different limits on how much property a debtor can keep when filing for bankruptcy. Although the rest of bankruptcy law is federal (meaning the same rules apply in all 50 states), exemption rules are made state by state.

Some states, like Florida, are quite liberal with their exemption laws. In Florida, there is no limit to the amount of home equity you can have when filing bankruptcy. You could own a $1 million house, file for bankruptcy, keep the house, and wipe out your other debts (of course, you would have to still continue to pay your mortgage). Other states are not so liberal. In New York, a single person can only exempt $10,000 worth of equity in a home, and a married couple can only exempt $20,000. In Delaware, there is no home equity exemption at all.

Note again that any federal changes in federal bankruptcy laws will surely change these exemption rules, so make sure when planning that you know what the limits are.

> **Money Talks**
>
> Some people contemplating bankruptcy go so far as to move from a restrictive state to a more liberal state in order to protect their property. Florida's liberal exemption laws were a main reason O. J. Simpson thought about moving there. Be careful, though: Not only is this action potentially fraudulent, but you have to live in the new state for at least six months before filing your case.

The reason that exemptions are probably the most critical element to your bankruptcy is because if you do not exempt your assets, or if your property is worth more than your state's exemptions allow, the trustee will take your nonexempt belongings, sell them, and use the money to pay back your creditors.

What Property Is Exempt?

Some states allow debtors to choose between the state's exemption system and the federal exemption system. Most states, however, have only one exemption system and no choice. Before you file, you must figure out whether your state's system would allow you to exempt all of your assets.

The federal exemption system is similar to those in use by the states and is therefore useful to explain what you can protect. Although only some states use this particular system, all states use a system that is at least very similar. The following items are exempt under the federal exemption rules.

Federal Exemption Rules

Property Protected	Amount Protected
Homestead (homes)	$17,425 equity if single, double that equity if married
Automobiles	$2,775 equity per car, only one car per person
Household goods and furnishings	$9,300 total

Property Protected	Amount Protected
Jewelry	$1,150 total
Tools of the trade	$1,750 total
Life Insurance	$9,300 in loan value
Alimony, child support	Unlimited
Payments due	Wrongful death payments, crime victims' compensation, public assistance, Social Security, unemployment compensation, veterans' benefits - unlimited
Health aids	Unlimited, if professionally prescribed
Pensions	ERISA-qualified pensions are totally exempt
Personal injury recoveries	$17,425
Wild card	Unused portion of homestead exemption, up to $8,725 per debtor

Your state will, in all likelihood, have a different list of items with different amounts, especially with regard to real estate. As indicated previously, some states are very generous when it comes to real estate, and others are not. (Protecting your real estate is discussed in detail later in the chapter.)

The important thing about any exemption system is that it is the equity in, not the gross value of, your property that is the critical factor. For example, Spencer has a home worth $100,000 with a $75,000 mortgage. Spencer thus has only $25,000 worth of equity in his home and needs to exempt only that amount. If he owes $9,000 on a car that is worth $10,000, then he needs to exempt only the $1,000 equity he has in the car in order to keep it. It is also important to understand that your equity is the amount you would get less any sales commissions and taxes due, which may reduce your actual equity even more.

The next thing to understand about exempting property is how the last item in this list, the wild card, works. The wild card is the key to keeping your assets when you file for bankruptcy. (Although most states have a wild card, not all states do, so be sure to find out the exact rules in your state. Ask a local bankruptcy attorney.)

Two Cents

Remember, it is just the equity in your property that you need to exempt.

The wild card is just like its poker namesake. You can play this card in the bankruptcy game to protect anything. You use it to protect home equity, cars over the $2,400 limit, cash in the bank (notice that money in the bank has no separate exemption in the preceding list), a boat, or any other item or items up to the wild card limit.

You will notice that in the preceding list, the wild card is the "unused portion of the homestead exemption, up to $8,300 per debtor." What this means is that if you have no home equity that you need to protect with your homestead exemption, you can use the $8,300 exemption to protect any other asset. If you have some home equity that needs protection, but it is less than $8,300, the difference is available as a wild card exemption.

Here are some examples of how the wild card might work:

◆ Cynthia's home is worth $100,000, and she owes $95,000 on it. She would use $5,000 of her homestead exemption to protect her home equity. The remaining $3,300 (remember, $8,300 total is available under this wild card system) could be used in wild card exemptions to protect other property.

◆ Sydney and Sierra don't own a home, but they do own a car that is paid off and is worth $10,000. They could use their $2,400 auto exemption, combine it with $7,600 from their wild card, and still have $9,000 to use to protect other property. (Remember, they each get $8,300 in wild card exemptions, for a total of $16,600.)

◆ Mara has $5,000 in the bank and owns no home (she's a renter). She could use her wild card exemption to protect her bank account and still have $3,300 left over to protect other property.

Again, because each state is different and allows exemptions and wild cards in different amounts, we strongly advise you to seek out a bankruptcy attorney to draft your bankruptcy paperwork, if for no other reason than to make sure that your property is protected.

How Much Is Your Property Really Worth?

Remember, if any of your property is over the corresponding limit, the trustee overseeing your case will take it and sell it. He will keep part of the proceeds and use the bulk of the money to pay back your creditors. Thus, a key to protecting assets in bankruptcy is to make sure that the values listed in your schedules are below the exemption limit, thereby giving your trustee no legal possibility of seizing your property.

Your attorney will probably advise you to list the lowest possible, albeit ostensibly reasonable, value for your assets. When valuing your car, he will recommend that you use the low blue book value instead of the high blue book value. Or you can use the price listed in the classified ads, as that is generally lower than even the low blue book value. Reduce the car's value even more for high mileage and problems in need of repair.

What you want to do is reduce the amount of equity you show in a piece of property that is potentially over the limit. Although your washer and dryer may have cost $1,000 new, what are they worth used? Maybe $200. Using a yard sale or liquidation value for your property in your schedules is both perfectly acceptable and intelligent.

We know that all of this is complicated. You really need an attorney to make sure your assets are properly protected. Your yellow pages will list all bankruptcy attorneys in your area. Make a couple of appointments with a few different ones; your initial consultation should be free. Find one you like, dicker about the fee a bit, and hire one to help you through this process. You don't perform surgery on yourself, and you shouldn't represent yourself in court either.

> **Money Talks**
>
> You should also ask yourself whether your trustee would bother taking and selling an item you own. An old aluminum fishing boat worth $200 may be of no interest to a trustee. How much would it cost him to get it and sell it? Who could he sell it to? How much time would it take? A vintage T-Bird over the limit is a different story.

> **Over Your Limit**
>
> The only way to get rid of mortgage arrears in a bankruptcy is to pay them off through a Chapter 13 plan. Mortgage arrears are not forgiven in a Chapter 7.

Protecting Your House

You may be concerned that your mortgage company will foreclose on your house if you file for bankruptcy, but that is usually a groundless fear. If you are current with your mortgage payments when you file and stay current throughout the case, then your lender cannot foreclose. It would be illegal. When your case is over, you will continue to make payments as if nothing has happened.

Things are a bit different if you are behind on your mortgage and you want to file a Chapter 7. In that case, you will need to make up the past-due amount within about a month or two from the date you file, as well as keep current throughout the entire case. If you remain in arrears after filing bankruptcy, your lender will eventually go before the bankruptcy court and ask for permission to foreclose on your house.

Exempting Your House

To figure out whether you will be able to fully exempt your house, you will need to do two things:

1. Figure out how much equity you have in your home. Look at what houses are selling for in your neighborhood to get a good idea of what your house is worth if you were to sell it today. Subtract the amount you owe your lender(s), and that is your equity.

2. Look up your equity limits and see whether you fall under the limit for your state.

As with your personal property, you want to show your home with the lowest possible, yet nevertheless reasonable, amount of equity so that you remain under your state's exemption limit.

If You Have Too Much Equity

First, value your home at the lowest reasonable amount. Look around your neighborhood, see what similar homes are selling for and use the lowest price you find in your paperwork.

Next, reduce your equity analysis for the potential cost of sale. We are not saying you are going to sell your home, you are merely trying to show the trustee how much he would get if he did sell your home. Because he would have to hire and pay for a real estate agent, you can reasonably reduce your equity, for these purposes, by that amount.

For example, Greg's home is worth $200,000, and he owes $150,000. That gives Greg $50,000 in equity. He's worried that if he files bankruptcy, he may lose his house because the equity limit in his state is $40,000. However, if Greg accounts for the cost of the sale of his home, he will be fine and can safely file his case. Typically, 8 percent is used to calculate the cost of sale. In Greg's case, this amount would equal $16,000. Thus Greg's actual equity is $50,000 less the $16,000 cost of sale, which means his equity is therefore really $34,000.

There is a lot to think about before filing bankruptcy. You must be sure that you have the type of debts that will get discharged. You must also be assured that most, if not all, of your assets will be protected. Make sure you figure this all out before you file.

The Least You Need to Know

◆ A bankruptcy wipes out your personal liability for your debts, but it doesn't wipe out any security interest.

◆ If you have a lot of credit card debt or other unsecured debt, a Chapter 7 bankruptcy makes sense.

◆ Make sure you will be able to exempt and protect your assets before you file your case.

◆ Do not lie on your paperwork, but be sure to value your assets as low as is reasonably possible.

◆ Don't forget to deduct the cost of sale from your home equity analysis.

Chapter 21

How a Chapter 7 Case Proceeds

In This Chapter

- Getting the case filed
- Understanding your paperwork
- The first meeting of creditors
- Amendments
- The discharge

The process of going through a Chapter 7 bankruptcy is surprisingly easy for most people. Life before bankruptcy is usually quite unpleasant: Creditors are calling, money is tight, and people are stressed and worried. But once you enter the bankruptcy process, all that changes. Almost magically, the phone stops ringing, and extra cash reappears.

Relief Is in Sight

The phone stops ringing because of the automatic stay that goes into effect when you file bankruptcy. You will recall that the stay stops all creditor collection activity, so once your case is filed, you don't have to worry about dealing with nasty creditors ever again.

Even better, money shows up. How? Because the money you previously spent paying your dischargeable debts every month is now yours to keep. If you have been paying $500 a month servicing your credit card debt, there is no need to pay that ever again once your bankruptcy case is filed. Voilá! The $500 a month is now yours to keep.

> **Over Your Limit**
>
> In 1998, Americans charged more than $400 billion on credit cards. They paid more than $40 billion in interest alone that year.

You will also find that, unlike your life today, life in bankruptcy is surprisingly nonadversarial. Throughout the process, you will be treated with respect and courtesy. Besides the fact that your creditors can no longer harass you, you will soon discover that civility is the rule in court.

Steps in the Process

There are basically four steps to the Chapter 7 process: hiring a lawyer (if you want one), filing your paperwork, going to a hearing, and obtaining your discharge.

"If It Pleases the Court ..."

The first thing to decide is whether you are going to hire an attorney to file your case for you, use a paralegal, or do it yourself. If at all possible, it is best to hire an attorney (and we're not just saying that because one of the authors of this book happens to be a bankruptcy attorney, honest!). You really need someone who can talk to the trustee and deal with the creditors if they contest the filing. Bankruptcy is serious business, and if something goes wrong, the consequences can be dire. You want to be sure that everything is handled correctly.

> **Two Cents**
>
> There are two fees to know about when filing bankruptcy. Filing fees paid to the court will run somewhere around $200. Attorney fees will cost you anywhere from $500 to $1,500. Be sure to try to get the attorney fees quoted to you reduced. Surprisingly, many lawyers will lower their fee, if asked, in order to keep you as a client.

On the other hand, avoid hiring a paralegal, if you can afford it. Sometimes you will see an ad in the paper like this: "Bankruptcy $75." That is an ad run by a paralegal. A paralegal *is not* an attorney. He cannot give legal advice and cannot go to the hearing with you. That is why his fees are so much less than a lawyer's. If you do decide to hire one, make sure that he has plenty of experience handling bankruptcies and be sure to get some referrals.

Finally, if you cannot afford a lawyer or a paralegal, then you can file your case on your own. There are several books, computer programs, and websites that can help you. Appendix E lists those resources.

Getting Your Case Filed

Whether you decide to go it alone or hire an attorney, the next step is also the most time-consuming. Because the court requires a lot of information from you before it will discharge your debts, you have to sit down and organize this information.

Among the things you will need to organize, and eventually list in your paperwork, are the following:

♦ **A list of all major assets.** This list includes everything of substance you own. All furniture? Yes. Every piece of silverware? No.

♦ **A list of all unsecured debts.** This list must include to whom the debts are owed, their addresses, and your account numbers.

♦ **A list of all secured debts.** This list would also include an indication of what property secures the debt and your intent with regard to the property: Do you want to keep it or give it back?

♦ **A list of income and expenses.** This list would comprise all sources of income and a list of average monthly expenses.

When you have all this information ready, either you, your attorney, or your paralegal will have to draft your petition and schedules. You will sign these under penalty of perjury.

A bankruptcy case is officially commenced when you file your petition and schedules with the court and pay the appropriate fee. Bankruptcy courts are divided into geographical districts and are normally located in the federal building of each particular district. The filing fee is the same whether you are filing alone or as husband and wife. After your case is filed, the automatic stay is issued and remains in effect for the duration of your case. Peace in our time!

Check It Out

Going to court without an attorney and representing yourself in a court proceeding is called **pro per** in legalese.

Over Your Limit

Bankruptcy fraud is a federal crime investigated by the FBI. Be sure to be thorough when you fill out your paperwork. Be sure to list all assets, even if doing so will put you over the exemption limit. Losing a car is preferable to going to jail.

The First Meeting of Creditors

After your petition and schedules are prepared and filed, the court sets a time for a hearing that you will need to attend, called the first meeting of creditors. That meeting usually occurs about a month or two after your case is filed. Notice that it is called a meeting. It is neither a trial nor a hearing before a judge. It is an informal meeting and usually quite painless.

At the meeting, you will meet your trustee. He or she is assigned by the Department of Justice to oversee your case. Your trustee will ask you a few questions about your assets (for example, whether you failed to list an asset or are hiding anything). The trustee will also probably have a few questions about your schedules. Although your lawyer (if you have one) will be present with you, he or she cannot answer for you.

You will not be unmercifully grilled or asked to explain why you are in bankruptcy. The trustee is far more interested in whether there may be some nonexempt assets to seize. Your entire meeting should last about five minutes.

> **Money Talks**
>
> The first meeting of creditors is poorly named. First of all, there is rarely a second meeting of creditors. Not only that, because there is nothing creditors can do to stop your case if you have acted legally, most don't bother to show up.

Normally, the only creditors who do bother to attend are secured creditors (like JC Penney) who hold a security interest in various items you may have recently purchased from them. It is important to understand that not everything you buy at Sears or JC Penney is secured. First, only items bought with their credit cards (that is, a JC Penney card) are secured. Second, only large items bought under these credit plans are secured. Items such as small household goods, clothes, and shoes, and other such things are not secured. Larger things like furniture, appliances, and electronic equipment are secured.

The Reality of Reaffirmation

All of your creditors are notified of your filing and the time and date of your meeting. A few may show up at the meeting to try to get you to sign reaffirmation agreements, but as we have said, it is not a good idea to sign such agreements if they can be avoided (sometimes they can and sometimes they can't).

Recall that debtors normally have three options with regard to secured merchandise: reaffirmation, redemption, and surrender. The problem with reaffirmation agreements is that they renew your personal liability for the debt, liability that is otherwise discharged in the bankruptcy.

Sears does have a security interest in your washer and dryer and does have the right, after the bankruptcy, to reclaim its property if you don't sign a reaffirmation (after all, that is the purpose of a security agreement). Certainly, Sears will tell you that the reaffirmation should be signed if you want to keep your washer and dryer. But you do not have to sign.

What happens if you do not reaffirm your debt? Once your case is over, Sears may come and try to get its washer and dryer back, and then again, it may not. Does it really want your old washer and dryer?

Two Cents

Debtors are not required by law to sign reaffirmation agreements.

Even if Sears does decide it wants your washer and dryer and does come to get them, you do not have to let the guys from Sears in your house. It is your house, and if they enter without your permission, they are trespassing. Sears (or any similar creditor) will have to have its attorney go to state court and get a judicial order allowing Sears to take back the property. How many thousands of dollars will that cost that creditor? What is a used washer and dryer worth? It is not cost-effective in most cases for Sears, or any secured creditor of fairly small amounts, to take its property back.

Money Talks
Sears was recently sued for what turned out to be illegal reaffirmation practices and had to pay millions in damages to bankrupt cardholders who felt forced to sign reaffirmation agreements. Today, Sears representatives are much more cautious when dealing with Chapter 7 clients. Now there really is a softer side of Sears.

The issue of whether you should sign the reaffirmation depends upon what kind of risk taker you are. If you are willing to gamble that your secured creditor will not go to the effort to get its merchandise back, then do not sign the reaffirmation. You may be able to keep the washer and dryer without paying a penny more. Then again, you may not.

If, on the other hand, you really want to keep the merchandise, and you do not want to take the chance of losing it later (or worry about doing so), then you should probably sign the new contract. If you do so, insist that the reaffirmed amount be only the fair market value of the property today (what a willing buyer would pay a willing seller for the merchandise today). Reaffirming for the entire amount is unnecessary.

Say that two years ago you bought a big-screen television at Circuit City and still owe $3,000 on the contract, but the set today is worth only $1,500. Then you need only reaffirm the $1,500. Here is why: Secured claims in bankruptcy are only secured up to the fair market value of the property. Even though you may owe Circuit City $3,000, if the fair market value of that television is $1,500, then the security interest is only that amount. The other $1,500 that you owe is considered unsecured, and as you know, unsecured debts are discharged in bankruptcy. If you sign a reaffirmation for the entire $3,000, you would be taking on $1,500 worth of debt that would otherwise be discharged. This is why you need a good attorney.

Many secured creditors of large items, such as cars and homes, do not ask for reaffirmation agreements, although some might. Those that do not require one assume that you will continue to make your scheduled monthly payments after the case is over. If you do not, they will take their property back.

What if you are going to surrender some property back to a secured lender? One surprising advantage of surrendering property is that it normally takes a few months to organize a time and date for the surrender. While you are waiting to give the property back, you can usually keep using it without paying for it. You can stay in your home without paying the mortgage for a few months. You can keep driving the car without making payments. The rule is that a debtor is supposed to act upon his statement of intention (reaffirm, redeem, or surrender) within 45 days of the filing, although it is a rarely enforced rule and one without penalty.

Understanding Your Paperwork

Bankruptcy paperwork may look intimidating, but it is quite easy to understand. A bankruptcy is made up of a petition, schedules that list your financial situation, a statement of financial affairs, an alphabetical listing of all creditors, and a summary.

Money Talks
Bankruptcy statutes in the United States are based upon English common law. In the United States, the first bankruptcy law was passed in 1898. The first bankruptcy statute in England dates back to 1542. In biblical times, ancient Israelites celebrated the Year of Jubilee every 50 years, whose provisions, among others, included the forgiveness of all debt.

Look at the top of any page in your bankruptcy, and you will see a headline in bold. That headline is then detailed in the rest of the page. For example, near the front of your paperwork will be a headline of "Schedule A—Real Property." Below the headline will be a detailed description of all real estate you own: where it is located, what it is worth, how much you owe, and so on. Each page of your bankruptcy is similarly laid out. (See Appendix A.)

Your bankruptcy paperwork will consist of the following:

- **Petition.** The petition is the first two pages of your bankruptcy document. It lists your name and that of your spouse, if filing jointly, your address, social security number, and other relevant information.

- **Schedule A—Real Property.** This schedule is where you list all real estate you own.

- **Schedule B—Personal Property.** Here you list household goods, bank accounts, clothes, jewelry, guns, IRAs, stocks, patents, cars, tools of the trade, animals, and everything else.

- **Schedule C—Property Claimed as Exempt.** As you know, this page is critical. Here you list all your exempt assets. If you do this well, you will exempt all of your assets listed on schedule A and B.

- **Schedule D—Creditors Holding Secured Claims.** Here you list all secured debts, such as car and home loans.

- **Schedule E—Creditors Holding Unsecured Priority Claims.** This seemingly confusing category includes taxes, government fines, alimony, child support, and that sort of thing. Although not normally dischargeable, these debts must be listed nonetheless.

- **Schedule F—Creditors Holding Unsecured Non-priority Claims.** These are the debts you will be getting rid of, your unsecured debts, such as credit cards and old medical bills.

- **Schedule G—Executory Contracts and Unexpired Leases.** Few consumer creditors have anything to report on this page. It consists of any leases that may be in effect at the time of filing or any contracts that have yet to be fulfilled (that is what *executory* means).

- **Schedule H—Codebtors.** A codebtor is someone who is also responsible for any of the debts you list, but who is not filing with you; for example, your husband (if you are filing separately) or your grandfather who co-signed a car loan for you. Although your bankruptcy will wipe out your responsibility for your debts, your codebtors (if any) remain liable for them.

> **Two Cents**
>
> Although bankruptcy information must be thorough and correct, here is an important tip: budgets (Schedule J) are flexible, and you want to show a budget that roughly equals your income, if at all possible, and stays within the bounds of truth and reasonableness.

- **Schedule I—Current Income of Individual Debtors.** Here you list your job, how much money you make every month, how much is taken out of your monthly paycheck, and sources of any other income.

- **Schedule J—Current Expenditures Of Individual Debtors.** Your last schedule requires that you give the court an idea of how much you spend every month on rent, utilities, food, recreation, insurance, car payments, and so on. You *do not* list what you have been spending on credit cards and other sorts of debts, because those will be discharged.

- **Declaration Concerning Debtor's Schedules.** You sign, under penalty of perjury, that the schedules are true, complete, and accurate.

These four documents come after your schedules:

- **Statement of Financial Affairs.** In this statement, you essentially give the court an idea of your recent financial dealings. You list your gross income for the past few years; any repossessions, foreclosures, or lawsuits in the past year; losses due to fire, theft, or gambling (which are dischargeable); transfers of property in the past year; property held in safe deposit boxes; and any recent prior addresses. Businesses must also list inventories, accountants, partners, and so on. This statement is also signed under penalty of perjury.

- **Statement of Intention.** With this statement, you indicate what you want to do with your secured property: Keep it or surrender it.

- **Matrix.** The court uses this alphabetical listing of all creditors to notify them of your bankruptcy.

- **Summary of Schedules.** This one-page sheet summarizes all preceding pages, especially your income, expenditures, assets, and debts, and is again signed under penalty of perjury.

Over Your Limit

Don't lie to the court. The penalty for perjury can include jail time and a fine of up to $500,000.

Amending Your Paperwork

Sometimes people discover a mistake or want to make a change in their paperwork after their case has been filed. Maybe you failed to list a creditor, or gave an incorrect address for one, or forgot to list an asset. Whatever the reason, bankruptcy procedure allows you to amend your schedules at any time before you receive your discharge.

Amending your papers is fairly simple. You will need to draft the amended schedule on an official bankruptcy form (like the one that was originally filed) and fill out an amendment cover sheet. Most local bankruptcy courts have one at the clerk's office. If you are adding a creditor, you will need to pay a little bit of money. Make five copies of the amendment and cover sheet and file it with the court.

If you are adding a creditor, and the creditors' meeting has already been held, then you may need to schedule a second meeting of creditors, although it depends upon the rules of the district where you live. If you do, either you or the court (again, depending upon your locale) will send a notice to all creditors of the new meeting time and date. Check with your court to find out the exact procedure.

You will also need to file a change of address form with the court if you move while you are in bankruptcy. Throughout your case, the court mails important information to you: a notice of filing (including the automatic stay order), a notice of no distribution (if your assets are completely exempt), and most importantly, your discharge order. The discharge order is something that you will want to keep safe for some time; it prevents any of your creditors whose debt was discharged from coming after you after the case is over. To send your discharge order to you, the court must be able to find you if you move.

The Discharge

The final step in this bankruptcy process occurs about two months after the creditors' meeting when your discharge comes in the mail, thereby ending your case and officially discharging you from your legal liability to repay the debts listed in your schedules. This entire process, from filing to meeting to discharge, normally takes about four months, sometimes three, and rarely six. That's it! Your case is over, your debts have been discharged, and you get your fresh start.

The Least You Need to Know

- ◆ From start to finish, your case should take roughly four months.

- ◆ The first meeting of creditors is poorly named; creditors rarely come, and there is rarely a second meeting.

- ◆ Make sure you understand the rules surrounding reaffirmation agreements before ever signing one.

- ◆ Almost all Chapter 7 debtors get their discharge without incident.

22

Chapter 13 Bankruptcy

In This Chapter

♦ Why Chapter 13?

♦ Requirements before filing

♦ How things proceed

♦ If you cannot finish the plan

Certainly, most people are better off by filing a Chapter 7 bankruptcy than a Chapter 13. Chapter 7s are relatively quick, simple, and easy to complete. Unfortunately, for some people, a Chapter 7 just will not work. Either it will not get rid of the type of debts they have, or it will cause them to lose nonexempt property. Chapter 13 was created for those people.

Although a Chapter 13 is neither quick, simple, nor easy to complete, it still can be a very useful debt-reduction tool in the right circumstances. Because most people do not want to be in bankruptcy for four months, let alone four years, you had better be sure that a Chapter 13 makes sense for you before plunging in. Furthermore, whereas a Chapter 7 can be handled without an attorney if need be, a Chapter 13 almost always requires the assistance of counsel, and attorneys' fees will probably cost at least $1,500.

Chapter 13 Overview

A Chapter 13 is generally similar to a Chapter 7, but the two are specifically different. As with a Chapter 7, the case begins when you file a petition and schedules, and an automatic stay is issued immediately. Schedules list all assets and debts. The discharge wipes out the debtor's personal liability for those debts. The difference between Chapter 7 and Chapter 13 relates mostly to the length of the case and the fact that debts will be repaid (at least partially) instead of wholly discharged in a Chapter 13.

Instead of wiping out all dischargeable debts in a few short months as a Chapter 7 does, a Chapter 13 lasts for at least three years and possibly up to five years, depending upon the circumstances. During that time, you promise to pay a certain amount of money every month through a Chapter 13 plan to the Chapter 13 trustee, who, in turn, uses the money to pay back your creditors. Think of a Chapter 13 as a legally sanctioned repayment plan.

> **Two Cents**
>
> A Chapter 13 is the only way to catch up with mortgage or auto arrears in a bankruptcy; a Chapter 7 will not wipe out those debts.

Generally speaking, there are three reasons to file a Chapter 13. Either you've fallen behind on your mortgage payments, fallen behind on taxes, or you have assets that would be considered nonexempt if you were to file a Chapter 7.

Dealing With Secured Creditors

Most people file a Chapter 13 because they are behind on a secured debt such as a car loan (but far more often, a home loan) and they see no way of catching up. This is the most common, and usually the best, reason that a person would choose to file a Chapter 13 bankruptcy instead of a Chapter 7.

> **Money Talks**
>
> At any given moment, 5 percent of all homeowners are behind on their mortgage payments. Although lenders are usually willing to work with a homeowner who is behind, for those in that 5 percent whose lenders are unreasonable, a Chapter 13 is a viable last resort.

What is great about a Chapter 13 bankruptcy insofar as mortgage arrears are concerned is that you can legally force your lender to accept a repayment plan, whether it wants to or not. You can bet that if you fall, say, four months behind on your mortgage payments, your lender would be highly unlikely to agree to a three-year repayment plan of those arrears. Instead, your lender will begin foreclosure proceedings long before it ever accepts such a repayment schedule. But by filing a Chapter 13 you can essentially force your lender to accept your proposed three-year repayment plan.

Is Your Home Worth Keeping?

If you want to file a Chapter 13 in order to catch up your mortgage arrears and keep your home, heed this warning: Fully 50 percent of all people who file a Chapter 13 never complete all plan payments. When that occurs, the Chapter 13 trustee dismisses the case and denies the debtor a discharge. When that happens, most Chapter 13 debtors convert their case to a Chapter 7, surrender their house, and lose all payments made to the Chapter 13 trustee. So you better be sure that you really want to keep your house and that your house is really worth keeping because paying the trustee a set amount every month is no easy task.

For example, Al fell three months behind on his mortgage payments for a total indebtedness of $5,000, including interest, penalties, and attorney fees. If Al wants to keep his house via Chapter 13, he will need to pay $168 per month for three years to the Chapter 13 trustee ($168 multiplied by 36 months equals $4,968) on top of all his normal monthly payments and his regular mortgage payment.

For many people, making this payment is no easy task. If extra money were around, they would not be filing Chapter 13 in the first place. Paying several hundred dollars to a trustee on top of all regular payments is difficult at best when money is tight.

Is your house worth keeping? If you have little equity, the answer may be no. Little equity is any amount under $10,000. Because staying current with Chapter 13 payment plans is so difficult, if you have less equity than that, it may just be best to file a Chapter 7 and surrender your house.

> **Two Cents**
>
> Losing your house in a Chapter 7 may not be the worst thing in the world, although it is certainly difficult. Many people can get a new mortgage loan only two short years after a Chapter 7 discharge.

> **Over Your Limit**
>
> If your budget will not allow you to repay all taxes due within 60 months, there is no point in filing a Chapter 13.

Taxes and Other Debts

Like mortgage lenders, sometimes Uncle Sam, too, is unwilling to work with you when you fall behind. If you owe on taxes that are not dischargeable in a Chapter 7 (see Chapter 21), you can always propose to repay them through a Chapter 13 plan.

The key to this is that you will have to propose a plan that would pay back all of the taxes, plus 10 percent interest, over a maximum of five years. If you cannot do that, your Chapter 13 trustee won't approve your case.

Also, a Chapter 13 might make sense if you are behind on child support, alimony, or student loans. If such problems cause your wages to be garnished or otherwise make your life difficult, a Chapter 13 would allow you to repay these debts over the course of your plan.

Again, these debts, just as with home arrears and taxes, must be repaid fully over the course of the plan to get a discharge. The rule here is that secured debts, such as mortgage arrears, and so-called priority debts, such as taxes, must be repaid fully over the course of a Chapter 13 case in order to get a discharge. We warned you this would not be easy.

Protecting Nonexempt Assets

Another common reason that a person may choose a Chapter 13 over a Chapter 7 is that a Chapter 13 allows the debtor to keep all assets, not just exempt assets. For example, Florence has $100,000 in credit card debt and has a BMW worth $20,000 that is paid off. If she filed Chapter 7, she would lose her car to the trustee because it is far above the exemption limit. However, if she filed a Chapter 13, she could keep the car because there is no limit on exemptions in a Chapter 13 case.

Is there a catch? But of course. One of the many requirements of a Chapter 13 is that your creditors receive at least what they would have received had you filed a Chapter 7. In the case of Florence, her creditors would have received at least $20,000, because that is the amount of her nonexempt assets.

Accordingly, she must present a Chapter 13 plan that proposes to pay back at least that much. Unlike the secured debts and priority debts mentioned previously, unsecured debts can be paid back less than 100 percent. Thus, Florence could offer a plan that would pay her creditors at least $20,000 over 60 months, or roughly $333 a month. Although this amount is still a hefty sum, she would get to keep her car and could wipe out her entire credit card debt for 20 cents on the dollar. At the end of her plan, the remainder of whatever Florence owed would be discharged, just as it would have been in a Chapter 7.

> **Two Cents**
>
> In 2002, more than 1.5 million bankruptcies were filed in the United States, the largest number of cases ever filed. Record numbers were also recorded in Great Britain and Japan.

Finally, the amount Florence (or any debtor) would have to pay back varies from district to district. The aforementioned test—creditors receiving at least what they would have received in a Chapter 7—is the minimum that a Chapter 13 debtor has to pay back to unsecured creditors. Some judicial districts require nothing more than that. Others mandate that unsecured creditors receive 100 percent of what they are owed. You need to find out the local rules in your area.

Other Reasons

Either of the following is also a legitimate reason for filing a Chapter 13:

◆ **You received a discharge in a bankruptcy within the past six years.** If you received a Chapter 7 discharge, you must wait at least six years before filing Chapter 7 again. If you received a Chapter 13 discharge, you must wait at least six years before filing a Chapter 7 (unless you repaid your creditors at least 70 percent of what you owed them). But in either case, you can file a Chapter 13 at any time.

◆ **You want to wipe out debts that cannot be discharged in a Chapter 7.** One of the true advantages of a Chapter 13 is that you can get debts discharged that cannot be discharged in a Chapter 7. Debts incurred by fraud, larceny, embezzlement, credit card fraud, assault, battery, false imprisonment, or defamation are not dischargeable in a Chapter 7. But in a Chapter 13, these debts can be repaid.

Bad Reasons for Choosing a Chapter 13

If you want to file a Chapter 13 because you feel a moral obligation to repay your debts and think that a Chapter 13 repayment plan would allow you to do that, don't. Although your intentions are admirable, that action would not be smart. You are better off paying the debts outside of bankruptcy. There is no point in harming your credit any more than you have to.

If you are contemplating filing a Chapter 13 instead of a Chapter 7 because you think it might look better to future creditors, you are mistaken. A bankruptcy is a bankruptcy is a bankruptcy. It matters little to anyone but you what chapter you choose to file under.

> **CAUTION**
>
> **Over Your Limit**
>
> More than 70 percent of all Americans have at least one negative notation on their credit reports. More than 40 million Americans are rejected for credit each year.

Pros and Cons to Filing Chapter 13

The advantages of filing Chapter 13 should be fairly apparent. You are able to keep your property, make up any arrears you may have on your own terms, rid yourself of debts that you could not get rid of in a Chapter 7, and discharge any other debts. Depending upon the circumstances and the laws in your district, you may be able to get rid of unsecured debts for pennies on the dollar. On the whole, a Chapter 13, if it applies to your situation, may be the best thing you can do for yourself.

Two Cents

Roughly 46 percent of all credit reports contain inaccurate information. The Federal Trade Commission receives more complaints related to credit-reporting abuses than all other items combined.

On the downside, paying the trustee back each month, every month, will surely get tiresome. Attorney fees are significantly higher in a Chapter 13 case than in a Chapter 7 case because a lot of work has to go into the plan and the various hearings. Also, your credit rating will be negatively affected. And what if you cannot finish your plan payments? You may end up in Chapter 7 anyway at that point. This possibility is discussed in detail at the end of this chapter.

Requirements

Unlike a Chapter 7, which permits anyone to file, regardless of employment status or debt levels, a debtor contemplating a Chapter 13 must meet certain requirements. Unless you meet these prerequisites, your case will be dismissed:

1. **Be an individual.** Only individuals can file a Chapter 13. The only business entity that can file a Chapter 13 is a sole proprietorship, and even then, it can do so only in the name of the individual who owns the business. Corporations and partnerships must either file a Chapter 7 (which would cause the business to be shut down) or a Chapter 11 (which allows the business to stay open but is quite expensive).

2. **Have regular income.** The individual who files must have a source of regular and stable income (usually a job) so that the court can be assured that the Chapter 13 plan payments can be made. Social security, welfare, or owning a small business would also constitute stable income, as would alimony, child support, or rental income. Because unemployment benefits are for a limited duration, they probably would not constitute stable income.

3. **Have disposable income.** The heart of a Chapter 13 is the repayment plan. As such, you must be able to afford plan payments. So not only must you have regular income, but your income must also exceed your expenses by enough so that

you will be able to repay your entire plan. When you fill out your budget (Schedules I and J), you must show that you have enough money left over at the end of every month to fund your plan. This strategy differs significantly from what you want to do in a Chapter 7.

4. **Be under the debt ceiling.** In a Chapter 7, there is no limit as to how much debt you can have. You can have $10,000 in unsecured debt or $500,000. You can have $10,000 in secured debts or one million. It makes no difference. In a Chapter 13, your unsecured debts cannot exceed $290,525, and your secured debts cannot exceed $871,550.

5. **Give your "best effort."** The plan has to be the very best effort that the debtor can put forth. That means that the debtor will live frugally, without expending money for luxuries. Beyond that, best effort varies from district to district. In some places, it means that all creditors, secured and unsecured alike, must be paid in full. In others, it means that the debtor will pledge all disposable income to the plan.

In most places, as long as you propose a budget that is fair and modest (but not necessarily Spartan), pledges all available extra capital to the plan, pays back secured and priority creditors 100 percent, and attempts to give your unsecured creditors something, the plan will be confirmed.

How Things Proceed

If you have determined that you fall within the Chapter 13 parameters and that it will solve your financial problems, things proceed in a somewhat similar fashion as in a Chapter 7. First of all, you will need to have your Chapter 13 petition and schedules drafted and filed.

You will also need to file a plan detailing how much you have to pay into the plan every month, how much total will be paid over the entire course of the plan, the percentage return you propose to pay your unsecured creditors, and how long the plan is expected to last. (See Appendix B.) You will need to make your first payment into the plan within a month of filing your documents. Failure to make plan payments will get your case dismissed.

A month or two after everything has been filed, you will attend the first meeting of creditors. Unlike Chapter 7 creditors' meetings, Chapter 13 creditors' meetings often require more than one appearance, and creditors often show up.

Unlike a Chapter 7 creditor meeting, which is intended to quickly discover if there are any unlisted assets or changes in the paperwork, a Chapter 13 meeting is a chance for the trustee to go over the plan in detail. He will ask questions such as …

- ◆ Does the plan meet all legal requirements?

- ◆ Is the plan proposed in good faith?

- ◆ Will the plan pay everyone back in the requisite number of months?

The trustee may request that the debtor make some changes to the plan or may ask that some documentation be provided.

Two Cents

Most districts cap the amount an attorney can charge up front for a Chapter 13 bankruptcy. Usually the limit is under $1,500. These courts do allow the attorney to add the remainder of any fees due into the plan. Thus, the attorney gets paid like all other creditors—through the plan when the Chapter 13 trustee sends him a check.

After the meeting of creditors has been concluded, you may be required to attend a valuation hearing, which occurs only if a creditor objects to the value you list in your schedules for its secured merchandise. For example, maybe you think that your car is worth only $4,000, and your lender thinks it is worth $8,000. A judge will decide who is right.

Finally, your plan must be confirmed by the bankruptcy court after the trustee signs off on it. If it is not confirmed, your case will be dismissed. In some jurisdictions, confirmation is accomplished without an actual hearing. Confirmation usually occurs about two months after filing the case.

Plan payments will be due every month, and payments are made to the trustee's office. Other than that, you will probably have little substantial interaction with the trustee for the duration of your case. After you have made all of your plan payments, you will get your discharge.

Failure to Complete the Plan

Again, only half of all Chapter 13 debtors complete their plan payments, although all assuredly enter the process with the best of intentions. In most cases, plan payments cease because the debtor or his spouse lost a job, the debtors get divorced, or some other situation renders further plan payments impossible.

When that happens, debtors have several options:

1. **Modify the plan.** It is always possible to modify the plan payments as circumstances dictate. As long as everyone will still get the amount required by law (for example, unsecured creditors receiving what they would have received in a Chapter 7, and so on), the modification should be acceptable to the trustee and creditors.

2. **Request a hardship discharge.** If a modification is not feasible, then you can apply for something called a *hardship discharge*. This discharge is possible when circumstances beyond your control significantly change your financial condition, such as the death of a mate or the permanent loss of a job. If this applies, the bankruptcy code provides for the possibility of a discharge, even if all plan payments have not been paid. The only hitch is that your unsecured creditors must receive, by the time of the hardship discharge, what they would have received in a Chapter 7. (The bankruptcy code likes that rule.)

> **Check It Out**
>
> One advantage of converting from a Chapter 13 to a Chapter 7 is that all debts that you have acquired since you filed the Chapter 13 (called **post-petition** debts) can be included in your new Chapter 7 case. In all other circumstances, both Chapter 7 and Chapter 13 alike, post-petition debts are non-dischargeable.

3. **Convert your case to a Chapter 7.** Debtors have the right to convert their case at any time. Although you may lose your house, your unsecured debts will be discharged, and you will be relieved of all further plan payments. The problem with a Chapter 13 conversion is that nonexempt assets, otherwise protected in your Chapter 13 case, will be sold in your Chapter 7 case.

4. **Have the case dismissed.** In a very small number of cases, having your case dismissed may be a good idea. A dismissal of the case puts the debtor and creditor back where they were before the case was filed (less any payments received). This option may be preferable, for example, where a desirable nonexempt asset would be sold in a Chapter 7 conversion.

Remember that, except in the special cases discussed in this chapter, a Chapter 7 bankruptcy is preferable to a Chapter 13 bankruptcy.

The Least You Need to Know

◆ Chapter 13 should be used to make up mortgage arrears, pay taxes, or protect nonexempt property.

◆ Certain requirements must be met for your plan to succeed.

◆ Payments must be made every month until the plan is paid in full.

◆ Having your Chapter 13 case converted to a Chapter 7 may be preferable to having it dismissed.

What Can Go Wrong?

In This Chapter

- ◆ Violations of the automatic stay
- ◆ A dismissed case
- ◆ A denied discharge
- ◆ Attempts to collect discharged debts
- ◆ Discrimination
- ◆ Unlisted debts or property

Most bankruptcies proceed without a hitch. If you are honest in your petition and schedules, your discharge will be granted. For most debtors, the process from filing to hearing to discharge is seamless and surprisingly simple. However, sometimes problems do arise, either during the case or soon after the discharge is granted. Most are fairly easy to deal with if you understand your rights.

Problems with the Automatic Stay

The automatic stay remains in effect for the duration of your case. Yet sometimes creditors want to continue collection activities despite the stay. Usually, they will request permission from the court to do so. That is legal. Sometimes, however, a creditor continues to proceed against a debtor, but it does so *without* court permission. Doing so is illegal. While this does happen, luckily it is a fairly rare occurrence.

Money Talks

The top 10 largest bankruptcies of all time:

10. M Corp, 1989, $20 billion in assets
 9. Pacific Gas & Electric, 2001, $21.5 billion in assets
 8. Adelpphia Communications, 2002, $21.5 billion in assets
 7. United Airlines, 2002, $25 billion in assets
 6. Global Crossing, 2002, $30 billion in assets
 5. Financial Corp of America, 1988, $34 billion in assets
 4. Texaco, 1987, $36 billion in assets
 3. Conseco Inc., 2002, $61 billion in assets
 2. Enron, 2002, $63 billion in assets
 1. Worldcom, 2002, $104 billion in assets

Of the top 10 bankruptcies, seven were filed in 2001 or 2002.

Relief from Stay Motions

When a creditor requests court permission to continue collection activities it is called a *relief from stay*. If the court grants the motion, the stay is lifted for this creditor only. A relief from stay motion cannot be sought just because a creditor is angry at being included in a bankruptcy. If that were true, then every creditor would file a similar motion. No, there are only a few, specific circumstances where a relief from stay will be sought and granted.

Two Cents

A creditor who brings a relief from stay motion against you is required to give you notice of the date and time for the hearing, and you have a right to defend yourself and oppose the relief from stay.

Normally, if you have no equity in a secured item, such as a car or house, and you stop making payments, the court will grant relief from stay because the lender's interest in the property is not being protected. For example, Vicky was two months behind on her mortgage and on the verge of foreclosure when she filed her Chapter 7. She intended to catch up her mortgage with the extra money she anticipated having after filing, but she never did. A month after filing, she was three months behind on her mortgage. In that case, her mortgage company would probably go to court and request relief from stay so that it could continue to foreclose. Because Vicky was continuing to fall behind on her mortgage, the court would likely grant the motion, and the automatic stay would be lifted pertaining to this creditor.

The stay stops all proceedings against you. If you are involved in a dispute unrelated to your bankruptcy, such as a divorce, the stay can be lifted as to that matter.

Acting Without Court Permission

Sometimes a creditor never requests relief from stay and continues to harass you as if nothing has happened. The collection agency keeps calling, or a creditor files suit. Such actions constitute contempt of court; the creditor has broken the law and can be fined by a bankruptcy judge for the violation.

If this happens to you, you have a few options. You could call the creditor and explain that he is violating a federal court order, which he may not know, and he may just stop. This action is certainly easier and cheaper than the second option: Your attorney may file a contempt of court motion against the creditor. A creditor, knowing of a bankruptcy, who continues to send the debtor a monthly bill will not get in trouble because that is not a significant violation. An auto repossession in the middle of the case, however, would be considered contempt of court.

> **Two Cents**
>
> For a contempt of court motion to succeed, the debtor must be able to prove that the creditor knew of the stay, that the creditor intentionally violated the stay, and that the violation was serious. This is not an easy three-part test to meet.

Bankruptcy Case Dismissals

Betty and Theo had their case dismissed. They came into Steve's office one day explaining that they needed to file bankruptcy. He prepared all of the paperwork, had them sign it, filed the case, and waited for the first meeting of creditors.

When they all went to the meeting a month later, the trustee asked Betty and Theo some seemingly very simple questions. Had they filed bankruptcy in the past two years? "No," they replied. Did they list all of their assets in their paperwork? "Of course!"

They were lying, and the trustee knew it. They had filed five bankruptcies in the previous four years, abusing the system and trying to keep their house out of foreclosure.

They also had a $10,000 car that they failed to disclose in their paperwork. The trustee dismissed their case, but not before seizing the car and selling it to pay back their creditors.

Dismissal of a case is an extreme circumstance that occurs very rarely. It only happens if your filing fees were never paid, if you fail to file all of your paperwork, if you fail to attend the first meeting of creditors, or if you filed your case in bad faith. Cases that are dismissed are usually dismissed "without prejudice," meaning you can file again. Just do it right the next time.

Denial of Discharge

Probably the worst possible thing that could happen to your case is to have your discharge denied, because the entire point of this exercise is to get the discharge. With a dismissal, you can normally file your case again fairly quickly. A denial of discharge is different. It means you had your chance, and you blew it; you don't have a chance to wipe out your debts with a bankruptcy for at least six years. A discharge can be denied for any of the following reasons:

◆ **Intentional concealment, transfer, or destruction of property.** The most common reason, this occurs when a debtor knowingly hides or sells nonexempt assets.

◆ **Dishonesty in connection with the bankruptcy case.** People who commit perjury (either in their paperwork or at their hearing), who conceal or destroy important financial documents, or who withhold records, can be denied a discharge.

◆ **Receipt of a discharge in the preceding six years.** You can file bankruptcy only every six years. If you received a discharge within the last six years, another one will be denied.

Denial of a discharge is a radical remedy used in only the most egregious of cases. Be honest, and all should go well.

Problems After the Discharge

Getting your discharge should be a big relief. It means the case is over, your unsecured debts are discharged, and it is time to move on. It is a time to begin anew financially, learn your lessons, and finally start to get ahead of the game. Living a life free from debt is a great joy. For most people who go through bankruptcy, that is exactly how it is. However, in a few cases, events occur after you have received your discharge that require some attention on your part.

Money Talks

If you have gone through bankruptcy, you should know that you are in good company. Even the Bible endorses the idea. In Deuteronomy 15:1-2, it is said, "At the end of every seven years, you are to cancel the debts of those who owe you money. This is how it is done. Everyone who has lent money to his neighbor is to cancel the debt: he must not try to collect the money: the Lord himself has declared the debt canceled."

Attempts to Collect Discharged Debts

Despite what the Bible says, creditors sometimes try and collect a debt that was discharged in bankruptcy. This is completely illegal. In most cases, the attempt to collect the debt is simply a mistake. Maybe the creditor did not know about the bankruptcy or possibly did not realize that it applied to the money he is owed.

A discharge is a federal court order. In it, all creditors are specifically told to cease all further collection activities. Like a violation of the automatic stay, violating this order also constitutes contempt of court and is illegal.

When it happens, the first thing to do is to write a letter to the creditor explaining that you filed for bankruptcy. Attach a copy of your discharge (always keep the original in your files), explain what a discharge is, tell him that his debt was in fact discharged, and demand to be left alone. If that does not work, it is time to get nasty.

For example, Beth owed a local department store $800; this debt had been included and was discharged in her bankruptcy. When the store still insisted on being paid after the case was over, Beth tried to explain nicely that she did not owe the money anymore. The store continued to harass her and finally sued her. Beth, having tried to explain politely that the debt had been discharged, had no choice but to file a contempt motion in bankruptcy court and was awarded $500. The store left her alone after that.

Two Cents

Even though your debt to your mom was discharged, you can still pay her back after your case is over if you want to. As long as you voluntarily choose to repay a debt, you can repay it. It is when you are forced to attempt to repay a discharged debt that a violation of the law has occurred.

Remember this though: Debts not listed in your bankruptcy paperwork are debts not discharged. You must have listed the debt in order to receive a discharge as to that debt. If you forgot to list a creditor whose debt would have been discharged had he been listed, see the "Debts Not Listed" section later in the chapter.

Finally, some debts are nondischargeable, and those creditors do have a right to get paid back once the case is concluded. There is nothing illegal about the IRS garnishing your wages to get back taxes paid after your case is over. Nondischargeable debts include ...

1. Taxes assessed within the last 3 years.

2. Debts arising from defrauding a bank.

3. Alimony, maintenance, or child support.

4. Debts resulting from injuries created by willful acts. (You shot someone, for example.)

5. Government fines and penalties.

6. Most student loans.

7. Drunk driving debts.

8. Debts denied or waived in a previous bankruptcy.

9. Debts incurred to pay nondischargeable taxes. (You used a credit card to pay off taxes before filing.)

10. Debts for various condominium and cooperative assessments.

Discrimination

It is illegal for the government to discriminate against you because you went through bankruptcy. A debtor who feels he or she has been illegally discriminated against because of a bankruptcy can have the offender sanctioned by the bankruptcy court.

Over Your Limit

Although the bankruptcy code protects you from discrimination, it offers no protection if you are denied benefits for reasons unrelated to your bankruptcy.

For example, Francesco was a licensed general contractor who built office buildings. Forced to file Chapter 7 because of his wife's illness, Francesco received his discharge about six months after he filed his case. A month after that, the State Contractors License Board wrote to him and said that it intended to revoke his contractor's license because of the bankruptcy. Francesco hired an attorney to write a letter back, explaining that it is generally illegal to discriminate against a debtor because of a bankruptcy and specifically illegal to revoke, suspend, or refuse to renew a license or permit because of a bankruptcy. The board immediately dropped the matter.

This protection from government discrimination based upon bankruptcy is fairly broad. Examples of impermissible actions include the following:

- Denying you a federally guaranteed student loan or grant because of a bank-ruptcy filing

- Refusing to issue a college transcript because of a bankruptcy

- Denying you accommodations in public housing

- Denying you any other government benefit or service, such as Social Security or welfare

---

Money Talks

The point of bankruptcy is to get a fresh start. It would be very hard to get one if a gov-ernment entity was able to hassle you because of a bankruptcy. So, for example, the Department of Motor Vehicles cannot withhold your driver's license because you owed it money and had that debt discharged. The DMV could, however, withhold your license if the reason is unrelated to the debt: a bad-driving record, for example. In that case, there is nothing discriminatory about withholding a license.

Protection from discrimination also extends to private employers. You cannot be fired if the reason for the firing is your bankruptcy. Knowing this can be especially helpful for Chapter 13 debtors because the trustee's payment is sometimes deducted from your paycheck. If an employer is unhappy about it, too bad. There is nothing he can do about it.

Debts Not Listed

Sometimes people forget to list a creditor on their schedules. If the mistake is discov-ered before the case is over, you can simply amend your schedules, pay a nominal fee to the bankruptcy clerk, file the amendment, and get the debt discharged.

If you discovered the problem after you received your discharge, then you have a problem. In that case, you are supposed to reopen your case and amend your sched-ules if you want to get the debt discharged. This will require hiring an attorney and having a motion filed with the court.

Another option, instead of choosing the costly and burdensome option of reopening the case, would be to write your creditor a letter. The Ninth Circuit Court of Appeals, for example, has stated that there is no need to reopen a case if the debt would have been discharged if it had been listed in the original filing. In the Ninth Circuit, the debt is treated *as if* it were discharged. In your letter, explain this to your creditor. In all likelihood, he will never know if you are in the Third District or the Eighth District or the Ninth District. Bluffing is not illegal.

Property Not Listed

If you forgot to list some property and realized it after your case was discharged, you have an obligation to tell your trustee about it. You still might be allowed to keep it.

Property You Already Owned Prior to Filing

If the property would have been exempt had you listed it, the trustee will take no action, and you can keep the property. Also, if the property is of no real value, the trustee will not take the time to reopen your case, take the property, sell it, and distribute the income to your creditors. But if you forgot to list that vintage Mercedes that you have in storage, you will not own it for long.

Property You Recently Inherited or Acquired

Certain property that you receive within six months from the date you filed your case must be disclosed to your trustee. Those items are as follows:

Inheritances: Any money you inherit within 180 days of filing becomes part of your bankruptcy estate.

Death benefits: Any money received from life insurance or a death benefit plan must also be disclosed.

Divorce settlements: Money or property received as a result of a divorce decree or a marital settlement agreement is part of your estate if it is received within 180 days of filing.

This means that even if you filed your case on January 1, received your discharge on May 1, and inherited $10,000 on June 1, you would have to tell the trustee about the money. To the extent that it is nonexempt, you may lose the money to the trustee.

In general, it should be clear now that the best thing to do is to be completely honest when you file for bankruptcy.

The Least You Need to Know

- Violations of the automatic stay are contempt of court if they are done without court permission.

- Having your case dismissed is usually a minor problem.

- Having your discharge denied is a major problem.

- Attempts to collect discharged debts can usually be dealt with by letter.

- Discrimination because of bankruptcy is illegal.

- Debts not listed are debts not discharged.

- Property not listed can be a problem.

Part 5

Getting Ahead of the Game

It's not over when the debt is gone! Remember everything you went through at the beginning of this book? Remember the lessons you learned, the ideas that you read about that seemed obvious when you learned them, but which were new to you nonetheless? Here's one more obvious idea: Just because you've beaten the debt you had does not mean you will never be in debt again.

We discuss ways of using debt in a positive manner, and ways of avoiding bad debt. We talk about maintaining your vigilance and planning for the future. Maintain your freedom! Invest for your future!

Chapter **24**

Getting Credit Again

In This Chapter

- ◆ Credit cards
- ◆ Auto loans
- ◆ Other bank loans
- ◆ Home loans

It will be difficult for you to reestablish a good credit rating and get credit again after a bankruptcy. That is a fact. But getting credit is not impossible; there are many creditors who still want your business. Credit will just be more expensive this time around. You will pay, literally, for your mistakes.

A Credit Card Society

As you near the end of the debt tunnel, you may never want to see another credit card again. Although we understand, appreciate, and empathize with that sentiment, living without a credit card in this world is difficult and almost unrealistic. Be that as it may, either through voluntarily cutting them up, having them cancelled, or because of a bankruptcy, many people have no credit cards whatsoever when they emerge from the bankruptcy tunnel.

As you know (only too well), our society is dependent upon credit cards. To do something as mundane as cash a check or rent a car while on vacation in some places, you must have a credit card. You probably need to get a credit card again. This time, though, you will use it differently.

What if you don't want a credit card? In that case, it is still possible to travel. Most large hotel chains will allow you to prepay for your hotel room, thereby obviating the need to reserve a room with a credit card. Many car rental companies will rent you a car without a credit card if you leave a hefty deposit (about $500).

Two Cents

If you don't have a credit card and you need to rent a car, go to Budget. Budget Rent a Car will let you rent a car with a debit card. Call 1-800-527-0700 or go to Budget.com.

Getting a credit card again can be a very positive step in your journey toward financial solvency. Getting a new card and not abusing it is a sign that lessons have been learned. The trick is in getting a new card.

Secured Credit Cards

Credit card companies want your business, despite your credit history. What they do for people like you is offer a credit card secured by money. In exchange for a card with, say, a $250 credit limit, the issuing bank requires that you open up a savings account in its institution with $250. If you fail to repay the debts incurred using the card, your account will be used to pay the debt.

A secured credit card looks just like any other credit card, with a Visa or MasterCard logo on the front. No one will know that it is a secured card. When you charge with it, the charge will go through just as it would with a "normal" credit card (assuming, of course, that you have room on the card).

Choosing a Secured Card

Choose a secured credit card based on these criteria:

♦ **The deposit requirement.** Usually, the minimum deposit required is $200, although it depends upon the institution. You can always deposit more and, by so doing, create a higher credit limit for yourself. A $500 deposit typically creates a $500 credit limit.

♦ **The grace period.** You need to become more familiar with this concept if you are going to become a more money-savvy individual. The grace period is the amount of time you are permitted to repay your balance without paying an additional finance charge. These time periods can range from 0 days to 30. More is obviously better, and we recommend finding a card with a 25- to 30-day grace period.

♦ **The interest rate.** Interest rates on secured cards can range anywhere from 10 percent or so to 20 percent and even higher. Go for the lowest rate you can find.

♦ **Matching funds.** Some cards will match your deposit with extra credit. For example, if you deposit $500, some cards will then give you a $1,000 credit limit.

♦ **A chance to get an unsecured card.** You really begin to establish good credit again when you have an unsecured credit card once more. Some secured credit card companies give you the chance to trade your secured card in (and thus get your deposit back) after a year of timely payments.

Decide which of these factors is most important to you. One thing you need to be sure of with any card you choose is that the issuing bank reports your payment history every month to the big three credit-reporting agencies: Equifax, TransUnion, and Experian. If it does not, you will not be reestablishing a new, good credit history.

Equally important is whether the issuing bank reports the card as secured to the credit-reporting agencies. You want a card that is not reported as secured. Why? A secured card that is not reported as secured (and not all are) looks like it is unsecured on your credit report. Other potential creditors who read the report will be more inclined to give you unsecured credit if it looks like you have unsecured credit already.

> **Money Talks**
>
> Maybe you're thinking to yourself, "What about TRW? I remember that they were a big credit-reporting agency at one time." TRW sold its credit reporting division and that area now goes under the name Experian.

So what you are looking for is a card that offers a "low" interest rate (remembering everything is relative), flexible terms, and reporting of the card as unsecured. There are several to choose from and their programs change, so look around. Some cards that we found that you may want to consider are:

♦ Universal Platinum MasterCard: According to the website, "The Universal Stored Value MasterCard is better than a secured card. It does not require you to open a bank account or put up a security deposit in order to obtain one. There are no interest charges associated with this card. 100 percent Guaranteed Approval."

♦ Orchard Bank MasterCard: Orchard Banks says that "The Orchard Bank MasterCard program was established to make credit cards available to those consumers unable to obtain them through traditional means."

◆ Centennial Card: Centennial says that "The Centennial VISA or MasterCard is especially designed for people who have had difficulties being approved for a major credit card. The Centennial Card is issued by First PREMIER Bank, one of the nation's leading credit card issuers specializing in MASTERCARD and VISA credit cards which help consumers re-establish their credit history."

Anyone, no matter how bad his or her credit history, should be able to get a secured credit card. Besides the ones mentioned here, you can find other secured credit cards through banks, credit unions, and in the classified sections of newspapers under "money to lend."

Saving the best for last, just recently we discovered a credit card company that will give practically anyone an unsecured card with a $250 limit. It's called the ARIA card, and the company can be reached at 1-888-237-4837 or on the Internet at ARIA.com.

Beware of Scams

Unscrupulous creditors are always looking to make a buck off of credit-hungry consumers. You must be very wary of this; Paula was not. After her bankruptcy, Paula received an offer from a company that said it would give her the chance to rebuild her credit and get a new credit card. For a $50 fee, she was sent something called a Universal Card and a catalog of overpriced merchandise. After she had bought $3,000 of this stuff using her new "credit card," she would be eligible for a Visa or MasterCard. I bet you can guess what happened $3,000 later. She was sent nothing more than a list of banks offering secured credit cards. Don't let this happen to you.

> **CAUTION**
>
> **Over Your Limit** _____
>
> The Federal Trade Commission (FTC) has recently taken legal action against several companies that are ripping off consumers with a secured credit card scam.
>
> The scam often works this way: An ad will offer a credit card to anyone if they call a number. But the number is not toll-free, rather it will be a '900' number, where you are billed up to $50 just for making the call.
>
> If you think you may have been a victim of such a scam, you can file a complaint with the FTC by calling 900-(just kidding!). The real number is 1-877-FTC-HELP.

A Tiger in Your Tank

Another way to reestablish credit is by getting a gasoline credit card. Normally, this would be difficult to do without good credit; however, there is a small loophole that you can jump through.

The first thing to do is find an oil company that is publicly traded that has a gas station near you. The trick is that you must buy stock in the gasoline company you want directly from the company. Call the company and say that you want to join its dividend reinvestment plan (DRIP). Do not say that you are applying for a credit card. You must buy at least $250 worth of stock to enroll in the company's DRIP.

Well-known companies offering DRIPs with stations in many places include the following:

◆ Exxon: 1-800-252-1800

◆ Mobil: 1-800-648-9291

◆ British Petroleum (BP)/Amoco: www.bpamoco.com

You will then get a packet in the mail explaining how to buy stock straight from the company. You will need to send in $250, and the company will enroll you in their DRIP and buy $250 worth of stock for you.

After about six months, the oil company will send you an application for a gas credit card. In essence, like a secured credit card, your stock will be securing your gas card, although the card will be reported as an unsecured card (which it is). So not only will you be getting a completely unsecured credit card, but you will also be starting your investment portfolio.

Check It Out

DRIPs get their name from the fact that they use dividends to purchase more stock. Thus "Dividend Reinvestment Plan." Whether or not you have to reinvest the dividends depends on the plan. A **dividend** is an annual payment to shareholders from company profits. You might make money through dividends and through a rising stock price.

Two Cents

According to investment guru the Motley Fool, DRIPs "are a way to begin investing with a very small amount of money while avoiding brokerage commissions and reinvesting dividends. In the long term, it's a great and 'patient' way to grow money."

Debit Cards

Another option (besides a credit card) for charging when the situation warrants is a debit card issued by your bank. A debit card is just like an ATM card, except that it also has a Visa or MasterCard logo on the front. It acts just like a credit card. You can charge with it just as you would a credit card, except that instead of using credit, you are using your checking account to immediately pay for the purchase. As long as you have money in the account, you can "charge."

Over Your Limit

If you lose your debit card, you must report it to the bank within two days. If you do, you will be liable for only up to $50. If you wait longer, that protection goes away (although most banks usually try to cover all losses). You might lose everything in your account.

The good thing about debit cards is that anyone can get one and there is no deposit requirement or credit check because the debit card is linked to your checking account. Yet because it looks just like a credit card, your business associate won't know the difference when you whip out your debit card to pay for lunch. On the downside, because you are not using credit, you are not reestablishing any credit.

Have We Got a Deal for You!

Another way to reestablish credit after a tough time is by getting a loan for a used car. You see ads all the time that say "Bad Credit? No Problem!" Of course it's no problem when you are charged 23 percent interest. Nevertheless, whether you filed bankruptcy or are just trying to reestablish a good credit file, a car loan is a good way to show that you can pay a bill on time.

There are three ways to get a car loan. First, you can go to your bank and try to get a loan. Second, you can buy from the dealer and have it locate financing for you. Lastly, you can buy from a dealer and finance it through that dealer.

No Money Down

Getting a loan from a bank is the best way to go, but of course, this only works if your credit rating is fairly good. The advantage of a direct bank loan is twofold. First, you will get a lower interest rate than you could find almost anywhere else. Second, you will be in a stronger bargaining position when you go to buy, because you can either buy from a private party (which is cheaper) or do without the dealer's help financing the car you like.

If you are unable to get a bank car loan, the next best option is to buy from a dealer and have it attempt to find financing for you through one of its sources. Depending upon your credit rating, your loan could run anywhere from 6 percent to 23 percent.

Although getting credit again is nice, be wary of falling into the same trap you were in before when you probably cared little about interest rates. It is that type of financial illiteracy that helped get you into debt in the first place.

Money Talks
By comparison, a $10,000, 6 percent auto loan, if it were to be paid back in three years, would cost you $11,800 (6 percent of $10,000 equals $600; $600 multiplied by three years equals $1,800; $10,000 added to $1,800 equals $11,800). The same loan, at 23 percent payable over three years, would cost $16,900.

Everyone Is Approved!

The last and worst option is a dealer-financed car loan. The key phrase to look for is "we carry our own papers." That means that the dealership does not use a bank to finance its used car loans. Instead, it finances the car itself. If you stop paying, they start repossessing.

The problem with dealer-financed auto loans is the extraordinarily high interest rate you will pay. But such loans are also an opportunity for people with bad credit to get a car and reestablish themselves financially.

After you have paid back the car loan faithfully, it will be far easier to get a loan in the future. Not only will the interest rate be lower the next time, but more dealers will be interested in selling you a car.

Two Cents
Want to pay cash for a car? A fine idea, but consider too that many car buyers prefer taking out loans to paying cash because (1) it builds credit; (2) cash may be better used for other purposes; (3) saving the cash enables them to build a cash cushion; or (4) the money might be needed for such things as emergencies or college tuition.

Insurance

A final thought about cars and money: The higher the deductible is on your car insurance, the lower your monthly payment. The monthly payment on a $100 deductible policy is far higher than on a $1,000 deductible policy. Considering the few times that you use your insurance and have to pay the deductible, you could pay for the $1,000 in a few months by getting the cheaper policy and banking the difference.

This decision would show real financial literacy. Say that your insurance with a $100 deductible is $200 a month, but that with a $1,000 deductible it would be $100 a month. If you purchased the insurance with the higher deductible, you could bank the extra $100 a month and in 10 months have enough to cover any future deductible. On top of that, you would earn interest on your money.

Passbook Loans

Getting a passbook loan to reestablish credit is similar to, but also distinct from, obtaining a secured credit card. The basic idea is the same: You use a savings account to establish credit. The execution is what differs.

To get a passbook loan, take a fair amount of money, $1,000 for example, and open up a passbook savings account (or any other type of savings account) at a bank. Add money to the account every so often for a few months. Then, ask the bank for a loan for an amount less than what is in your savings account and secured by that account. The bank will loan the money to you because the loan is secured by the savings account.

Right off the bat you have convinced a major financial institution to give you a loan. That the loan is usually not reported as secured is icing on the cake. Anyone reading your credit report will be far more likely to extend you credit when he or she sees that a conservative institution like a bank was willing to take a risk on you and lend you money.

A Mortgage?

As strange as it may sound, you can get a mortgage after you have cleaned up your debt problems or received a discharge in bankruptcy. It usually takes about two years of clean credit to get one.

The reason you can get a mortgage is that it is usually quite a bit easier to pay bills in a timely manner after you have gotten out of debt. A record of paying bills on time again is the key to getting a home loan after debt. You need to have established a new history of good credit, instead of your old history of bad credit. Paying bills on time and rebuilding your credit with the techniques outlined in this chapter will help make you a more attractive candidate to a lender.

How Much House Can You Afford?

Lenders will pre-approve a loan whose annual payments equal up to 28 percent of your pretax annual income, but that amount may be more house than you need. For example, 28 percent of $50,000 in annual pretax income would result in a loan payment of about $1,150 per month. A 20 percent loan, however, results in a more manageable monthly mortgage payment of only $833 a month. In your post-debt era, less may be more.

Keeping Costs Down

You want to put as little money down and pay as little per month as possible on your new house. Federal Housing Authority (FHA) or Veteran's Administration (VA) loans are your best bet. With these loans, you need only put down 3 percent.

The two main things to consider when looking for a mortgage are the points you will pay for the loan and your closing costs (things like escrow fees, real estate agent fees, and recording costs). A point is 1 percent of the loan value, so the lower the points, the better. Closing costs can be outrageous. Here are some tips for keeping closing costs down:

- ◆ **Split the closing costs with the seller.** As the buyer, you would normally pay the closing costs, but an anxious seller will happily share these with you if it makes the sale.

- ◆ **Add the closing costs into the price of the home.** If, for example, your closing costs are going to be $10,000, ask the seller to add that amount into the price he is asking for the house so that you can add them into the mortgage. Your loan

Two Cents

Want to keep your credit outstanding? Follow these rules: 1) Pay all of your bills on time. All of your bills. You would be surprised at the kind of bills that might show up on a credit report if you pay them late. 2) Once a year, get a copy of your credit report and make sure that there are no errors on it.

Money Talks

The FHA's primary objective is to assist in providing housing opportunities for low- to moderate-income families. The agency does not generally provide the funds for the mortgages directly, but rather insures home mortgage loans made by private lenders such as mortgage bankers, savings and loans, and banks.

Check It Out

If you can come up with a hefty down payment, say 25 percent or more, the bank will ignore your past credit problems. The bank does not document your credit history for this type of loan, which is why it is called a **no-documentation loan.**

will be slightly higher, but you will pay less out of pocket. You must understand though, that over the life of the loan, your closing costs will end up being much higher (because you'll pay interest on the closing costs, which you would avoid if you paid the closing costs up front).

◆ **Have the seller pay for repairs.** Often, a house will need some work done to it before closing. Give the seller the option of fixing these things himself or paying for your cost of repair. That way, when the house is yours, you won't have to dip into your pocket to fix all of the initial little problems.

Finding Money for a Down Payment

Even with an FHA or VA loan, you will need to come up with several thousand dollars for a down payment, which can be difficult. Here are two ways to get the money:

Withdraw money from your 401(k) at work. You are legally entitled to withdraw up to 80 percent of your 401(k) to pay for a down payment on your primary residence. If you borrow against your 401(k), instead of just withdrawing the money, you can only borrow 50 percent.

Buy the house with a lease-option. In this scenario, you lease the house from the seller for a year or two and the seller agrees to earmark part of the money for your down payment. If you pay $1,000 a month for two years and the seller agrees to utilize 50 percent of that as your down payment, then after two years you have put $12,000 down on the house. This is how one of your authors bought their first home.

Whatever you do with your new credit, do not make the same mistakes you made before. Make sure that any debt you acquire is manageable.

The Least You Need to Know

◆ Secured credit cards are one of the best ways to begin to reestablish a good credit rating.

◆ Car loans are also a good way to get credit again, but they can be very expensive.

◆ You can get a mortgage even with a few black marks on your credit report.

Chapter 25

What the Rich Know That You Don't

In This Chapter

- ◆ Assets versus liabilities
- ◆ Investment basics
- ◆ Investing versus speculating
- ◆ Determining long-term goals
- ◆ The 10 percent solution

Becoming intelligent with money requires more than just getting out of debt. It also means making your money work for you instead of you working for it. It means earning interest instead of paying interest. It means buying assets instead of liabilities.

All of these things are true even if you are not out of debt yet. Even if you are diligently repaying your debts, it is still time to begin to think and act like the rich do; not because being rich is the goal (it may or may not be), but because rich people understand money.

Beginning with this chapter, and for the next few chapters, we will show you how money works for the wealthy and how you can begin to make more of it. Not only will this enable you to get out of debt more quickly, it just makes life easier. As John Lennon once said, "I'd rather be rich and unhappy than poor and unhappy."

Start Now

It is easy to say that you can't begin to invest until you are out of debt. That is commendable. It is also wrong. If we are looking at how wealthy people treat money, do you think that they don't have debts or that they don't have bills to pay? Of course, they do. Their bills would dwarf yours by comparison because their overhead is so much higher than yours. But that does not stop them from using their money wisely.

They buy cattle ranches, collect art, invest in businesses, dabble in the stock market, and gobble up real estate because they know that money invested is money returned.

Despite mortgages, credit card bills, family members needing help, and huge tax liabilities, most wealthy people make sure to invest at least 10 percent of their income. Investing is how rich people stay ahead.

It doesn't matter what type of investment you pick; you could choose to start your own business or buy some mutual funds. The important thing is to shift your thinking from just getting out of debt to getting ahead.

We are not saying that you have to get rich. You don't. What we are saying is that if you are in debt, then maybe there are a few things you could learn about money, and rich people are the best role models.

Take Jill, for example. A writer and producer for the television show *Cheers*, she made a lot of money and now lives the good life. But she does not just have her money sitting in the bank. Jill owns six in-and-out auto lube franchises. Her money makes money.

You need to begin to do the same. Sure, money is tight, but there are ways for you to create investment capital without changing your life. We explain how to do so at the end of the chapter, so read on.

> **Money Talks**
>
> In 1963, John Lennon and Paul McCartney formed Northern Songs, a corporation that would own the rights to Beatles songs. The company was formed with assets of a little more than $200. In the late 1980s, Michael Jackson gained control of the company, paying more than $60 million for it.

> **Money Talks**
>
> The World Bank Atlas estimates that the total value of all assets owned by individuals in the world is between 500 trillion and one quadrillion dollars. (That's $1,000,000,000,000,000.) This amount does not include assets owned by governments or religions.

Assets and Liabilities

In the movie *The Edge*, Anthony Hopkins and Alec Baldwin played two men stranded in the Alaskan outback. Armed with only a few knives, a book about survival in the wilderness, and their wits, the two had to find a way to live and make it out.

At one point a grizzly bear began to stalk them. The survival book had a chapter on how to kill a bear. Baldwin was convinced they could not do it without a gun. Hopkins thought otherwise. His motto was, "What one man can do another can do." He read the book, learned how to kill a bear, believed that what one man could do another could do, and made Baldwin believe it, too. It was not easy, but they killed the bear.

Only a movie, yes, but it's a powerful lesson nonetheless. What one man can do, another can do. If those men can slay a movie bear, you can slay the money bear. What the financially literate can do, you can do, too—if you learn how they do it. Do you want to know how the wealthy became rich in the first place? They bought assets.

Liabilities Are Not Assets

We all think we know the difference between an asset and a liability, but sometimes the most obvious thing is the most difficult. The problem for most people who fall into debt is that they buy liabilities, but think they are assets. The first thing to understand then is the difference between an asset and a liability and how they affect your bottom line.

There are many ways to define what assets and liabilities are. Accountants have definitions, as do business people and investors, but let's keep it simple:

◆ An asset makes you money.

◆ A liability costs you money.

If you want to get rich, or out of debt, you will buy assets instead of liabilities. Let's say that you and your sister Sydney both just inherited $5,000. What would you do with that money? If you are like most people, you would buy a liability. Maybe you would use it as a down payment on a new car or use it to take your mate on a nice trip. Those are fine things, but they just don't make you money. They cost you money.

Look at the facts. If you put that $5,000 down on a new car, you would be creating more debt in the form of monthly payments. Sure, the car would be an "asset" in the conventional sense of the word, but a car and a car loan don't make you any money. They cost you money. The same is true for a trip. These things look like assets, but they are liabilities insofar as money goes, see? (This is not to say that you shouldn't buy a new car when you need one.)

Over Your Limit

A $20,000 car loan at 15 percent interest payable over five years would end up costing you over $33,000.

Let's also assume Sydney is a bit more financially literate than you and that she decides to do something different with her $5,000. She wants to buy an asset. She might buy some stocks or mutual funds, or she might invest it in some real estate. Maybe she will decide to expand her business with it. She would use the money in such a way that it would make her more money instead of cost her money.

Consider the difference. Even if you got a low interest rate, your new car would end up costing you maybe another $20,000. Five years from today, you would be another $25,000 in the hole (with a five-year-old car to show for it). Conversely, $5,000 put in a mutual fund might make Sydney another $3,000. Five years later, she would be $8,000 ahead. There's a big difference between $25,000 down versus $8,000 ahead.

This, then, creates a cycle. With $8,000 to use, Sydney might be able to purchase a small rental property and thereby create even more income for herself. You would have an older car with probably 75,000 miles on it that is worth one third of what it cost you and no way to create more money.

Multiply this time and again, and you will begin to see why the rich do indeed get richer. Assets make money; liabilities cost money. Wealthy people buy assets. The poor and middle class buy liabilities thinking they are assets.

Types of Assets

Of course, you need a new car sometimes (well, maybe you don't need a new car; maybe a used car would do, and you could pocket the difference). The point is, if you are going to get out of debt, get ahead, and make more money, you need to buy some assets; you need to invest some money.

Consider the following investments:

Two Cents

During one three-year stretch, the stock with the best return on investment was Dell Computer, growing an astounding 2,862 percent.

- ◆ **The stock market:** You can buy stocks, bonds, or mutual funds.

- ◆ **Real estate:** Someone owns all of those rentals people live in. With federally guaranteed loan programs, qualifying for a loan is not so far-fetched.

- ◆ **A new business:** We all know the economy is changing. Home-based businesses and other entrepreneurial activities are the jobs of the future.

Investing 101

So just what is investing? It is putting something of value into something else with the expectation that the end result will be bigger and better. You can invest your time in a good cause, you can invest your energy in your job, or you can invest yourself in a relationship. When you invest in these things, you expect that something good will come of your effort. Likewise, when you invest your money in stocks, mutual funds, real estate, or a business, you do so because you think your money will grow over time.

The magic in investing is in something called *compounding*. As you earn investment returns, your returns begin to gain returns as well, allowing you to turn a measly dollar into thousands of dollars if you leave it invested long enough.

You saw this concept in action with the example of Sydney earlier. Her $5,000 became $8,000. If she continued to invest the $8,000, it would soon be worth $12,000, and so on. The more money you save and invest today, the more you'll have in the future. Real wealth is created almost miraculously through investing and the most mundane and commonplace principles of time, patience, and the power of compounding.

Compounding is so magical that you can fairly easily double and triple your money over long periods of time. When you hear someone brag about doubling his money in 10 years, you should know that you only need a 7.1 percent annual return to double your money in 10 years. If the Standard and Poor's 500 (a widely used barometer of the stock market) had gone up 10.6 percent a year, the poor fellow who doubled his money in 10 years under-performed compared to the market.

Check It Out

Compound interest occurs when the interest you are paid on an asset is allowed to become part of that asset (think interest on a saving account), so that your interest begins to earn interest.

Two Cents

A hundred dollars a month invested at 7 percent for 15 years, compounded annually, would return $31,696. Invested for 30 years, it would become $121,997.

Investing Is Not Speculating

With compounding, you have to wait patiently for years for your riches to accumulate. But why put your money in slow-and-steady investment vehicles that merely promise double-digit returns when (according to some infomercials) you could have near-instant riches? What if you want it all now?

Then speculating is for you. Speculating is the art of taking your hard-earned money and putting it in a scheme that promises potential amazing returns. The key word is potential. What are the odds of winning the lottery? Probably something like one in seven million. What about Vegas? Your odds of walking out a winner are less than 50/50. These are extreme examples of speculating. Speculating is like gambling.

According to the dictionary, a speculative investment is a "transaction or venture the profits of which are conjectural or subject to chance; to buy or sell with the hope of profiting by fluctuations in price." To invest, though, is to "commit capital in business in order to earn a financial return; the outlay of money for income or profit."

Understanding the difference between speculating and investing is simple once you focus on the difference between two words in the definitions of these concepts. The key word in the definition of speculation is *hope*. The key word in the definition of invest is *earn*.

> **CAUTION**
>
> **Over Your Limit**
>
> You have a greater chance of dying from flesh-eating bacteria (about one in a million) than you do of winning the Powerball Lotto jackpot.

Let's say that you hear your dentist telling a patient about a company that is "going to go through the roof in the next few months." If you call your broker the first thing the next morning and place an order for 100 shares, you've just speculated. Do you know anything about the company? Are you familiar with its competition? What were its earnings last quarter? Are you not just hoping that your dentist knows what he is talking about? That's speculation.

> **Money Talks**
>
> Tulips were introduced in the Netherlands in 1593. In 1636, trading in tulips rapidly increased, and more and more people started speculating. Bulbs of one or two guilders could be worth a hundred a few months later. Fortunes were being made, and people from all walks of life who knew nothing of tulips became swept up in the gamble. "Tulipomania" was in full bloom. In 1637, prices spiraled to a ridiculous level. The market finally collapsed in 1637, leaving many people bankrupt.

Investing, on the other hand, requires research, expertise, and patience on your part. If you do your homework and learn about where and how to invest your money, the chances that you will lose it are quite small. Yes, all investing requires some element of risk. The difference is, real investing takes a lot of the risk out of the equation (but even with investing, there's always at least a little risk, except when you invest in a federally insured bank account).

Setting Your Investment Goals

Deciding how you are going to become an investor and what types of investments you will make requires planning. You need to answer these sorts of questions:

◆ What do you want to accomplish by investing? Is this money to get you out of debt? A down payment on a house? Your child's education? A home? Income to live on in retirement?

◆ What is your investment time frame? Five years? Tenx? Twenty?

◆ How much money will you need to reach your goals?

Don't let yourself get away with nonspecific answers, either. In the end, investing is about numbers, and you need to get used to that. That is a good thing. Real numbers let you see exactly what you need in order to get to your financial destination. How much do you need to get out of debt? How much will college cost when your child needs to go? How much yearly income is reasonable for your retirement?

After you have a rough idea of how much money you will need, you can start to think about what investment vehicles might be right for you and what kind of returns you can reasonably expect to make from them. Take a look at how various types of investments have performed historically:

◆ Putting your money into cash reserves, such as U.S. Treasury bills or money market funds, has yielded roughly 4.2 percent per year during this century.

◆ Long-term government bonds have returned around 4.0 percent per year since 1900.

◆ Overall, stocks have returned an average of 9.8 percent per year since 1900.

> **Money Talks**
>
> The best decades for stocks have been the 1950s, when stocks increased by 18.23 percent annually; the 1980s, when stocks increased by 16.64 percent annually; and the 1990s, during which stocks increased by 17.3 percent annually. But don't ask about the 2000s!

Taking the Plunge

The two major variables in figuring out your investment plan are your risk tolerance and the amount of time you can dedicate to investing. In our capitalistic society, the biggest rewards are given to those who take the biggest risks—the entrepreneurs.

Rather than being risk takers, most of us have gotten into the habit of putting in eight hours a day working for someone else. At the end of the week, we cash our paycheck and do it all over again. It's called the rat race.

But think about the guy who owns the company you work for. He's not hurting for money, is he? He knows something you are just figuring out: Working for someone else doesn't make you rich. Being the employee just makes you the employee. Being the boss is more risky, but it can also make you rich.

You need to become the boss of your own financial world. It need not be a full-time position, and you certainly do not have to quit your job tomorrow because you have decided to become an investor today. What it will require is learning the entrepreneurial skills necessary to take back control of your financial house. It is going to require taking chances with both your time and money and possibly being told by your loved ones that it cannot be done. But it can.

So what kind of financial investment is right for you? Here are the pros and cons of each possible investment option:

- Stocks are fairly risky, but they can easily be done on a part-time basis and have historically given good returns.

- Bonds are much less risky than stocks and can also be done part-time, but they give smaller returns.

- Real estate can be risky if you buy the wrong piece of property or buy at the wrong time, but generally speaking, it can be a great way to make extra money part-time. For some people, however, the hassles of dealing with tenants are not worth the possible return.

- Starting your own business is probably a full-time venture, and both the risks and rewards are high.

The 10 Percent Solution

You are probably thinking that this all sounds well and good, but where will you find any extra money to invest? We are here to tell you that you can create it, but we warn you: It will not be easy.

Of course, you have lots of bills; that's why you bought this book. You have a list of things and people you need to pay: rent, mortgages, car payments, dad, credit cards, and household goods. Pay them. But you need to add one more category to that list: you. We are not advising you to be irresponsible. Pay your bills. Get out of debt. But as you do, pay yourself first.

First? Yes, first. You need to take a fixed amount of your income every month, put it in savings, and not touch it. Saving 10 percent of your income would be great, but 5 percent would do for starters. Do it every month. As we said, this will not be easy. It will take self-discipline. But it's the best way to be sure you have money to invest.

Say that you bring home $2,000 a month. Of that amount, $600 is paid toward rent, $300 goes for the car payment, food takes up another $500, and utilities take another $300. You have $300 left over for everything else. Now, take a percentage of the total, say 5 percent ($100), and stick it in the bank. Besides getting into the habit of saving, you will begin to create a nest egg.

At the end of a year, how much would you have? $1,200? Nope. You would have more. Why? Because you would have begun to act like the rich do, and you would have been compounding your money and earning interest instead of paying interest. That $1,200 might be worth $1,300 at the end of the year. It would be a small, but very significant, milestone.

Over Your Limit

The current savings rate of households in the United States, on average, is less than 4 percent of income after taxes.

You don't need a lot to get started in the world of investing. You can buy plenty of mutual funds for $1,000. A total of $3,000 can be the down payment on a duplex. You could live in half, rent out the other half, and begin a real estate investment career.

The secret, and the hard part, is to put away money every month and to pay yourself before all others. There will be months where you are sure you cannot do it, but who is more important to pay than you? If you don't prioritize your finances, who will? Pay yourself first, and you will thank yourself later.

If you do this, you will begin to act like the rich. You will be creating the means to buy some real assets instead of frittering a measly $100 away on liabilities. You will earn interest instead of pay interest. You will be acting like the financially literate. Remember: What one man can do, another can do.

The Least You Need to Know

- ◆ Liabilities are not assets if they cost you money.
- ◆ Compounding your money is the secret to getting ahead.
- ◆ Investing and speculating are very different.
- ◆ Saving money every month is how you can get started.

Chapter 26

Staying Out of Trouble

In This Chapter

- ◆ Creating an asset protection plan
- ◆ Insurance
- ◆ Protecting your homestead
- ◆ Prenuptial agreements
- ◆ Living trusts
- ◆ Incorporating
- ◆ Family Limited Partnerships and LLCs

As most of us know only too well, debt can sneak up on you when you least expect it. Sometimes it comes on quietly and slowly, ensnaring you before you realize it. Other times, it attacks suddenly, as in the case of a lost job, divorce, or illness.

And when debt does attack, it can consume your assets—including your home, car, or business. So in this chapter we want to show you several ways to protect those assets so that if debt does attack again, you can fend it off.

The Need for a Plan

Let's assume that things are better financially, or that they will soon get better. The purpose of this book has not just been to help you get out of debt, but to help you prosper, too. Once that happens, however, you may become a bigger target, as people are much more apt to sue someone who has assets than someone who does not.

Indeed, there is a phenomenon in this country known as the "litigation explosion," referring to the many lawsuits that Americans file—some valid, others not. The problem is, it is difficult and time consuming for courts to separate the legitimate from frivolous lawsuits, and by the time they do, defendants (potentially you) have usually already spent a lot of money.

Similarly, creditors may be less inclined to sue if your property is legally protected from their long arm. You can take steps to protect what you have worked so hard to get. In this chapter, we'll take a look at some ways that you can protect your assets from creditors.

Insurance

Maybe the easiest way to protect your assets and financial health is to be properly insured. Countless Americans are forced into bankruptcy because of uninsured medical problems or by being underinsured with their automobile insurance.

What sort of insurance do you need? Here are your options:

- **Health:** If you are self-employed, or if your employer doesn't provide adequate insurance, then it is vital to your economic well-being that you get health insurance. In some cases, you may be eligible for COBRA (the Consolidated Omnibus Budget Reconciliation Act of 1985). This law allows you to personally continue your employer-sponsored group medical insurance, dental, and prescription drug coverage on an individual basis after you leave that place of employment. Another way to find reasonable health care insurance is simply by shopping around. Try ehealthinsurance.com.

- **Disability:** Disability insurance covers you when you can't work because you are disabled due to injury.

- **Automobile:** If you are underinsured and you injure someone, that party can come after your home, bank accounts, and so on, after the policy limits have been reached. Similarly, if your auto insurance doesn't cover the cost of a replacement car in case yours is ruined, you could get stuck with no car at all, or for paying for an old loan of a car that has been totaled. Adequate car insurance is important.

- ◆ **Home/Property:** If you have a mortgage, then homeowner's insurance is probably required by your lender. But if your home is paid off or if you rent, you should consider getting your personal property insured. Losing your life's possessions to a flood, fire, or theft is a disaster in more ways than one.

- ◆ **Life:** We think that getting life insurance is one of the most important things you can do. Adults normally want to provide a good life for their spouse and children. Well, what happens to that dream if you die? The dream will likely die, too. Life insurance keeps the dream alive.

Homesteading

One of the simplest things you can do to protect your home is to file what is known as a "homestead exemption" with the county recorder where you live. Most states allow it, and doing so protects at least some of the equity that you build in your home from creditors.

For example, say that you live in a state that allows for a $15,000 homestead exemption, and you file it. Thereafter, if someone sues you, wins, and attaches a lien on your home for $100,000, you would be paid $15,000 from the sale of your home before any payment is made on the lien, as long as you recorded the homestead exemption first. It's a simple way to protect home equity from creditors, and may even scare a few off.

Amounts of the homestead protection vary by state; sometimes it's as little as $3,500, and in other states it is unlimited. You will need to do a little research to see how much it is in your state.

The Prenup

A prenuptial agreement or premarital agreement is an agreement between a couple made prior to marriage that states their plan for the marriage and what should happen should the marriage fail.

Although they sometimes get a bad rap, prenups can actually be of use to almost anyone contemplating marriage. For instance, a prenup can be used to ensure that one party will be liable for certain debts, or to make sure that the new spouse will not become responsible for an old debt of her betrothed.

Two Cents

To be valid, the prenup must be in writing, both parties must make a full and complete disclosure of all property and other assets, and both parties must be adequately protected by the agreement. "Full disclosure" means that both parties have revealed their significant assets and debts. Failure to do so constitutes fraud, and fraud invalidates contracts.

Here's an example: Cindy is about to marry Ray, a nice man with exorbitant architecture school bills. The prenup could spell out that even though Cindy may benefit from Ray's education, the couple agrees that the debt shall remain Ray's sole responsibility.

Because a prenuptial agreement is a contract, like any contract, it creates a set of "laws" between the parties who sign it. It can stay in effect as long as the couple stays married, or it can terminate on a predetermined date if both parties agree, on their fifth wedding anniversary, for example. It can deal with one main asset, several small debts, or future alimony. It is all up to the couple. If you need a prenup, you would be wise to consult with an attorney.

The Recoverable Living Trust

Imagine that you (or you and your spouse) are about to take a long trip overseas without your children. Before departure, you would probably plan ahead, anticipating any possible problems. Of course, you would arrange for someone you love and trust to care for your children while you were away, making sure to leave him or her with enough money, and you also would probably leave a set of instructions as to how to care for each child.

In other words, you would have planned ahead to make sure that your children are supported and cared for. However, accidents don't just happen while we're on long trips. For instance, each time you get into your car for the commute to work, there's a chance you won't be coming back. Who knows what tomorrow will bring? So why not plan ahead for the care and support or your children?

Over Your Limit

Aside from attorney fees, other fees involved in probating an estate include accountants to handle tax issues and appraisers if real estate or a business is involved. Fees will also need to be paid for death certificates, filing of legal documents, legal publication charges, recording, fax and phone, postage, and so on.

How do you do that? Simple: You create a living trust.

A living trust is a message to those around you explaining how you want things handled when you are gone. Ideally, it would be funded with enough money to give your loved ones the money they would need should something happen to you.

Having a living trust is one more way to avoid racking up big bills and throwing your family into debt. How? In this case, the bills would be those owed by your spouse or children should you pass away with no will, or a will, but no living trust. Dying without one can easily end up costing your loved ones tens of thousands of dollars.

Wills vs. Living Trusts

The legal process whereby your property is distributed to heirs and your debts to your creditors are paid is called probate. Probate is an expensive, time-consuming process that can end up costing your estate roughly 10 percent of its gross value in fees.

Think about that. If you own a home worth $250,000 (owing $200,000), and have a $50,000 life insurance policy, then the gross value of your estate is $300,000. Without doing some simple, proper estate planning, probate can eat up approximately $30,000 of that estate. Instead of leaving your loved ones with enough to start again, you leave them with a measly $20,000. How long will that last?

But that's what will happen if you die with only a will. A will guarantees that your assets will go through probate; that's how it works. But a living trust allows you to legally circumvent probate.

How? A living trust is a separate legal entity, set up by you, owned by you, and controlled by you, which holds your property for your benefit during your life. But because this "entity" owns your property, when you die, there is nothing of yours to probate. It is simple, elegant, and highly effective.

Even better: Because you own and control the trust during your life, you continue to have control of your property. Then, upon your death, your successor trustee will transfer your property to whomever you want, just as a will would, but without any fees or costs. You will be ensuring that your loved ones don't go into debt because you died.

Living Trust Benefits

A living trust is really quite an easy thing to create. It shouldn't be intimidating nor complex. It need not change how you use your property. It is nothing more than a legal entity created by you to hold your property for your use while you are alive, and then it becomes a mechanism to transfer that property to your loved ones after you pass away, without court supervision and without any expensive legal fees.

Two Cents

Creating a living trust is one area where you might consider playing lawyer. It need not be a very complicated document, and there are several very good legal software programs that walk you through the process. Quicken Family Lawyer is one such program.

Obviously, one of the main advantages of a living trust is that it allows your assets to transfer to your beneficiaries without probate, without lawyers, and without high fees. Other advantages are as follows:

♦ Because it is a private document, a living trust also protects your privacy. No one need ever know the size of your estate and to whom you left it.

♦ If the value of your estate is more than $650,000, significant tax savings can be had as well. If this is important to you, see a lawyer.

The Beauty of Incorporating

If you are in some way self-employed, then one of the easiest and best ways to shield yourself from lawsuits is by incorporating. By conducting your business as a corporation, you set up a wall between you, your assets, and the outside world.

A corporation is a separate legal entity, and one of the very best aspects of having your own, personal corporation is that it limits your personal liability.

For example, say that you own a business and that your business signs what seems to be a lucrative contract. Later it turns out that you made a big mistake and your business owes the other party $500,000. If you were not incorporated, the other side could come after you personally for money damages. This means that you could lose your business, your house—everything.

That would not be true if you incorporated. Creditors are limited to the assets of the corporation only for payment and may not collect directly from the shareholders.

Over Your Limit

A corporation does not protect you from personal debts and personal lawsuits. It only protects you when acting in a business capacity.

Similarly, when your business takes on debt, and it is a corporation, it is the business that owes the debt, not you personally, and creditors can only sue the business, and not you. Do you see, then, how incorporating can protect you?

If you do incorporate, all of your business should be done in the name of the business—purchases, contracts, leases, sales, loans—everything.

Pros and Cons of Incorporating

Incorporating isn't for everyone, as the following list of pros and cons should make clear.

Pros:

◆ The corporation limits one's personal liability.

◆ The corporation is a separate legal entity: The corporation has its own tax identification number and is its own legal entity, separate and apart from the owners.

◆ Others may take your business more seriously if it is incorporated.

◆ A corporation has numerous tax advantages, including pension and profit sharing options.

Cons:

◆ It is expensive to create, and possibly, depending upon the situation, to maintain. Incorporating may cost $1,000 or $10,000, depending upon the type and complexity.

◆ A corporation is subject to greater governmental regulation and control than other sorts of business entities.

There are three common types of corporations to choose from (we're leaving out a discussion of C corporations, which aren't intended for small businesses whose stock isn't publicly traded): limited liability companies, professional corporations, and S corporations.

Limited Liability Companies

Limited liability companies (or LLCs) combine many of the advantages of a corporation and a partnership without the disadvantages. Like a corporation, an LLC provides the limited personal liability that is so attractive in corporations. An LLC is a separate legal entity that can sue and be sued as well as buy and own property.

Similar to a corporation, "articles of incorporation" must be filed with the Secretary of State of each state where the LLC does business, and a registered agent must be named for *service of process*.

Check It Out

The name of a person who can be served with a lawsuit on behalf of a corporation is called the **agent for service of process.**

Two Cents

A C corporation (S and C are tax code names) is your basic large corporation. Microsoft and Ford are C corporations. The reason why businesses choose this form of corporation is that its shares (its stock) are easily transferable, which is not true for other forms of corporations.

Professional Corporations

A professional corporation is a specific type of corporation for the professionally licensed only. The professional is the sole shareholder. The type of permissible professional varies by state, but usually includes doctors, lawyers, veterinarians, dentists, psychologists, and accountants. Note, though, that a professional corporation cannot normally shield you from a malpractice award.

S Corporations

S corporations are intended for smaller enterprises. Like an LLC, an S corporation is informal, but still limits your personal liability.

Obviously, incorporating only makes sense if you have some sort of business that you carry on, in which you might face some sort of liability. If that is the case, you would be silly not to incorporate.

Family Limited Partnerships and LLCs

Family Limited Partnerships and Family LLCs are specific tools used by high-income people who are engaged in fairly high-risk occupations vis-à-vis liability: surgeons, lawyers, etc. If that doesn't apply to you, skip this section, but if it does, read on.

Let's first talk about partnerships generally. There are two classes of partnerships—general partnerships and limited partnerships. In a general partnership, all partners are equal. Each partner has equal power to incur obligations on behalf of the partnership, and each partner has unlimited liability for the debts of that partnership. Because each partner in a general partnership is equal vis-à-vis power and liabilities, some partnerships decide to form as a limited partnership instead.

In a limited partnership, there is usually only one general partner (although there could be more). The other partners are called limited partners, hence the name limited partnership.

In a limited partnership, the general partner or partners have full management responsibility and control of the partnership business on a day-to-day basis. The general partner runs the show and makes the decisions. A limited partner cannot incur obligations on behalf of the partnership and does not participate in the daily operations and management of the partnership.

The participation of a limited partner in the partnership is usually nothing more than initially contributing capital and hopefully later receiving a proportionate share of the profits. A limited partner is essentially a passive investor with its attendant diminished liability.

Limited Partnerships for Individuals and Families

There is a special class of limited partnership called a "Family Limited Partnership" (FLP). In a FLP, either a husband and wife would be the general partners, or a single person would be the general partner of his or her FLP. All valuable assets are transferred to the FLP—cars, homes, stocks and bonds, savings, etc.

The reason for this is that state laws prohibit a creditor of one partner from taking the assets of the whole partnership to satisfy claims. All a creditor can seize are distributions made by the partnership, but if the partnership makes no distributions, there are no assets to seize.

Assume that the husband is in a high-risk occupation, vis-à-vis liability—say that he is a surgeon. A FLP might be a great planning tool for him. For example, it might make sense to have the husband own a one percent interest in the FLP as the general partner and the wife own a 99 percent interest. Assuming that distributions are made to pay the bills, etc., creditors would only have a right to the husband's 1 percent, not the wife's 99 percent.

What if the husband gets hit with a $1 million malpractice judgment and the creditor comes after the husband and discovers that he has no assets in his name? Can the creditor then take the assets of the FLP to satisfy the judgment? The answer is no. Under the Uniform Limited Partnership Act, a creditor of a partner cannot seize partnership assets to satisfy that partner's debts.

Money Talks

The Uniform Limited Partnership Act (ULPA) originally dates back to 1916. It was extensively revised in 1976, and amended in 1985. In 2001, it was amended extensively again, according to The National Conference of Commissioners on Uniform State Laws, "to reflect modern business practices and developments in the law." According to Howard J. Swibel, chair of the committee that drafted the new ULPA, "The new Uniform Limited Partnership Act recognizes modern-day uses of limited partnerships by providing greater flexibility and protection."

It should also be noted that a Limited Liability Company could be used to the same effect as a FLP (called, not surprisingly therefore, a FLLC), and with similar results.

Because FLLCs also offer limited personal liability, the result is often similar. Note, however, that while there may be other benefits when creating either a FLP or a FLLC (mostly tax considerations), there are also some potential liabilities. As such, some cautionary advice is warranted.

A Word of Caution

Obviously, FLLCs and FLPs are excellent ways to protect yourself from future liability. To do so effectively, however, two precautions are needed:

- **Avoid fraudulent conveyances:** It is illegal to transfer assets with the intent to defraud a creditor. This happens most often when, on the eve of a lawsuit, all assets are transferred into a FLP or FLLC. That will not stand. You must have a legitimate reason for creating your FLP or LLC, other than hiding assets from a creditor.

  The best time, therefore, to create either entity is when there are no legal hassles or creditors on the horizon. That way, there can be no legitimate challenge arguing a fraudulent conveyance.

> **Over Your Limit**
>
> Make sure that you hire a lawyer who is well-versed in asset protection law. Also, avoid lawyers who encourage you to violate tax laws or otherwise bend the rules.

- **Hire a lawyer:** You don't perform surgery on yourself, and you shouldn't perform legal surgery on yourself, either. Creating a Family Limited Partnership or Limited Liability Company is a complicated matter and should only be done with the assistance of an attorney.

Now, Therefore

The purpose of this chapter is to give you some ideas about the various methods available to you to protect your assets and avoid future debts. The important thing is to work with a lawyer and plan ahead. Doing so can save you and your loved ones from much future grief.

The Least You Need to Know

- Creating an asset protection plan makes good financial sense.
- Getting proper insurance is a basic requirement for staying out of debt.

◆ Living Trusts can protect your family.

◆ Prenuptial agreements protect you.

◆ Incorporating is one of the smartest things you can do for your business.

◆ Family Limited Partnerships and LLCs can protect your assets.

Chapter 27

Life After Debt

In This Chapter

- ◆ Money management
- ◆ Rules for the proper use of credit
- ◆ Help beyond this book

Whew. If you have gotten this far, you have absorbed a lot of information. You may be out of debt by now, or you may be just beginning the process. Either way, we salute you. Changing habits, especially financial ones, is no easy task.

Keep in mind three things if you are to get out and stay out of debt. The first is use money intelligently. Second, as you progress, you must be concerned with the proper use of credit. Finally, utilize resources beyond this book to help you when you need it.

Be Smart with Your Money

Getting out of debt and staying out of debt demands that you respect how important each dollar is. One less dollar owed to a creditor is a dollar that you can put to more selfish goals. As Ben Franklin said, "A penny saved is a penny earned."

When it comes to using and spending money, the essential idea boils down to this: You must watch what you spend and what you make. If you spend more than you make, you go back into debt; if you make more than you spend, you stay out of debt.

Money Talks

A study was made of a graduating class at Yale one year. Upon graduation, students were polled to see how many had specific goals and how many had those goals written down. Only 3 percent had written down their goals. That study found that at the 20-year class reunion, the 3 percent who had written down their goals were the most accomplished personally, professionally, and financially.

Keep Track of Your Spending

If you keep track of how much you are spending, the odds are greatly increased that you will get out of debt. Probably the best way to keep track is to have some sort of budget. As discussed in detail in Chapter 7, you need not create a budget that immobilizes you. In fact, creating an impossible budget is the worst thing you can do. A budget that enables you to prioritize your expenditures is all you need.

Call it whatever you want—a plan, a budget, a priority list—it doesn't matter. What matters is what this thing can do for you:

♦ It can free up money and let you spend it in accordance with what matters to you most.

♦ It may nudge you toward being a bit more conservative with money, which may not be altogether bad.

♦ It can help you free up some money to earmark toward getting out of debt or saving up for some investments.

♦ Most importantly, it takes the blinders off.

Two Cents

Cosmetics pioneer Madame C. J. Walker was once asked how she got her start. "I got a start by giving myself a start," she replied.

Even just keeping closer track of what comes in and where it goes out will allow you to make better, more informed decisions about your money. You begin to turn the money tide when you stop going into debt and start getting out of debt. A budget can help do that.

Staying Out of Debt

Why is it so easy to go into debt, but so difficult to get out of debt? For the same reason it's easier to gain weight than lose weight. We don't know exactly what that reason is. Someone must know, but it sure isn't us.

What we do know is that as you work your plan, following these three simple rules will ensure that you stay out of debt.

Rule Number 1: If you can't afford it, don't buy it or do it.

Going into debt with a well-thought-out plan for how you will pay it back is one thing. That is debt you can afford. Going into debt with no plan and no means of paying it back is another matter altogether. One helps; one hinders. One is good debt; the other is bad debt.

Hector and his brother Jaime are a good contrast. Hector wanted to start his own import-export business. He created a budget and a business plan and figured that he needed $10,000 to get started. His best friend was willing to lend Hector the money on two conditions. First, Hector had to agree to repay $500 a month. Second, the debt would be secured by a lien on Hector's house. Hector's business projections concluded that he would be able to afford the $500 payment, so he agreed to the deal, got the loan, and started his business.

Jaime makes about $2,000 a month and saves nothing because his combined bills total what he earns. Nevertheless, Jaime, depressed over Hector's newfound success, wanted to show his brother that he was making money, too, so he charged a $1,500 big-screen television. He had no means and no plan for paying it back. If you can't afford it, don't buy it (unless it is an emergency, of course).

Rule Number 2: Make more than you spend.

This rule is a corollary to rule number 1. If you do nothing but follow this rule, you need never have unnecessary debt again.

Rule Number 3: Just say no.

Staying out of debt requires self-discipline. Say no to the enormous pressure all around you to go into debt. Say no to your child who wants that new Nintendo that you can't afford. Say no to yourself. The only way to go into debt is to say yes to debt. By saying no to debt you cannot afford, you are saying yes to prosperity and abundance, which is ironic. By saying no to debt, you create prosperity and thereby are still able to get and do what you want, only without any debt.

Ten Percent Is All We Ask

The budget solution works best when you combine it with what we have called the "Ten percent solution." If you are able to save 10 percent of your net take-home pay, you are on the way to financial prosperity.

Budgeting will allow you to get out of debt, but saving and investing allows you to get ahead. You can do whatever you want with that 10 percent: leave it in the bank, start a business, or invest it in the stock market, for example. That's your choice. The important thing is that you begin to make your money grow.

The thought of saving 10 percent of your income may still seem impossible, but getting rid of, say, $20,000 in credit card debts probably seemed impossible at one time, too. Both goals are a matter of priorities. When you went into debt, whatever it was you wanted or did to create that debt was more important than the debt itself. That was your priority at that time. That's fine; you're human; we're human. Debt happens.

By buying this book, you have decided that it is now time for different priorities. Certainly, if you want to get out of debt, then not incurring more debt will have to be more important than things you want to purchase or do. For example, staying out of debt has to be more important than charging a trip to the Bahamas that you can't afford. It's a matter of priorities. What's more important: the trip or the debt? In order for you to stay out of debt, the answer has to be the debt.

> **Two Cents**
>
> If you were 60 years old, cut your spending by $5 a day, and began to invest that money getting a 6 percent return, then by the time you turned 65 you would have $10,500. If you began at age 50, you would have $43,000, and if you started at age 30, you would have $203,000.

One of these priorities should be to pay yourself 10 percent of your income before you pay anyone else. If that seems impossible, just pretend that you are another one of your creditors whom you are committed to repaying. Pay your bill to yourself first.

If you get out of debt, watch what you spend, and invest for the future, your financial prosperity is almost assured.

On the Proper Use of Credit

We have said all along that not all debt is bad debt. When you do, consciously, choose to go into debt again, there are ways to do so wisely:

1. Exercise caution when taking on debt. Think twice. Is there a way to do this (whatever it is) without incurring more debt?

2. If you do go into debt, borrow when it's free or practically free. Remember that most credit cards charge no interest if you pay the balance once the bill comes. That means you are borrowing money for free. By the same token, if you are going to keep a running balance, do so on the card with the lowest interest rate.

3. Use credit to create a good credit rating. The better your credit rating, the less it will cost you to borrow money when you do need it in the future. Use a credit card and pay it off consistently. Pay your car loan and mortgage on time. Pay off a loan. The better a credit risk you become, the more money you will save down the road.

4. Debt is best when it funds investments rather than consumption. You will have something to show for the invested debt.

If you value your money, you will not make the same debt mistakes twice.

Help Beyond This Book

We hope that we have given you a lot of help, tools, ideas, and ways to get out of debt. Yet that may not be enough. There are people and groups you can contact that may be of great assistance. But exercise caution, some of these organizations seem more helpful than they are.

Debt Counseling

When you get deep in debt and there seems to be no way out, it is good to know that help is available. There are many debt counseling services out there these days that can help you restructure your debt, reduce or eliminate late charges and high interest rates, and generally get you back on the road to prosperity.

The thing to realize is that not all debt counseling services are created equally. Some have strong relationships with the banks and credit card companies, know what they are doing, and put you on a smart repayment plan that both you and your creditors can live with.

Others are not so good. For example, some debt counseling services practice something called "front-loading." This means that they create a repayment plan for you, but take their entire fee out of your first payment, thus putting you a never-ending month behind on your payments to creditors. You want to be sure to avoid outfits like these.

 Two Cents

After creditors have received three on-time payments through CCCS, they usually stop the phone calls on good faith that the debt is being repaid in a timely manner.

One way to know when you are dealing with a reputable debt counseling agency is that it will be a member of Independent Consumer Credit Counseling Agencies (AICCCA). This is a national organization that is dedicated to integrity and honesty in the delivery of debt counseling services. By creating standards and practices that all members must adhere to (for example, prohibiting front-loading), AICCCA helps ensure that you get what you are paying for—professional debt counseling and debt relief.

So look around and do some shopping before you choose a debt counseling agency. One of those that we have found that we like a lot is Debt Free: 1-800-354-1781, www.debtfreetoday.com.

Counseling

Sometimes, debt is about more than money; it's about anger and stress, anxiety and depression. Indeed, money problems are among the most stressful problems a person can have. They can be injurious to your mental health, your physical health, and your relationship. Dealing with the stress of money and its attendant problems sometimes requires professional help, and we wholeheartedly recommend it in the right circumstances.

Besides helping with the stress of the matter, money counseling can also help uncover other issues that the money problems may be masking. Sometimes, money is the symptom and not the cause. Various resources for counseling are listed in the appendixes.

And Now, the End (or a New Beginning) Is Near

Thank you for allowing us to help guide you through what is likely a tough situation. We hope that we have provided solutions, made the journey easier to understand, and maybe put a smile on your face a time or two. You deserve a life of prosperity and abundance. If we made that more likely, then we have all done our jobs.

Live long and prosper!

The Least You Need to Know

- Cutting back, staying out of debt, and saving a little bit are the keys to long-term financial health.
- Using credit wisely is important if you want to stay out of debt.
- Debt Counseling can help a lot, as long as you choose the right counselors.

Bankruptcy Petition and Schedules

FORM B1	United States Bankruptcy Court	Voluntary Petition
	EASTERN District of _CALIFORNIA_	

Name of Debtor (if individual, enter Last, First, Middle): _Columbus, Christopher_	Name of Joint Debtor (Spouse)(Last, First, Middle):
All Other Names used by the Debtor in the last 6 years (include married, maiden, and trade names): _NONE_	All Other Names used by the Joint Debtor in the last 6 years (include married, maiden, and trade names):
Soc. Sec./Tax I.D. No. (if more than one, state all): _555-55-5555_	Soc. Sec./Tax I.D. No. (if more than one, state all):
Street Address of Debtor (No. & Street, City, State & Zip Code): _555 55th Ave_ _Lisbon, America_ _Phone: 555-5555_	Street Address of Joint Debtor (No. & Street, City, State & Zip Code):
County of Residence or of the Principal Place of Business: _Lisbon_	County of Residence or of the Principal Place of Business:
Mailing Address of Debtor (if different from street address): _SAME_	Mailing Address of Joint Debtor (if different from street address):

Location of Principal Assets of Business Debtor
(If different from street address above): _NOT APPLICABLE_

Information Regarding the Debtor (Check the Applicable Boxes)

Venue (Check any applicable box)

- [X] Debtor has been domiciled or has had a residence, principal place of business, or principal assets in this District for 180 days immediately preceding the date of this petition or for a longer part of such 180 days than in any other District.
- [ ] There is a bankruptcy case concerning debtor's affiliate, general partner, or partnership pending in this District.

Type of Debtor (Check all boxes that apply)		**Chapter or Section of Bankruptcy Code Under Which the Petition is Filed** (Check one box)
[X] Individual(s) [ ] Railroad [ ] Corporation [ ] Stockbroker [ ] Partnership [ ] Commodity Broker [ ] Other _____		[X] Chapter 7 [ ] Chapter 11 [ ] Chapter 13 [ ] Chapter 9 [ ] Chapter 12 [ ] Sec. 304 - Case ancillary to foreign proceeding

Nature of Debts (Check one box)	**Filing Fee** (Check one box)
[X] Consumer/Non-Business [ ] Business	[X] Full Filing Fee attached.
Chapter 11 Small Business (Check all boxes that apply) [ ] Debtor is a small business as defined in 11 U.S.C. § 101 [ ] Debtor is and elects to be considered a small business under 11 U.S.C. § 1121(e) (Optional)	[ ] Filing Fee to be paid in installments (Applicable to individuals only) Must attach signed application for the court's consideration certifying that the debtor is unable to pay fee except in installments. Rule 1006(b). See Official Form No. 3.

Statistical/Administrative Information (Estimates only)

- [ ] Debtor estimates that funds will be available for distribution to unsecured creditors.
- [X] Debtor estimates that, after any exempt property is excluded and administrative expenses paid, there will be no funds available for distribution to unsecured creditors.

THIS SPACE FOR COURT USE ONLY

Estimated Number of Creditors	1-15	16-49	50-99	100-199	200-999	1000-over
	[X]	[ ]	[ ]	[ ]	[ ]	[ ]

Estimated Assets							
$0 to $50,000	$50,001 to $100,000	$100,001 to $500,000	$500,001 to $1 million	$1,000,001 to $10 million	$10,000,001 to $50 million	$50,000,001 to $100 million	More than $100 million
[ ]	[ ]	[X]	[ ]	[ ]	[ ]	[ ]	[ ]

Estimated Debts							
$0 to $50,000	$50,001 to $100,000	$100,001 to $500,000	$500,001 to $1 million	$1,000,001 to $10 million	$10,000,001 to $50 million	$50,000,001 to $100 million	More than $100 million
[ ]	[ ]	[X]	[ ]	[ ]	[ ]	[ ]	[ ]

Voluntary Petition	Name of Debtor(s):	FORM B1, Page 2

Voluntary Petition
(This page must be completed and filed in every case)

Name of Debtor(s):

Christopher Columbus

FORM B1, Page 2

Prior Bankruptcy Case Filed Within Last 6 Years (If more than one, attach additional sheet)		
Location Where Filed: *NONE*	Case Number:	Date Filed:

Pending Bankruptcy Case Filed by any Spouse, Partner or Affiliate of this Debtor (If more than one, attach additional sheet)		
Name of Debtor: *NONE*	Case Number:	Date Filed:
District:	Relationship:	Judge:

Signatures

Signature(s) of Debtor(s) (Individual / Joint)

I declare under penalty of perjury that the information provided in this petition is true and correct.
[If petitioner is an individual whose debts are primarily consumer debts and has chosen to file under chapter 7] I am aware that I may proceed under chapter 7, 11, 12 or 13 of title 11, United States Code, understand the relief available under each such chapter, and choose to proceed under chapter 7.
I request relief in accordance with the chapter of title 11, United States Code, specified in this petition.

X _____
Signature of Debtor *Christopher Columbus*

X _____
Signature of Joint Debtor

_____
Telephone Number (if not represented by attorney)

July 4, 2000
Date

Signature of Debtor (Corporation/ Partnership)

I declare under penalty of perjury that the information provided in this petition is true and correct, and that I have been authorized to file this petition on behalf of the debtor.

The debtor requests relief in accordance with the chapter of title 11, United States Code, specified in this petition.

X _____
Signature of Authorized Individual

_____
Printed Name of Authorized Individual

_____
Title of Authorized Individual

_____
Date

Signature of Attorney

X _____
Signature of Attorney for Debtor(s)

_____
Printed Name of Attorney for Debtor(s)

_____
Firm Name

_____
Address

_____

_____

_____   *July 4, 2000*
Telephone Number   Date

Exhibit A
(To be completed if debtor is required to file periodic reports (e.g., forms 10K and 10Q) with the Securities and Exchange Commission pursuant to Section 13 or 15(d) of the Securities Exchange Act of 1934 and is requesting relief under chapter 11)
☐ Exhibit A is attached and made a part of this petition.

Exhibit B
(To be completed if debtor is an individual whose debts are primarily consumer debts)
I, the attorney for the petitioner named in the foregoing petition, declare that I have informed the petitioner that [he or she] may proceed under chapter 7, 11, 12, or 13 of title 11, United States Code, and have explained the relief available under each such chapter.

X _____
Attorney

July 4, 2000
Date

Signature of Non-Attorney Petition Preparer

I certify that I am a bankruptcy petition preparer as defined in 11 U.S.C. § 110, that I prepared this document for compensation, and that I have provided the debtor with a copy of this document.

_____
Printed Name of Bankruptcy Petition Preparer

_____
Social Security Number

_____
Address

_____

_____

Names and Social Security numbers of all other individuals who prepared or assisted in preparing this document:

If more than one person prepared this document, attach additional sheets conforming to the appropriate official form for each person.

X _____
Signature of Bankruptcy Petition Preparer

_____
Date

A bankruptcy petition preparer's failure to comply with the provisions of title 11 and the Federal Rules of Bankruptcy Procedure may result in fines or imprisonment or both 11 U.S.C. § 110; 18 U.S.C. § 156.

UNITED STATES BANKRUPTCY COURT

NOTICE TO INDIVIDUAL CONSUMER DEBTOR

The purpose of this notice is to acquaint you with the four chapters of the federal Bankruptcy Code under which you may file a bankruptcy petition. The bankruptcy law is complicated and not easily described. Therefore, you should seek the advice of an attorney to learn of your rights and responsibilities under the law should you decide to file a petition with the court. Court employees are prohibited from giving you legal advice.

Chapter 7: Liquidation ($130 filing fee plus $45 administrative fee)

1.   Chapter 7 is designed for debtors in financial difficulty who do not have the ability to pay their existing debts.

2.   Under chapter 7 a trustee takes possession of all your property. You may claim certain of your property as exempt under governing law. The trustee then liquidates the property and uses the proceeds to pay your creditors according to priorities of the Bankruptcy Code.

3.   The purpose of filing a chapter 7 case is to obtain a discharge of your existing debts. If, however, you are found to have committed certain kinds of improper conduct described in the Bankruptcy Code, your discharge may be denied by the court, and the purpose for which you filed the bankruptcy petition will be defeated.

4.   Even if you receive a discharge, there are some debts that are not discharged under the law. Therefore, you may still be responsible for such debts as certain taxes and student loans, alimony and support payments, criminal restitution, and debts for death or personal injury caused by driving while intoxicated from alcohol or drugs.

5.   Under certain circumstances you may keep property that you have purchased subject to valid security interest. Your attorney can explain the options that are available to you.

Chapter 13: Repayment of All or Part of the Debts of an Individual with Regular Income ($130 filing fee plus $30 administrative fee)

1.   Chapter 13 is designed for individuals with regular income who are temporarily unable to pay their debts but would like to pay them in installments over a period of time. You are only eligible for chapter 13 if your debts do not exceed certain dollar amounts set forth in the Bankruptcy Code.

2.   Under chapter 13 you must file a plan with the court to repay your creditors all or part of the money that you owe them, using your future earnings. Usually, the period allowed by the court to repay your debts is three years, but no more than five years. Your plan must be approved by the court before it can take effect.

3.   Under chapter 13, unlike chapter 7, you may keep all your property, both exempt and non-exempt, as long as you continue to make payments under the plan.

4.   After completion of payments under the plan, your debts are discharged except alimony and support payments, student loans, certain debts including criminal fines and restitution and debts for death or personal injury caused by driving while intoxicated from alcohol or drugs, and long term secured obligations.

Chapter 11: Reorganization ($800 filing fee plus $30 administrative fee)

Chapter 11 is designed primarily for the reorganization of a business but is also available to consumer debtors. Its provisions are quite complicated, and any decision by an individual to file a chapter 11 petition should be reviewed with an attorney.

Chapter 12: Family farmer ($200 filing fee plus $30 administrative fee)

Chapter 12 is designed to permit family farmers to repay their debts over a period of time from future earnings and is in many ways similar to chapter 13. The eligibility requirements are restrictive, limiting its use to those whose income arises primarily from a family-owned farm.

I, the debtor, affirm that I have read this notice.

July 4, 2000
_____
Date

_____
Signature of Debtor

_____
Case Number

DEBTOR COPY   COURT COPY
(circle one)

STATEMENT OF INFORMATION REQUIRED BY 11 U.S.C. § 341

INTRODUCTION

Pursuant to the Bankruptcy Reform Act of 1994, the Office of the United States Trustee, United States Department of Justice, has prepared this information sheet to help you understand some of the possible consequences of filing a bankruptcy petition under chapter 7 of the Bankruptcy Code. This information is intended to make you aware of—

(1) the potential consequences of seeking a discharge in bankruptcy, including the effects on credit history;

(2) the effect of receiving a discharge of debts;

(3) the effect of reaffirming a debt; and

(4) your ability to file a petition under a different chapter of the Bankruptcy Code.

There are many other provisions of the Bankruptcy Code that may affect your situation. This information sheet contains only general principles of law and is not a substitute for legal advice. If you have questions or need further information as to how the bankruptcy laws apply to your specific case, you should consult with your lawyer.

WHAT IS A DISCHARGE?

The filing of a chapter 7 petition is designed to result in a discharge of most of the debts you listed on your bankruptcy schedules. A discharge is a court order that says you do not have to repay your debts, but there are a number of exceptions. Debts which may not be discharged in your chapter 7 case include, for example, most taxes, child support, alimony, and student loans; court-ordered fines and restitution; debts obtained through fraud or deception; and personal injury debts caused by driving while intoxicated or taking drugs. Your discharge may be denied entirely if you, for example, destroy or conceal property; destroy, conceal or falsify records; or make a false oath. Creditors cannot ask you to pay any debts which have been discharged. You can only receive a chapter 7 discharge once every six (6) years.

WHAT ARE THE POTENTIAL EFFECTS OF A DISCHARGE?

The fact that you filed bankruptcy can appear on your credit report for as long as 10 years. Thus, filing a bankruptcy petition may affect your ability to obtain credit in the future. Also, you may not be excused from repaying any debts that were not listed on your bankruptcy schedules or that you incurred after you filed bankruptcy.

WHAT ARE THE EFFECTS OF REAFFIRMING A DEBT?

After you file your petition, a creditor may ask you to reaffirm a certain debt or you may seek to do so on your own. Reaffirming a debt means that you sign and file with the court a legally enforceable document, which states that you promise to repay all or a portion of the debt that may otherwise have been discharged in your bankruptcy case. Reaffirmation agreements must generally be filed with the court within 60 days after the first meeting of creditors.

Reaffirmation agreements are strictly voluntary — they are not required by the Bankruptcy Code or other state or federal law. You can voluntarily repay any debt instead of signing a reaffirmation agreement, but there may be valid reasons for wanting to reaffirm a particular debt.

Reaffirmation agreements must not impose an undue burden on you or your dependents and must be in your best interest. If you decide to sign a reaffirmation agreement, you may cancel it at any time before the court issues your discharge order or within sixty (60) days after the reaffirmation agreement was filed with the court, whichever is later. If you reaffirm a debt and fail to make the payments required in the reaffirmation agreement, the creditor can take action against you to recover any property that was given as security for the loan and you may remain personally liable for any remaining debt.

OTHER BANKRUPTCY OPTIONS

You have a choice in deciding what chapter of the Bankruptcy Code will best suit your needs. Even if you have already filed for relief under chapter 7, you may be eligible to convert your case to a different chapter.

Chapter 7 is the liquidation chapter of the Bankruptcy Code. Under chapter 7, a trustee is appointed to collect and sell, if economically feasible, all property you own that is not exempt from these actions.

Chapter 11 is the reorganization chapter most commonly used by businesses, but it is also available to individuals. Creditors vote on whether to accept or reject a plan, which also must be approved by the court. While the debtor normally remains in control of the assets, the court can order the appointment of a trustee to take possession and control of the business.

Chapter 12 offers bankruptcy relief to those who qualify as family farmers. Family farmers must propose a plan to repay their creditors over a three-to-five year period and it must be approved by the court. Plan payments are made through a chapter 12 trustee, who also monitors the debtors' farming operations during the pendency of the plan.

Finally, chapter 13 generally permits individuals to keep their property by repaying creditors out of their future income. Each chapter 13 debtor writes a plan which must be approved by the bankruptcy court. The debtor must pay the chapter 13 trustee the amounts set forth in their plan. Debtors receive a discharge after they complete their chapter 13 repayment plan. Chapter 13 is only available to individuals with regular income whose debts do not exceed $1,077,000 ($269,250 in unsecured debts and $807,750 in secured debts).

AGAIN, PLEASE SPEAK TO YOUR LAWYER IF YOU NEED FURTHER INFORMATION OR EXPLANATION, INCLUDING HOW THE BANKRUPTCY LAWS RELATE TO YOUR SPECIFIC CASE.

In re _Christopher Columbus_ _____ / Debtor   Case No. _____

(If known)

SCHEDULE A-REAL PROPERTY

Except as directed below, list all real property in which the debtor has any legal, equitable, or future interest, including all property owned as a cotenant, community property, or in which the debtor has a life estate. Include any property in which the debtor holds rights and powers exercisable for the debtor's own benefit. If the debtor is married, state whether the husband, wife, or both own the property by placing an "H,""W,""J," or "C"in the column labeled "Husband, Wife, Joint, or Community." If the debtor holds no interest in real property, write "None" under "Description and Location of Property."

Do not include interests in executory contracts and unexpired leases on this schedule. List them in Schedule G-Executory Contracts and Unexpired Leases.

If an entity claims to have a lien or hold a secured interest in any property, state the amount of the secured claim. See schedule D. If no entity claims to hold a secured interest in the property, write "None" in the column labeled "Amount of Secured Claim."

If the debtor is an individual or if a joint petition is filed, state the amount of any exemption claimed in the property only in Schedule C-Property Claimed as Exempt.

Description and Location of Property	Nature of Debtor's Interest in Property Husband—H Wife—W Joint—J Community—C	Current Market Value of Debtor's Interest, in Property without Deducting any Secured Claim or Exemption	Amount of Secured Claim
Residence		$ 120,000	$ 120,000

_NO_   continuation sheets attached

TOTAL $ 120,000
(Report also on Summary of Schedules.)

In re _Christopher Columbus_ _____ / Debtor   Case No. _____

(If known)

SCHEDULE B-PERSONAL PROPERTY

Except as directed below, list all personal property of the debtor of whatever kind. If the debtor has no property in one or more of the categories, place an "X" in the appropriate position in the column labeled "None." If additional space is needed in any category, attach a separate sheet properly identified with the case name, case number, and the number of the category. If the debtor is married, state whether husband, wife, or both own property by placing an "H","W","J," or "C" in the column labeled "Husband, Wife, Joint, or Community." If the debtor is an individual or a joint petition is filed, state the amount of any exemptions claimed only in Schedule C-Property Claimed as Exempt.

Do not list interests in executory contracts and unexpired leases on this schedule. List them in Schedule G-Executory Contracts and Unexpired Leases.

If the property is being held for the debtor by someone else, state that person's name and address under "Description and Location of Property."

Type of Property	None	Description and Location of Property	Husband—H Wife—W Joint—J Community—C	Current Market Value of Debtor's Interest in Property, without Deducting any Secured Claim or Exemption
1. Cash on hand.	X			
2. Checking, savings or other financial accounts, certificates of deposit, or shares in banks, savings and loan, thrift, building and loan, and homestead associations, or credit unions, brokerage houses, or cooperatives.		_Bank of Lisbon_		$ 100
3. Security deposits with public utilities, telephone companies, landlords, and others.	X			
4. Household goods and furnishings, including audio, video, and computer equipment.		_Household goods. None more than $400._		$ 2,500
5. Books, pictures and other art objects, antiques, stamp, coin, record, tape, compact disc, and other collections or collectibles.		_Books_		$ 100
6. Wearing apparel.		_Clothes_		$ 400
7. Furs and jewelry.		_Misc. Jewelry_		$ 500
8. Firearms and sports, photographic, and other hobby equipment.	X			
9. Interests in insurance policies. Name insurance company of each policy and itemize surrender or refund value of each.		_Term Policy – $0 cash value_		
10. Annuities. Itemize and name each issuer.	X			
11. Interests in IRA, ERISA, Keogh, or other pension or profit sharing plans. Itemize.		_401(k)_		$ 15,000
12. Stock and interests in incorporated and unincorporated businesses. Itemize.	X			
13. Interests in partnerships or joint ventures. Itemize.	X			
14. Government and corporate bonds and other negotiable and non-negotiable instruments.	X			
15. Accounts Receivable.	X			
16. Alimony, maintenance, support, and property settlements to which the debtor is or may be entitled. Give particulars.	X			
17. Other liquidated debts owing debtor include tax refunds. Give particulars.	X			

Page __1__ of __2__

In re _Christopher Columbus_ _____ / Debtor   Case No. _____
(If known)

SCHEDULE B-PERSONAL PROPERTY
(Continuation Sheet)

Type of Property	N o n e	Description and Location of Property	Husband—H Wife—W Joint—J Community—C	Current Market Value of Debtor's Interest in Property, without Deducting any Secured Claim or Exemption
18. Equitable or future interests, life estates, and rights or powers exercisable for the benefit of the debtor other than those listed in Schedule of Real Property.	X			
19. Contingent and non-contingent interests in estate of a decedent, death benefit plan, life insurance policy, or trust.	X			
20. Other contingent and unliquidated claims of every nature, including tax refunds, counterclaims of the debtor, and rights to setoff claims. Give estimated value of each.	X			
21. Patents, copyrights, and other intellectual property. Give particulars.	X			
22. Licenses, franchises, and other general intangibles. Give particulars.	X			
23. Automobiles, trucks, trailers and other vehicles.		1997 Honda Prelude 1992 Toyota Camry 1994 Suzuki Motorcycle		$ 15,000 $ 5,000 $ 2,000
24. Boats, motors, and accessories.	X			
25. Aircraft and accessories.	X			
26. Office equipment, furnishings, and supplies.	X			
27. Machinery, fixtures, equipment and supplies used in business.	X			
28. Inventory.	X			
29. Animals.	X			
30. Crops - growing or harvested. Give particulars.	X			
31. Farming equipment and implements.	X			
32. Farm supplies, chemicals, and feed.	X			
33. Other personal property of any kind not already listed. Itemize.	X			

Page __2__ of __2__

Total → $ 40,600

(Report total also on Summary of Schedules)

In re _Christopher Columbus_ _____ / Debtor   Case No. _____

(If known)

SCHEDULE C-PROPERTY CLAIMED EXEMPT

Debtor elects the exemptions to which debtor is entitled under:

(Check one box)

☐ 11 U.S.C. § 522(b)(1): Exemptions provided in 11 U.S.C. § 522(d). Note: These exemptions are available only in certain states.

☒ 11 U.S.C. § 522(b)(2): Exemptions available under applicable nonbankruptcy federal laws, state or local law where the debtor's domicile has been located for the 180 days immediately preceding the filing of the petition, or for a longer portion of the 180-day period than in any other place, and the debtor's interest as a tenant by the entirety or joint tenant to the extent the interest is exempt from process under applicable nonbankruptcy law.

Description of Property	Specify Law Providing each Exemption	Value of Claimed Exemption	Current Value of Property without Deducting Exemption
Residence	Calif. C.C.P. S703.140(b)(1)	$ 0	$ 120,000
Bank of Lisbon	Calif. C.C.P. S703.140(b)(5)	$ 100	$ 100
Household goods. None more than $400.	Calif. C.C.P. S703.140(b)(3)	$ 2,500	$ 2,500
Books	Calif. C.C.P. S703.140(b)(5)	$ 100	$ 100
Clothes	Calif. C.C.P. S703.140(b)(3)	$ 400	$ 400
	Calif. C.C.P. S703.140(b)(4)	$ 500	$ 500
401(k)	Calif. C.C.P. S703.140(b)(10)(E)	$ 15,000	$ 15,000
1997 Honda Prelude	Calif. C.C.P. S703.140(b)(2)	$ 0	$ 15,000
1992 Toyota Camry	Calif. C.C.P. S703.140(b)(5)	$ 5,000	$ 5,000
1994 Suzuki Motorcycle	Calif. C.C.P. S703.140(b)(5)	$ 2,000	$ 2,000

Page No. ___1___ of ___1___

In re _Christopher Columbus_ _____ / Debtor   Case No. _____
                                                                    (If known)

SCHEDULE D-CREDITORS HOLDING SECURED CLAIMS

State the name, mailing address, including zip code, and account number, if any, of all entities holding claims secured by property of the debtor as of the date of filing of the petition. List creditors holding all types of secured interests such as judgment liens, garnishments, statutory liens, mortgages, deeds of trust, and other security interests. List creditors in alphabetical order to the extent practicable. If all secured creditors will not fit on this page, use the continuation sheet provided.

If any entity other than a spouse in a joint case may be jointly liable on a claim, place an "X" in the column labeled "Codebtor," include the entity on the appropriate schedule of creditors and complete Schedule H - Codebtors. If a joint petition is filed, state whether husband, wife, both of them, or the marital community may be liable on each claim by placing an "H," "W," "J," or "C" in the column labeled "Husband, Wife, Joint, or Community."

If the claim is contingent, place and "X" in the column labeled "Contingent." If the claim is unliquidated, place an "X" in the column labeled "Unliquidated." If the claim is disputed, place an "X" in the column labeled "Disputed." (You may need to place an "X" in more than one of these three columns.)

Report the total of all claims listed on this schedule in the box labeled "Total" on the last sheet of the completed schedule. Report this total also on the Summary of Schedules.

☐ Check this box if debtor has no creditors holding secured claims to report on this Schedule D.

Creditor's Name and Mailing Address including Zip Code	Codebtor	Date Claim was Incurred, Nature of Lien, and Description and Market Value of Property Subject to Lien H—Husband W—Wife J—Joint C—Community	Contingent	Unliquidated	Disputed	Amount of Claim without Deducting Value of Collateral	Unsecured Portion, if any
Account No. _4444_ Creditor #: 1 Lisbon Cars of America P.O. Box 4444 Lisbon, America		1998 Auto Loan 1997 Honda Prelude Value: $ 15,000.00				$ 20,000.00	$ 5,000.00
Account No. 55555 Creditor #: 2 Lisbon Financial P.O. Box 2222 Lisbon, America		1990 First Deed of Trust Residence Value: $ 120,000.00				$120,000.00	$ 0.00
Account No. 		Value:					
Account No. 		Value:					
Account No. 		Value:					

_No_ continuation sheets attached

Subtotal $ 140,000.00
(Total of this page)

Total $ 140,000.00
(Use only on last page and on Summary of Schedules)

In re *Christopher Columbus* _____ / Debtor   Case No. _____

                                                                                          (If known)

SCHEDULE E-CREDITORS HOLDING UNSECURED PRIORITY CLAIMS

A complete list of claims entitled to priority, listed separately by type of priority, is to be set forth on the sheets provided. Only holders of unsecured claims entitled to priority should be listed on this schedule. In the boxes provided on the attached sheets, state the name and mailing address, including zip code, and account number, if any, of all entities holding priority claims against the debtor or the property of the debtor, as of the date of the filing of this petition.

If any entity other than a spouse in a joint case may be jointly liable on a claim, place an "X" in the column labeled "Codebtor," include the entity on the appropriate schedule of creditors, and complete Schedule H-Codebtors. If a joint petition is filed, state whether husband, wife, both of them, or the marital community may be liable on each claim by placing an "H,""W,""J," or "C" in the column labeled "Husband, Wife, Joint, or Community."

If the claim is contingent, place an "X" in the column labeled "Contingent." If the claim is unliquidated, place an "X" in column labeled "Unliquidated." If the claim is disputed, place an "X" in the column labeled "Disputed." (You may need to place an "X" in more than one of these three columns.)

Report the total of claims listed on each sheet in the box labeled "Subtotal" on each sheet. Report the total of all claims listed on this Schedule E in the box labeled "Total" on the last sheet of the completed schedule. Repeat this total also on the Summary of Schedules.

☐ Check this box if debtor has no creditors holding unsecured priority claims to report on this Schedule E.

TYPES OF PRIORITY CLAIMS

☐ **Extensions of credit in an involuntary case**
Claims arising in the ordinary course of the debtor's business or financial affairs after the commencement of the case but before the earlier of the appointment of a trustee or the order for relief. 11 U.S.C. § 507(a)(2).

☐ **Wages, salaries, and commissions**
Wages, salaries, and commissions, including vacation, severance, and sick leave pay owing to employees and commissions owing to qualifying independent sales representatives up to $4300* per person earned within 90 days immediately preceding the filing of the original petition, or the cessation of business, whichever occurred first, to the extent provided in 11 U.S.C. § 507(a)(3).

☐ **Contributions to employee benefit plans**
Money owed to employee benefit plans for services rendered within 180 days immediately preceding the filing of the original petition, or the cessation of business, whichever occurred first, to the extent provided in 11 U.S.C. § 507(a)(4).

☐ **Certain farmers and fishermen**
Claims of certain farmers and fishermen, up to $4300* per farmer or fisherman, against the debtor, as provided in 11 U.S.C. § 507(a)(5).

☐ **Deposits by individuals**
Claims of individuals up to $1,950* for deposits for the purchase, lease, or rental of property or services for personal, family, or household use, that were not delivered or provided. 11 U.S.C. § 507(a)(6).

☐ **Alimony, Maintenance or Support**
Claims of a spouse, former spouse, or child of the debtor, for alimony, maintenance or support, to the extent provided in 11 U.S.C. § 507(a)(7).

☒ **Taxes and Certain Other Debts Owed to Governmental Units**
Taxes, customs duties, and penalties owing to federal, state, and local governmental units as set forth in 11 U.S.C. § 507(a)(8).

☐ **Commitments to Maintain the Capital of an Insured Depository Institution**
Claims based on commitments to FDIC, RTC, Director of the Office of Thrift Supervision, Comptroller of the Currency, or Board of Governors of the Federal Reserve System, or their predecessors or successors, to maintain the capital of an insured depository institution. 11 U.S.C. § 507 (a)(9).

*Amounts are subject to adjustment on April 1, 2001, and every three years thereafter with respect to cases commenced on or after the date of adjustment.

_____*1*_ continuation sheets attached

In re _Christopher Columbus_ _____ / Debtor   Case No. _____
                                                                    (If known)

SCHEDULE E-CREDITORS HOLDING UNSECURED PRIORITY CLAIMS

(Continuation Sheet)

TYPE OF PRIORITY: _Taxes and Certain Other Debts Owed to Governmental Units_

Creditor's Name and Mailing Address including Zip Code	Codebtor	Date Claim was Incurred, and Consideration for Claim H—Husband W—Wife J—Joint C—Community	Contingent	Unliquidated	Disputed	Total Amount of Claim	Amount Entitled to Priority
Account No. _2543849_ Creditor #: 1 Waste Disposal 1324 Paddock Pl Lisbon, America		_1999_ Arrears				$ 750.00	$ 750.00
Account No.							
Account No.							
Account No.							
Account No.							
Account No.							
Account No.							

Sheet No. ___1___ of ___1___ continuation sheets attached to
Schedule of Creditors holding Unsecured Priority Claims

Subtotal $ (Total of this page)   750.00

Total $ (Use only on last page and on Summary of Schedules)   750.00

In re _Christopher Columbus_ _____ / Debtor   Case No. _____
(If known)

SCHEDULE F-CREDITORS HOLDING UNSECURED NONPRIORITY CLAIMS

State the name, mailing address, including zip code, and account number, if any, of all entities holding unsecured claims without priority against the debtor or the property of the debtor, as of the date of filing of the petition. Do not include claims listed in Schedules D and E. If all creditors will not fit on this page, use the continuation sheet provided.

If any entity other than a spouse in a joint case may be jointly liable on a claim, place an "X" in the column labeled "Codebtor," include the entity on the appropriate schedule of creditors, and complete Schedule H - Codebtors. If a joint petition is filed, state whether husband, wife, both of them, or the marital community may be liable on each claim by placing an "H," "W," "J," or "C" in the column labeled "Husband, Wife, Joint, or Community."

If the claim is contingent, place an "X" in the column labeled "Contingent." If the claim is unliquidated, place an "X" in the column labeled "Unliquidated." If the claim is disputed, place an "X" in the column labeled "Disputed." (You may need to place an "X" in more than one of these three columns.)

Report total of all claims listed on this schedule in the box labeled "Total" on the last sheet of the completed schedule. Report this total also on the Summary of Schedules.

☐ Check this box if debtor has no creditors holding unsecured nonpriority claims to report on this Schedule F.

Creditor's Name and Mailing Address including Zip Code	Codebtor	Date Claim was Incurred, and Consideration for Claim. If Claim is Subject to Setoff, so State. H—Husband W—Wife J—Joint C—Community	Contingent	Unliquidated	Disputed	Amount of Claim
Account No. _4444_ Creditor #: 1 American Express Suite 0001 Chicago, IL 60679-0001		1996 Credit card purchases				$ 4,900.00
Account No. _4444444_ Creditor #: 2 Bank of America P O Box 53132 Phoenix, AZ 85072-3132		1996 Credit card purchases				$ 5,100.00
Account No. _4444_ Creditor #: 3 JC Penney P.O. Box 3665 Portland, OR 97208		1999 Credit card purchases				$ 450.00
Account No. _4444_ Creditor #: 4 Macy's P.O. Box 4582 Carol Stream, IL 60197		1997 Credit card purchases				$ 875.00
Account No. _4444_ Creditor #: 5 Mervyns c/o Retailers Natl. Bank P.O. Box 59287 Minneapolis, MN 55459-0287		1993 Credit card purchases				$ 4,500.00

_1_ continuation sheets attached

Subtotal $ $ 15,825.00
(Total of this page)

Total $
(Use only on last page and on Summary of Schedules)

In re _Christopher Columbus_ _____ / Debtor   Case No. _____
                                                                                  (If known)

SCHEDULE F-CREDITORS HOLDING UNSECURED NONPRIORITY CLAIMS
(Continuation Sheet)

Creditor's Name and Mailing Address including Zip Code	Codebtor	Date Claim was Incurred, and Consideration for Claim. If Claim is Subject to Setoff, so State. H—Husband W—Wife J—Joint C—Community	Contingent	Unliquidated	Disputed	Amount of Claim
Account No. 44444 Creditor #: 6 Providian P.O. Box 4017 Woburn, MA 01888		1997 Credit card purchases				$ 3,300.00
Account No. 4444 Creditor #: 7 Saks Fifth Ave. Dept. 0034 Palantine, IL 60055		1005 Credit card purchases				$ 1,020.00
Account No. 4444 Creditor #: 8 Sears P.O. Box 5000 Rancho Cucamonga, CA 91729		1997 Credit card purchases				$ 920.00
Account No. 44444 Creditor #: 9 Wachovia P.O. Box 15515 Wilmington, DE 19886-5515		1990 Credit card purchases				$ 10,900.00
Account No.						
Account No.						
Account No.						

Sheet no. _1_ of _1_ sheets attached to Schedule of
Creditors Holding Unsecured Nonpriority Claims

Subtotal $ (Total of this page) $ 16,140.00

Total $
(Use only on last page and on Summary of Schedules) $ 31,965.00

In re *Christopher Columbus* _____ / Debtor   Case No. _____

                                                                             (If known)

SCHEDULE G-EXECUTORY CONTRACTS AND UNEXPIRED LEASES

Describe all executory contracts of any nature and all unexpired leases of real or personal property. Include any timeshare interests.
State nature of debtor's interest in contract, i.e., "Purchaser," "Agent," etc. State whether debtor is the lessor or lessee of a lease.
Provide the names and complete mailing addresses of all other parties to each lease or contract described.

NOTE: A party listed on this schedule will not receive notice of the filing of this case unless the party is also scheduled in the appropriate schedule of creditors.

☒ Check this box if the debtor has no executory contracts or unexpired leases.

Name and Mailing Address, including Zip Code, of other Parties to Lease or Contract	Description of Contract or Lease and Nature of Debtor's Interest. State whether Lease is for Nonresidential Real Property. State Contract Number of any Government Contract.

Page *1* of *1*

In re *Christopher Columbus* _____ / Debtor   Case No. _____

(If known)

SCHEDULE H-CODEBTORS

Provide the information requested concerning any person or entity, other than a spouse in a joint case, that is also liable on any debts listed by debtor in the schedules of creditors. Include all guarantors and co-signers. In community property states, a married debtor not filing a joint case should report the name and address of the nondebtor spouse on this schedule. Include all names used by the nondebtor spouse during the six years immediately preceding the commencement of this case.

☒ Check this box if the debtor has no codebtors.

Name and Address of Codebtor	Name and Address of Creditor

Page ___<u>1</u>___ of ___<u>1</u>___

In re _Christopher Columbus_ _____/ Debtor   Case No. _____

SCHEDULE I-CURRENT INCOME OF INDIVIDUAL DEBTOR(S)

The column labeled spouse must be completed in all cases filed by joint debtors and by a married debtor in a chapter 12 or 13 case whether or not a joint petition is filed, unless the spouses are separated and a joint petition is not filed.

Debtor's Marital Status: _Single_	DEPENDENTS OF DEBTOR AND SPOUSE		
	NAMES	AGE	RELATIONSHIP
	Francesco	_12_	
	Dominque	_6_	

EMPLOYMENT:	DEBTOR	SPOUSE
Occupation	_Adventurer_	
Name of Employer	_Queen of Spain_	
How Long Employed	_4 years_	
Address of Employer	_Lisbon, America_	

Income: (Estimate of average monthly income)	DEBTOR		SPOUSE	
Current Monthly gross wages, salary, and commissions (pro rate if not paid monthly)	$	_3,500.00_	$	
Estimated Monthly Overtime	$	_0.00_	$	
SUBTOTAL	$	_3,500.00_	$	
LESS PAYROLL DEDUCTIONS				
a. Payroll Taxes and Social Security	$	_750.00_	$	
b. Insurance	$	_35.00_	$	
c. Union Dues	$	_25.00_	$	
d. Other (Specify):	$	_0.00_	$	
SUBTOTAL OF PAYROLL DEDUCTIONS	$	_810.00_	$	
TOTAL NET MONTHLY TAKE HOME PAY	$	_2,690.00_	$	
Regular income from operation of business or profession or farm (attach detailed statement)	$	_0.00_	$	
Income from Real Property	$	_0.00_	$	
Interest and dividends	$	_0.00_	$	
Alimony, maintenance or support payments payable to the debtor for the debtor's use or that of dependents listed above.	$	_0.00_	$	
Social Security or other government assistance Specify:	$	_0.00_	$	
Pension or retirement income	$	_0.00_	$	
Other monthly income Specify:	$	_0.00_	$	
TOTAL MONTHLY INCOME	$	_2,690.00_	$	

TOTAL COMBINED MONTHLY INCOME $ ____ _2,690.00_
(Report also on Summary of Schedules)

Describe any increase or decrease of more than 10% in any of the above categories anticipated to occur within the year following the filing of this document:

In re *Christopher Columbus* _____ / Debtor   Case No. _____
(If known)

SCHEDULE J-CURRENT EXPENDITURES OF INDIVIDUAL DEBTOR

Complete this schedule by estimating the average monthly expenses of the debtor and the debtor's family. Pro rate any payments made bi-weekly, quarterly, semi-annually, or annually to show monthly rate.

☐ Check this box if a joint petition is filed and debtor's spouse maintains a separate household. Complete a separate schedule of expenditures labeled "Spouse."

Rent or home mortgage payment (include lot rented for mobile home)	$ 900.00
Are real estate taxes included? Yes ☐ No ☒	
Is property insurance included? Yes ☐ No ☒	
Utilities: Electricity and heating fuel	$ 125.00
Water and sewer	$ 25.00
Telephone	$ 75.00
Other *cable TV*	$ 50.00
Other	$ 0.00
Home maintenance (repairs and upkeep)	$ 25.00
Food	$ 600.00
Clothing	$ 75.00
Laundry and Dry cleaning	$ 25.00
Medical and Dental expenses	$ 25.00
Transportation (not including car payments)	$ 150.00
Recreation, clubs, and entertainment, newspapers, magazines, etc.	$ 100.00
Charitable contributions	$ 20.00
Insurance (not deducted from wages or included in home mortgage payments)	
Homeowner's or renter's	$ 100.00
Life	$ 50.00
Health	$ 0.00
Auto	$ 100.00
Other:	$ 0.00
Taxes (not deducted from wages or included in home mortgage)	
Specify:	$ 0.00
Installment payments: (In chapter 12 and 13 cases, do not list payments to be included in the plan)	
Auto	$ 290.00
Other:	$ 0.00
Alimony, maintenance, and support paid to others	$ 0.00
Payments for support of additional dependents not living at your home	$ 0.00
Regular expenses from operation of business, profession, or farm (attach detailed statement)	$ 0.00
Other:	$ 0.00
TOTAL MONTHLY EXPENSES (Report also on Summary of Schedules)	$ 2,735.00

[FOR CHAPTER 12 AND 13 DEBTORS ONLY]
Provide the information requested below, including whether plan payments are to be made bi-weekly, monthly, annually, or at some other regular interval.

A. Total projected monthly income	$
B. Total projected monthly expenses	$
C. Excess Income (A minus B)	$
D. Total amount to be paid into plan each:	$

UNITED STATES BANKRUPTCY COURT
EASTERN DISTRICT OF CALIFORNIA
SACRAMENTO DIVISION

In re *Christopher Columbus*

Case No.
Chapter   7

_____ / Debtor

Attorney for Debtor: _____

STATEMENT OF FINANCIAL AFFAIRS

This statement is to be completed by every debtor. Spouses filing a joint petition may file a single statement on which the information for both spouses is combined. If the case is filed under chapter 12 or chapter 13, a married debtor must furnish information for both spouses whether or not a joint petition is filed, unless the spouses are separated and a joint petition is not filed. An individual debtor engaged in business as a sole proprietor, partner, family farmer, or self-employed professional, should provide the information requested on this statement concerning all such activities as well as the individual's personal affairs.

Questions 1 - 15 are to be completed by all debtors. Debtors that are or have been in business, as defined below, also must complete Questions 16 - 21. **If the answer to any question is "None," or the question is not applicable, mark the box labeled "None."** If additional space is needed for the answer to any question, use and attach a separate sheet properly identified with the case name, case number (if known), and the number of the question.

DEFINITIONS

"In business." A debtor is "in business" for the purpose of this form if the debtor is a corporation or partnership. An individual debtor is "in business" for the purpose of this form if the debtor is or has been, within the two years immediately preceding the filing of this bankruptcy case, any of the following: an officer, director, managing executive, or person in control of a corporation; a partner, other than a limited partner, of a partnership; a sole proprietor or self-employed.

"Insider." The term "insider" includes but is not limited to: relatives of the debtor; general partners of the debtor and their relatives, corporations of which the debtor is an officer, director, or person in control; officers, directors, and any person in control of a corporate debtor and their relatives; affiliates of the debtor and insiders of such affiliates; any managing agent of the debtor. 11 U.S.C. §101(30).

1. **Income from employment or operation of business.**
State the gross amount of income the debtor has received from employment, trade, or profession, or from operation of the debtor's business from the beginning of this calendar year to the date this case was commenced. State also the gross amounts received during the two years immediately preceding this calendar year. (A debtor that maintains, or has maintained, financial records on the basis of a fiscal rather than a calendar year may report fiscal year income. Identify the beginning and ending dates of the debtor's fiscal year.) If a joint petition is filed, state income for each spouse separately. (Married debtors filing under chapter 12 or chapter 13 must state income of both spouses whether or not a joint petition is filed, unless the spouses are separated and a joint petition is not filed.)

<u>AMOUNT</u>   <u>SOURCE (if more than one)</u>

Year to date:$24,300

* Last year:$32,000*

Year before:$31.500

2. **Income other than from employment or operation of business.**
State the amount of income received by the debtor other than from employment, trade, profession, or operation of the debtor's business during the **two years** immediately preceding the commencement of this case. Give particulars. If a joint petition is filed, state income for each spouse separately. (Married debtors filing under chapter 12 or chapter 13 must state income for each spouse whether or not a joint petition is filed, unless the spouses are separated and a joint petition is not filed.)

☒ NONE

3a. Payments to creditors.
List all payments on loans, installment purchases of goods or services, and other debts, aggregating more than $600 to any creditor, made within **90 days** immediately preceding the commencement of this case. (Married debtors filing under chapter 12 or chapter 13 must include payments by either or both spouses whether or not a joint petition is filed, unless the spouses are separated and a joint petition is not filed.)

☒ NONE

3b. List all payments made within **one year** immediately preceding the commencement of this case to or for the benefit of creditors who are or were insiders. (Married debtors filing under chapter 12 or chapter 13 must include payments by either or both spouses whether or not a joint petition is filed, unless the spouses are separated and a joint petition is not filed.)

☒ NONE

4a. Suits and administrative proceedings, executions, garnishments and attachments.
List all suits and administrative proceedings to which the debtor is or was a party within **one year** immediately preceding the filing of this bankruptcy case. (Married debtors filing under chapter 12 or chapter 13 must include information concerning either or both spouses whether or not a joint petition is filed, unless the spouses are separated and a joint petition is not filed.)

☒ NONE

4b. Describe all property that has been attached, garnished or seized under any legal or equitable process within **one year** immediately preceding the commencement of this case. (Married debtors filing under chapter 12 or chapter 13 must include information concerning property of either or both spouses whether or not a joint petition is filed, unless the spouses are separated and a joint petition is not filed.)

☒ NONE

5. Repossessions, foreclosures and returns.
List all property that has been repossessed by a creditor, sold at a foreclosure sale, transferred through a deed in lieu of foreclosure or returned to the seller, within **one year** immediately preceding the commencement of this case. (Married debtors filing under chapter 12 or chapter 13 must include information concerning property of either or both spouses whether or not a joint petition is filed, unless the spouses are separated and a joint petition is not filed.)

☒ NONE

6a. Assignments and receiverships.
Describe any assignment of property for the benefit of creditors made within **120 days** immediately preceding the commencement of this case. (Married debtors filing under chapter 12 or chapter 13 must include any assignment by either or both spouses whether or not a joint petition is filed, unless the spouses are separated and a joint petition is not filed.)

☒ NONE

6b. List all property which has been in the hands of a custodian, receiver, or court-appointed official within **one year** immediately preceding the commencement of this case. (Married debtors filing under chapter 12 or chapter 13 must include information concerning property of either or both spouses whether or not a joint petition is filed, unless the spouses are separated and a joint petition is not filed.)

☒ NONE

7. Gifts
List all gifts or charitable contributions made within **one year** immediately preceding the commencement of this case except ordinary and usual gifts to family members aggregating less than $200 in value per individual family member and charitable contributions aggregating less than $100 per recipient. (Married debtors filing under chapter 12 or chapter 13 must include gifts or contributions by either or both spouses whether or not a joint petition is filed, unless the spouses are separated and a joint petition is not filed.)

☒ NONE

8. Losses
List all losses from fire, theft, other casualty or gambling within **one year** immediately preceding the commencement of this case **or since the commencement of this case.** (Married debtors filing under chapter 12 or chapter 13 must include losses by either or both spouses whether or not a joint petition is filed, unless the spouses are separated and joint petition is not filed.)

☒ NONE

9. Payments related to debt counseling or bankruptcy.
List all payments made or property transferred by or on behalf of the debtor to any persons, including attorneys, for consultation concerning debt consolidation, relief under the bankruptcy law or preparation of a petition in bankruptcy within **one year** immediately preceding the commencement of this case.

☒ NONE

10. Other transfers
List all other property, other than property transferred in the ordinary course of the business or financial affairs of the debtor, transferred either absolutely or as a security within **one year** immediately preceding the commencement of this case. (Married debtors filing under chapter 12 or chapter 13 must include transfers by either or both spouses whether or not a joint petition is filed, unless the spouses are separated and a joint petition is not filed.)

☒ NONE

---

11. Closed financial accounts
List all financial accounts and instruments held in the name of the debtor or for the benefit of the debtor which were closed, sold, or otherwise transferred within **one year** immediately preceding the commencement of this case. Include checking, savings, or other financial accounts, certificates of deposit, or other instruments; shares and share accounts held in banks, credit unions, pension funds, cooperatives, associations, brokerage houses and other financial institutions. (Married debtors filing under chapter 12 or chapter 13 must include information concerning accounts or instruments held by or for either or both spouses whether or not a joint petition is filed, unless spouses are separated and a joint petition is not filed.)

☒ NONE

---

12. Safe deposit boxes
List each safe deposit or other box or depository in which the debtor has or had securities, cash, or other valuables within **one year** immediately preceding the commencement of this case. (Married debtors filing under chapter 12 or chapter 13 must include boxes or depositories of either or both spouses whether or not a joint petition is filed, unless the spouses are separated and a joint petition is not filed.)

☒ NONE

---

13. Setoffs
List all setoffs made by any creditor, including a bank, against a debt or deposit of the debtor within **90 days** preceding the commencement of this case. (Married debtors filing under chapter 12 or chapter 13 must include information concerning either or both spouses whether or not a joint petition is filed, unless the spouses are separated and a joint petition is not filed.)

☒ NONE

---

14. Property held for another person
List all property owned by another person that the debtor holds or controls.

☒ NONE

---

15. Prior address of debtor.
If the debtor has moved within the **two years** immediately preceding the commencement of this case, list all premises which the debtor occupied during that period and vacated prior to the commencement of this case. If a joint petition is filed, report also any separate address of either spouse.

☒ NONE

The following questions are to be completed by every debtor that is a corporation or partnership and by any individual debtor who is or has been, within two years immediately preceding the commencement of this case, any of the following: an officer, director, managing executive, or owner of more than 5 percent of the voting securities of a corporation; a partner, other than a limited partner, of a partnership; a sole proprietor or otherwise self-employed.

(An individual or joint debtor should complete this portion of the statement **only** if the debtor is or has been in business, as defined above, within the two years immediately preceding the commencement of this case.)

16. Nature, location and name of business

a. If the debtor is an individual, list the names and addresses of all businesses in which the debtor was an officer, director, partner, or managing executive of a corporation, partnership, sole proprietorship, or was a self-employed professional within the **two years** immediately preceding the commencement of this case, or in which the debtor owned 5 percent or more of the voting or equity securities within the two years immediately preceding the commencement of this case.

b. If the debtor is a partnership, list the names and addresses of all businesses in which the debtor was a partner or owned 5 percent or more of the voting securities, within the **two years** immediately preceding the commencement of this case.

c. If the debtor is a corporation, list the names and addresses of all businesses in which the debtor was a partner or owned 5 percent or more of the voting securities within the two years immediately preceding the commencement of this case.

☒ NONE

17a. Books, records and financial statements
List all bookkeepers and accountants who within the **six years** immediately preceding the filing of this bankruptcy case kept or supervised the keeping of books of account and records of the debtor.

☒ NONE

17b. List all firms or individuals who within the **two years** immediately preceding the filing of this bankruptcy case have audited the books of account and records, or prepared a financial statement of the debtor.

☒ NONE

17c. List all firms or individuals who at the time of the commencement of this case were in possession of the books of account and records of the debtor. If any of the books of account and records are not available, explain.

☒ NONE

17d. List all financial institutions, creditors and other parties, including mercantile and trade agencies, to whom a financial statement was issued within **two years** immediately preceding the commencement of this case by the debtor.

☒ NONE

18a. Inventories
List the dates of the last two inventories taken of your property, the name of the person who supervised the taking of each inventory, and the dollar amount and basis of each inventory.

☒ NONE

18b. List the name and address of the person having possession of the records of each of the two inventories reported in a., above.

☒ NONE

19a. Current Partners, Officers, Directors and Shareholders
If the debtor is a partnership, list the nature and percentage of partnership interest of each member of the partnership.

☒ NONE

19b. If the debtor is a corporation, list all officers and directors of the corporation, and each stockholder who directly or indirectly owns, controls, or holds 5 percent or more of the voting securities of the corporation.

☒ NONE

20a. Former partners, officers, directors and shareholders.
If the debtor is a partnership, list each member who withdrew from the partnership within **one year** immediately preceding the commencement of this case.

☒ NONE

20b. If the debtor is a corporation, list all officers, or directors whose relationship with the corporation terminated within **one year** immediately preceding the commencement of this case.

☒ NONE

21. Withdrawals from a partnership or distribution by a corporation
If the debtor is a partnership or corporation, list all withdrawals or distributions credited or given to an insider, including compensation in any form, bonuses, loans, stock redemptions, options exercised and any other prerequisite during **one year** immediately preceding the commencement of this case.

☒ NONE

STATEMENT OF FINANCIAL AFFAIRS

DECLARATION UNDER PENALTY OF PERJURY BY INDIVIDUAL DEBTOR

I declare under penalty of Perjury that I have read the answers contained in the foregoing statement of financial affairs and any attachments thereto and that they are true and correct.

Date _July 4, 2000_   Signature _____
                                                        Christopher Columbus

Date _____   Signature _____

Penalty for making a false statement: Fine of up to $500,000 or imprisonment for up to 5 years or both. 18 U.S.C. §152 and §3571.

Statement of Financial Affairs (Declaration) -- Page 5

UNITED STATES BANKRUPTCY COURT
EASTERN DISTRICT of CALIFORNIA
SACRAMENTO DIVISION

In re *Christopher Columbus*

Case No.
Chapter 7

_____ / Debtor

Attorney for Debtor:

CHAPTER 7 INDIVIDUAL DEBTOR'S STATEMENT OF INTENTION

1. I have filed a schedule of assets and liabilities which includes consumer debts secured by property of the estate.

2. I intend to do the following with respect to the property of the estate which secures those consumer debts:

a. **Property to Be Surrendered.**

Description of Property	Creditor's Name
None	

b. **Property to Be Retained.**   [Check any applicable statement.]

Description of Property	Creditor's Name	Property is claimed as exempt	Property will be redeemed pursuant to §722	Debt will be reaffirmed pursuant to §524(c)
1997 Honda Prelude	*Lisbon Cars of America*			X
Residence	*Lisbon Financial*			X

Signature of Debtor(s)

Date: _____   Debtor: _____

Page _1_ of _1_

**UNITED STATES BANKRUPTCY COURT
EASTERN DISTRICT of CALIFORNIA
SACRAMENTO DIVISION**

In re *Christopher Columbus*

Case No.
Chapter   7

_____ / Debtor

Attorney for Debtor: *Steven D. Strauss*

CERTIFICATION OF CREDITOR MATRIX

     I hereby certify that the attached matrix includes the names and addresses of all creditors listed on the debtor's schedules.

Date: *July 4, 2000*

_____ __

Debtor's Attorney

```
American Express
Acct: 4444
Suite 0001
Chicago, IL  60679-0001


Bank of America
Acct: 4444444
P.O. Box 53132
Phoenix, AZ  85072-3132


JC Penney
Acct: 4444
P.O. Box 3665
Portland, OR  97208


Lisbon Cars of America
Acct: 4444
P.O. Box 4444
Lisbon, America


Lisbon Financial
Acct: 55555
P.O. Box 2222
Lisbon, America


Macy's
Acct: 4444
P.O. Box 4582
Carol Stream, IL  60197


Mervyns
Acct: 4444
c/o Retailers Natl. Bank
P.O. Box 59287
Minneapolis, MN  55459-0287
```

```
Providian
Acct: 44444
P.O. Box 4017
Woburn, MA   01888



Saks Fifth Ave.
Acct: 4444
Dept. 0034
Palantine, IL   60055



Sears
Acct: 4444
P.O. Box 5000
Rancho Cucamonga, CA   91729



Wachovia
Acct: 44444
P.O. Box 15515
Wilmington, DE   19886-5515



Waste Disposal
Acct: 2543849
1324 Paddock Pl
Lisbon, America
```

UNITED STATES BANKRUPTCY COURT
EASTERN DISTRICT of CALIFORNIA
SACRAMENTO DIVISION

In re *Christopher Columbus*

Case No.
Chapter   7

_____ / Debtor

Attorney for Debtor:

SUMMARY OF SCHEDULES

Indicate as to each schedule whether that schedule is attached and state the number of pages in each. Report the totals from Schedules A, B, D, E, F, I, and J in the boxes provided. Add the amounts from Schedules A and B to determine the total amount of the debtor's assets. Add the amounts from Schedule D, E, and F to determine the total amount of the debtor's liabilities.

NAME OF SCHEDULE	Attached (Yes/No)	No. of Sheets	AMOUNTS SCHEDULED		
			ASSETS	LIABILITIES	OTHER
A-Real Property	Yes	1	$ 120,000.00		
B-Personal Property	Yes	2	$ 40,600.00		
C-Property Claimed as Exempt	Yes	1			
D-Creditors Holding Secured Claims	Yes	1		$ 140,000.00	
E-Creditors Holding Unsecured Priority Claims	Yes	2		$ 750.00	
F-Creditors Holding Unsecured Nonpriority Claims	Yes	2		$ 31,965.00	
G-Executory Contracts and Unexpired Leases	Yes	1			
H-Codebtors	Yes	1			
I-Current Income of Individual Debtor(s)	Yes	1			$ 2,690.00
J-Current Expenditures of Individual Debtor(s)	Yes	1			$ 2,735.00
Total Number of Sheets in All Schedules ▸		13			
Total Assets ▸			$ 160,600.00		
Total Liabilities ▸				$ 172,715.00	

In re _Christopher Columbus_ _____ / Debtor Case No. _____
                                                            (If known)

DECLARATION CONCERNING DEBTOR'S SCHEDULES

DECLARATION UNDER PENALTY OF PERJURY BY INDIVIDUAL DEBTOR

I declare under penalty of perjury that I have read the foregoing Summary and Schedules, consisting of ___14___ sheets, and that they are true and correct to the best of my knowledge, information and belief.   (Total shown on summary page plus 1)

Date: _July 4, 2000_____   Signature _____
                                          Christopher Columbus

Date: _____   Signature _____

Penalty for making a false statement or concealing property: Fine of up to $500,000 or imprisonment for up to 5 years or both. 18 U.S.C. §152 and §3571.

Appendix B

Sample Chapter 13 Plan

UNITED STATES BANKRUPTCY COURT

NORTHERN DISTRICT OF CALIFORNIA

In Re: Christopher Columbus (Chapter 13 debtor), Chapter 13 Plan

Case No: 03-9999

1. The future earnings of the debtor are submitted to the supervision and control of the bankruptcy trustee, and the debtor shall pay to the trustee the sum of $665 a month for 36 months or until all allowed claims are paid.

2. From the payments so received, the trustee shall make disbursements as follows:

    a. For trustee and administration expenses required by 11 USC 507 (a)(1)

    b. To secured creditors whose claims are allowed as follows:

Arrears on home:	$1,645
Homeowners Association arrears:	$204
Auto:	$3,870

    c. To priority creditors (the IRS) in the amount of $5,000

    d. To unsecured creditors: zero cents on the dollar

3. The debtor shall pay directly the following fully secured creditors and lessors: None

4. The date this case was filed shall be the effective date of the Plan as well as the date when interest ceases accruing on unsecured claims.

5. The Court may, after hearing upon such notice as the Court may designate, increase or reduce the amount or the time for payments where it appears that circumstances so warrant.

Dated: 9/10/03_____

Debtor

Appendix C

Fair Debt Collection Practices Act: Relevant Sections

The Fair Debt Collection Practices Act (FDCPA) was enacted in 1977 to protect consumers from unfair and abusive collection practices. The law regulates professional, third-party collection businesses, agents, and attorneys, but not "in-house" collectors or employees of creditors who collect their own debts. The FDCPA is enforced on the federal level by the Federal Trade Commission. The state where you live may have regulations that provide further consumer protection. State laws vary.

The following sections are taken directly from *Title 15, United States Code, Commerce And Trade, Chapter 41—Consumer Credit Protection Subchapter V—Debt Collection Practices.*

1692b. Acquisition of Location Information

Any debt collector communicating with any person other than the consumer for the purpose of acquiring location information about the consumer shall

1. identify himself, state that he is confirming or correcting location information concerning the consumer, and, only if expressly requested, identify his employer;

2. not state that such consumer owes any debt;

3. not communicate with any such person more than once unless requested to do so by such person or unless the debt collector reasonably believes that the earlier response of such person is erroneous or incomplete and that such person now has correct or complete location information;

4. not communicate by postcard;

5. not use any language or symbol on any envelope or in the contents of any communication affected by the mails or telegram that indicates that the debt collector is in the debt collection business or that the communication relates to the collection of a debt; and

6. after the debt collector knows the consumer is represented by an attorney with regard to the subject debt and has knowledge of, or can readily ascertain, such attorney's name and address, not communicate with any person other than that attorney, unless the attorney fails to respond within a reasonable period of time to communication from the debt collector.

1692c. Communication in Connection with Debt Collection

Communication with Consumer Generally

Without the prior consent of the consumer given directly to the debt collector or the express permission of a court of competent jurisdiction, a debt collector may not communicate with a consumer in connection with the collection of any debt

1. at any unusual time or place or a time or place known or which should be known to be inconvenient to the consumer. In the absence of knowledge of circumstances to the contrary, a debt collector shall assume that the convenient time for communicating with a consumer is after 8 o'clock antemeridian and before 9 o'clock postmeridian, local time at the consumer's location;

2. if the debt collector knows the consumer is represented by an attorney with respect to such debt and has knowledge of, or can readily ascertain, such attorney's name and address, unless the attorney fails to respond within a reasonable period of time to a communication from the debt collector or unless the attorney consents to direct communication with the consumer; or

3. at the consumer's place of employment if the debt collector knows or has reason to know that the consumer's employer prohibits the consumer from receiving such communication.

Communication with Third Parties

Except as provided in section 1692b of this title, without the prior consent of the consumer given directly to the debt collector, or the express permission of a court of competent jurisdiction, or as reasonably necessary to effectuate a postjudgment judicial remedy, a debt collector may not communicate, in connection with the collection of any debt, with any person other than the consumer, his attorney, a consumer reporting agency if otherwise permitted by law, the creditor, the attorney of the creditor, or the attorney of the debt collector.

Ceasing Communication

If a consumer notifies a debt collector in writing that the consumer refuses to pay a debt or that the consumer wishes the debt collector to cease further communication with the consumer, the debt collector shall not communicate further with the consumer with respect to such debt, except

1. to advise the consumer that the debt collector's further efforts are being terminated;

2. to notify the consumer that the debt collector or creditor may invoke specified remedies which are ordinarily invoked by such debt collector or creditor; or

3. where applicable, to notify the consumer that the debt collector or creditor intends to invoke a specified remedy.

If such notice from the consumer is made by mail, notification shall be complete upon receipt.

Consumer Defined

For the purpose of this section, the term *consumer* includes the consumer's spouse, parent (if the consumer is a minor), guardian, executor, or administrator.

1692d. Harassment or Abuse

A debt collector may not engage in any conduct the natural consequence of which is to harass, oppress, or abuse any person in connection with the collection of a debt. Without limiting the general application of the foregoing, the following conduct is a violation of this section:

1. The use or threat of use of violence or other criminal means to harm the physical person, reputation, or property of any person.

2. The use of obscene or profane language or language the natural consequence of which is to abuse the hearer or reader.

3. The publication of a list of consumers who allegedly refuse to pay debts, except to a consumer reporting agency or to persons meeting the requirements of section 1681a(f) or 1681b(3) of this title.

4. The advertisement for sale of any debt to coerce payment of the debt.

5. Causing a telephone to ring or engaging any person in telephone conversation repeatedly or continuously with intent to annoy, abuse, or harass any person at the called number.

6. Except as provided in section 1692b of this title, the placement of telephone calls without meaningful disclosure of the caller's identity.

1692e. False or Misleading Representations

A debt collector may not use any false, deceptive, or misleading representation or means in connection with the collection of any debt. Without limiting the general application of the foregoing, the following conduct is a violation of this section:

1. The false representation or implication that the debt collector is vouched for, bonded by, or affiliated with the United States or any State, including the use of any badge, uniform, or facsimile thereof.

2. The false representation of

   A. the character, amount, or legal status of any debt; or

   B. any services rendered or compensation which may be lawfully received by any debt collector for the collection of a debt.

3. The false representation or implication that any individual is an attorney or that any communication is from an attorney.

4. The representation or implication that nonpayment of any debt will result in the arrest or imprisonment of any person or the seizure, garnishment, attachment, or sale of any property or wages of any person unless such action is lawful and the debt collector or creditor intends to take such action.

5. The threat to take any action that cannot legally be taken or that is not intended to be taken.

6. The false representation or implication that a sale, referral, or other transfer of any interest in a debt shall cause the consumer to

    A. lose any claim or defense to payment of the debt; or

    B. become subject to any practice prohibited by this subchapter.

7. The false representation or implication that the consumer committed any crime or other conduct in order to disgrace the consumer.

8. Communicating or threatening to communicate to any person credit information which is known or which should be known to be false, including the failure to communicate that a disputed debt is disputed.

9. The use or distribution of any written communication which simulates or is falsely represented to be a document authorized, issued, or approved by any court, official, or agency of the United States or any State, or which creates a false impression as to its source, authorization, or approval.

10. The use of any false representation or deceptive means to collect or attempt to collect any debt or to obtain information concerning a consumer.

11. The failure to disclose in the initial written communication with the consumer and, in addition, if the initial communication with the consumer is oral, in that initial oral communication, that the debt collector is attempting to collect a debt and that any information obtained will be used for that purpose, and the failure to disclose in subsequent communications that the communication is from a debt collector, except that this paragraph shall not apply to a formal pleading made in connection with a legal action.

12. The false representation or implication that accounts have been turned over to innocent purchasers for value.

13. The false representation or implication that documents are legal process.

14. The use of any business, company, or organization name other than the true name of the debt collector's business, company, or organization.

15. The false representation or implication that documents are not legal process forms or do not require action by the consumer.

16. The false representation or implication that a debt collector operates or is employed by a consumer reporting agency as defined by section 1681a(f) of this title.

1692f. Unfair Practices

A debt collector may not use unfair or unconscionable means to collect or attempt to collect any debt. Without limiting the general application of the foregoing, the following conduct is a violation of this section:

1. The collection of any amount (including any interest, fee, charge, or expense incidental to the principal obligation) unless such amount is expressly authorized by the agreement creating the debt or permitted by law.

2. The acceptance by a debt collector from any person of a check or other payment instrument postdated by more than five days unless such person is notified in writing of the debt collector's intent to deposit such check or instrument not more than ten nor less than three business days prior to such deposit.

3. The solicitation by a debt collector of any postdated check or other postdated payment instrument for the purpose of threatening or instituting criminal prosecution.

4. Depositing or threatening to deposit any postdated check or other postdated payment instrument prior to the date on such check or instrument.

5. Causing charges to be made to any person for communications by concealment of the true purpose of the communication. Such charges include, but are not limited to, collect telephone calls and telegram fees.

6. Taking or threatening to take any nonjudicial action to effect dispossession or disablement of property if

   A. there is no present right to possession of the property claimed as collateral through an enforceable security interest;

   B. there is no present intention to take possession of the property; or

   C. the property is exempt by law from such dispossession or disablement.

7. Communicating with a consumer regarding a debt by postcard.

8. Using any language or symbol, other than the debt collector's address, on any envelope when communicating with a consumer by use of the mails or by telegram, except that a debt collector may use his business name if such name does not indicate that he is in the debt collection business.

1692g. Validation of Debts

Notice of Debt; Contents

Within five days after the initial communication with a consumer in connection with the collection of any debt, a debt collector shall, unless the following information is contained in the initial communication or the consumer has paid the debt, send the consumer a written notice containing

1. the amount of the debt;

2. the name of the creditor to whom the debt is owed;

3. a statement that unless the consumer, within thirty days after receipt of the notice, disputes the validity of the debt, or any portion thereof, the debt will be assumed to be valid by the debt collector;

4. a statement that if the consumer notifies the debt collector in writing within the thirty-day period that the debt, or any portion thereof, is disputed, the debt collector will obtain verification of the debt or a copy of a judgment against the consumer and a copy of such verification or judgment will be mailed to the consumer by the debt collector; and

5. a statement that, upon the consumer's written request within the thirty-day period, the debt collector will provide the consumer with the name and address of the original creditor, if different from the current creditor.

Disputed Debts

If the consumer notifies the debt collector in writing within the thirty-day period described in subsection (a) of this section that the debt, or any portion thereof, is disputed, or that the consumer requests the name and address of the original creditor, the debt collector shall cease collection of the debt, or any disputed portion thereof, until the debt collector obtains verification of the debt or a copy of a judgment, or the name and address of the original creditor, and a copy of such verification or judgment, or name and address of the original creditor, is mailed to the consumer by the debt collector.

Admission of Liability

The failure of a consumer to dispute the validity of a debt under this section may not be construed by any court as an admission of liability by the consumer.

1692j. Furnishing Certain Deceptive Forms

a. It is unlawful to design, compile, and furnish any form knowing that such form would be used to create the false belief in a consumer that a person other than the creditor of such consumer is participating in the collection of or in an attempt to collect a debt such consumer allegedly owes such creditor, when in fact such person is not so participating.

b. Any person who violates this section shall be liable to the same extent and in the same manner as a debt collector is liable under section 1692k of this title for failure to comply with a provision of this subchapter.

1692k. Civil Liability

Amount of Damages

Except as otherwise provided by this section, any debt collector who fails to comply with any provision of this subchapter with respect to any person is liable to such person in an amount equal to the sum of

1. any actual damage sustained by such person as a result of such failure;

2. A. in the case of any action by an individual, such additional damages as the court may allow, but not exceeding $1,000; or

   B. in the case of a class action,

      i. such amount for each named plaintiff as could be recovered under subparagraph (A), and

      ii. such amount as the court may allow for all other class members, without regard to a minimum individual recovery, not to exceed the lesser of $500,000 or 1 per centum of the net worth of the debt collector; and

3. in the case of any successful action to enforce the foregoing liability, the costs of the action, together with a reasonable attorney's fee as determined by the court. On a finding by the court that an action under this section was brought in bad faith and for the purpose of harassment, the court may award to the defendant attorney's fees reasonable in relation to the work expended and costs.

Factors Considered by Court

In determining the amount of liability in any action under subsection (a) of this section, the court shall consider, among other relevant factors,

1. in any individual action under subsection (a)(2)(A) of this section, the frequency and persistence of noncompliance by the debt collector, the nature of such non-compliance, and the extent to which such noncompliance was intentional; or

2. in any class action under subsection (a)(2)(B) of this section, the frequency and persistence of noncompliance by the debt collector, the nature of such noncompliance, the resources of the debt collector, the number of persons adversely affected, and the extent to which the debt collector's noncompliance was intentional.

Intent

A debt collector may not be held liable in any action brought under this subchapter if the debt collector shows by a preponderance of evidence that the violation was not intentional and resulted from a bona fide error notwithstanding the maintenance of procedures reasonably adapted to avoid any such error.

Jurisdiction

An action to enforce any liability created by this subchapter may be brought in any appropriate United States district court without regard to the amount in controversy, or in any other court of competent jurisdiction, within one year from the date on which the violation occurs.

Advisory Opinions of Commission

No provision of this section imposing any liability shall apply to any act done or omitted in good faith in conformity with any advisory opinion of the Commission, notwithstanding that after such act or omission has occurred, such opinion is amended, rescinded, or determined by judicial or other authority to be invalid for any reason.

1692I. Administrative Enforcement

Federal Trade Commission

Compliance with this subchapter shall be enforced by the Commission, except to the extent that enforcement of the requirements imposed under this subchapter is specifically committed to another agency under subsection (b) of this section. For purpose of the exercise by the Commission of its functions and powers under the Federal Trade Commission Act, a violation of this subchapter shall be deemed an unfair or deceptive act or practice in violation of that Act. All of the functions and powers of the Commission under the Federal Trade Commission Act are available to the Commission to enforce compliance by any person with this subchapter, irrespective of whether that person is engaged in commerce or meets any other jurisdictional tests in the Federal Trade Commission Act, including the power to enforce the provisions of this subchapter in the same manner as if the violation had been a violation of a Federal Trade Commission trade regulation rule.

Applicable Provisions of Law

Compliance with any requirements imposed under this subchapter shall be enforced under

1. section 8 of the Federal Deposit Insurance Act [12 U.S.C.A. 1818], in the case of

   A. national banks, and Federal branches and Federal agencies of foreign banks, by the Office of the Comptroller of the Currency;

   B. member banks of the Federal Reserve System (other than national banks), branches and agencies of foreign banks (other than Federal branches, Federal agencies, and insured State branches of foreign banks), commercial lending companies owned or controlled by foreign banks, and organizations operating under section 25 or 25(a) of the Federal Reserve Act [12 U.S.C.A. 601 et seq., 611 et seq.], by the Board of Governors of the Federal Reserve System; and

   C. banks insured by the Federal Deposit Insurance Corporation (other than members of the Federal Reserve System) and insured State branches of foreign banks, by the Board of Directors of the Federal Deposit Insurance Corporation;

2. section 8 of the Federal Deposit Insurance Act [12 U.S.C.A. 1818], by the Director of the Office of Thrift Supervision, in the case of a savings association the deposits of which are insured by the Federal Deposit Insurance Corporation;

3. the Federal Credit Union Act, by the National Credit Union Administration Board with respect to any Federal credit union;

4. subtitle IV of Title 49, by the Secretary of Transportation, with respect to all carriers subject to the jurisdiction of the Surface Transportation Board;

5. the Federal Aviation Act of 1958, by the Secretary of Transportation with respect to any air carrier or any foreign air carrier subject to that Act; and

6. the Packers and Stockyards Act, 1921 (except as provided in section 406 of that Act), by the Secretary of Agriculture with respect to any activities subject to that Act. The terms used in paragraph (1) that are not defined in this subchapter or otherwise defined in section 3(s) of the Federal Deposit Insurance Act (12 U.S.C. 1813(s)) shall have the meaning given to them in section 1(b) of the International Banking Act of 1978 (12 U.S.C. 3101).

Agency Powers

For the purpose of the exercise by any agency referred to in subsection (b) of this section of its powers under any Act referred to in that subsection, a violation of any requirement imposed under this subchapter shall be deemed to be a violation of a requirement imposed under that Act. In addition to its powers under any provision of law specifically referred to in subsection (b) of this section, each of the agencies referred to in that subsection may exercise, for the purpose of enforcing compliance with any requirement imposed under this subchapter any other authority conferred on it by law, except as provided in subsection (d) of this section.

Rules and Regulations

Neither the Commission nor any other agency referred to in subsection (b) of this section may promulgate trade regulation rules or other regulations with respect to the collection of debts by debt collectors as defined in this subchapter.

Appendix D

Fair Credit Reporting Act: Relevant Sections

Section 604, 1681b. Permissible Purposes of Reports

a. In General

A consumer reporting agency may only furnish a consumer report under the following circumstances and no other:

1. In response to the order of a court having jurisdiction to issue such an order, or a subpoena issued in connection with proceedings before a Federal grand jury.

2. In accordance with the written instructions of the consumer to whom it relates.

3. To a person which it has reason to believe

   A. intends to use the information in connection with a credit transaction involving the consumer on whom the information is to be furnished and involving the extension of credit to, or review or collection of an account of, the consumer; or

   B. intends to use the information for employment purposes; or

C. intends to use the information in connection with the underwriting of insurance involving the consumer; or

D. intends to use the information in connection with a determination of the consumer's eligibility for a license or other benefit granted by a governmental instrumentality required by law to consider an applicant's financial responsibility or status; or

E. otherwise has a legitimate business need for the information in connection with a business transaction involving the consumer; intends to use the information as a potential investor or servicer or current insurer in connection with a valuation of, or an assessment of the credit or prepayment risks associated with, an existing credit obligation; or

F. otherwise has a legitimate business need for the information

  i. in connection with a business transaction that is initiated by the consumer;

  or

  ii. to review an account to determine whether the consumer continues to meet the terms of the account.

4. In response to a request by the head of a state or local child support enforcement agency (or a state or local government official authorized by the head of such an agency), if the person making the request certifies to the consumer reporting agency that

A. the consumer report is needed for the purpose of establishing an individual's capacity to make child support payments or determining the appropriate level of such payments;

B. the paternity of the consumer for the child to which the obligation relates has been established or acknowledged by the consumer in accordance with state laws under which the obligation arises (if required by those laws);

C. the person has provided at least 10 days' prior notice to the consumer whose report is requested, by certified or registered mail to the last known address of the consumer, that the report will be requested; and

D. the consumer report will be kept confidential, will be used solely for a purpose described in subparagraph (A), and will not be used in connection with any other civil, administrative, or criminal proceeding, or for any other purpose.

5. To an agency administering a state plan under Section 454 of the Social Security Act (42 U.S.C. 654) for use to set an initial or modified child support award.

b. Conditions for Furnishing and Using Consumer Reports for Employment Purposes

1. Certification from User

A consumer reporting agency may furnish a consumer report for employment purposes only if

    A. the person who obtains such report from the agency certifies to the agency that

        i. the person has complied with paragraph (2) with respect to the consumer report, and the person will comply with paragraph (3) with respect to the consumer report if paragraph (3) becomes applicable; and

        ii. information from the consumer report will not be used in violation of any applicable federal or state equal employment opportunity law or regulation; and

    B. the consumer reporting agency provides with the report or has previously provided a summary of the consumer's rights under this title, as prescribed by the Federal Trade Commission under Section 609(c)(3). /fcra609.htm – (c)(3) fcra609.htm – (c)(3)

2. Disclosure to Consumer

    A. A person may not procure a consumer report, or cause a consumer report to be procured, for employment purposes with respect to any consumer, unless

        i. a clear and conspicuous disclosure has been made in writing to the consumer at any time before the report is procured or caused to be procured, in a document that consists solely of the disclosure, that a consumer report may be obtained for employment purposes; and

        ii. the consumer has authorized in writing (which authorization may be made on the document referred to in clause (A)) the procurement of the report by that person.

    B. Application by mail, telephone, computer, or other similar means: If a consumer described in subparagraph (C) applies for employment by mail, telephone, computer, or other similar means, at any time before a consumer report is procured or caused to be procured in connection with that application

        i. the person who procures the consumer report on the consumer for employment purposes shall provide to the consumer, by oral, written, or electronic means, notice that a consumer report may be obtained for employment purposes, and a summary of the consumer's rights under section 615(a)(3); and

ii. the consumer shall have consented, orally, in writing, or electronically to the procurement of the report by that person.

C. Scope: Subparagraph (B) shall apply to a person procuring a consumer report on a consumer in connection with the consumer's application for employment only if

i. the consumer is applying for a position over which the Secretary of Transportation has the power to establish qualifications and maximum hours of service pursuant to the provisions of section 31502 of title 49, or a position subject to safety regulation by a State transportation agency; and

ii. as of the time at which the person procures the report or causes the report to be procured the only interaction between the consumer and the person in connection with that employment application has been by mail, telephone, computer, or other similar means.

3. Conditions on Use for Adverse Actions

A. In general: Except as provided in subparagraph (B), in using a consumer report for employment purposes, before taking any adverse action based in whole or in part on the report, the person intending to take such adverse action shall provide to the consumer to whom the report relates

i. a copy of the report; and

ii. a description in writing of the rights of the consumer under this title, as prescribed by the Federal Trade Commission under Section 609(c)(3). /fcra609.htm – (c)(3) fcra609.htm – (c)(3)

B. Application by mail, telephone, computer, or other similar means:

i. If a consumer described in subparagraph (C) applies for employment by mail, telephone, computer, or other similar means, and if a person who has procured a consumer report on the consumer for employment purposes takes adverse action on the employment application based in whole or in part on the report, then the person must provide to the consumer to whom the report relates, in lieu of the notices required under subparagraph (A) of this section and under section 615(a), within three business days of taking such action, an oral, written or electronic notification

        I. that adverse action has been taken based in whole or in part on a consumer report received from a consumer reporting agency;

      II. of the name, address, and telephone number of the consumer reporting agency that furnished the consumer report (including a toll-free telephone number established by the agency if the agency compiles and maintains files on consumers on a nationwide basis);

    III. that the consumer reporting agency did not make the decision to take the adverse action and is unable to provide to the consumer the specific reasons why the adverse action was taken; and

    IV. that the consumer may, upon providing proper identification, request a free copy of a report and may dispute with the consumer reporting agency the accuracy or completeness of any information in a report.

  ii. If, under clause (B)(i)(IV), the consumer requests a copy of a consumer report from the person who procured the report, then, within three business days of receiving the consumer's request, together with proper identification, the person must send or provide to the consumer a copy of a report and a copy of the consumer's rights as prescribed by the Federal Trade Commission under section 609(c)(3).

C. Scope: Subparagraph (B) shall apply to a person procuring a consumer report on a consumer in connection with the consumer's application for employment only if

  i. the consumer is applying for a position over which the Secretary of Transportation has the power to establish qualifications and maximum hours of service pursuant to the provisions of section 31502 of title 49, or a position subject to safety regulation by a State transportation agency; and

  ii. as of the time at which the person procures the report or causes the report to be procured the only interaction between the consumer and the person in connection with that employment application has been by mail, telephone, computer, or other similar means.

4. Exception for National Security Investigations

A. In general: In the case of an agency or department of the United States Government which seeks to obtain and use a consumer report for employment purposes, paragraph (3) shall not apply to any adverse action by such agency or department which is based in part on such consumer report, if the head of such agency or department makes a written finding that

     i. the consumer report is relevant to a national security investigation of such agency or department;

     ii. the investigation is within the jurisdiction of such agency or department;

     iii. there is reason to believe that compliance with paragraph (3) will

        I. endanger the life or physical safety of any person;

        II. result in flight from prosecution;

        III. result in the destruction of, or tampering with, evidence relevant to the investigation;

        IV. result in the intimidation of a potential witness relevant to the investigation;

        V. result in the compromise of classified information; or

        VI. otherwise seriously jeopardize or unduly delay the investigation or another official proceeding.

B. Notification of consumer upon conclusion of investigation: Upon the conclusion of a national security investigation described in subparagraph (A), or upon the determination that the exception under subparagraph (A) is no longer required for the reasons set forth in such subparagraph, the official exercising the authority in such subparagraph shall provide to the consumer who is the subject of the consumer report with regard to which such finding was made

     i. a copy of such consumer report with any classified information redacted as necessary;

     ii. the identification with reasonable specificity of the nature of the investigation for which the consumer report was sought.

C. Delegation by head of agency or department: For purposes of subparagraphs (A) and (B), the head of any agency or department of the United States Government may delegate his or her authorities under this paragraph to an official of such agency or department who has personnel security responsibilities and is a member of the Senior Executive Service or equivalent civilian or military rank.

D. Report to the congress: Not later than January 31 of each year, the head of each agency and department of the United States Government that exercised authority under this paragraph during the preceding year shall submit a report to the Congress on the number of times the department or agency exercised such authority during the year.

E. Definitions: For purposes of this paragraph, the following definitions shall apply:

   i. Classified information: The term *classified information* means information that is protected from unauthorized disclosure under Executive Order No. 12958 or successor orders.

c. Furnishing Reports in Connection with Credit or Insurance Transactions That Are Not Initiated by the Consumer

1. In General

A consumer reporting agency may furnish a consumer report relating to any consumer pursuant to subparagraph (A) or (C) of subsection (a)(3) in connection with any credit or insurance transaction that is not initiated by the consumer only if

A. the consumer authorizes the agency to provide such report to such person; or

   i. the transaction consists of a firm offer of credit or insurance;

   ii. the consumer reporting agency has complied with subsection (e); and

   iii. there is not in effect an election by the consumer, made in accordance with subsection (e), to have the consumer's name and address excluded from lists of names provided by the agency pursuant to this paragraph.

2. Limits on Information Received Under Paragraph (1)(b)

A person may receive pursuant to paragraph (1)(B) only

A. the name and address of a consumer;

B. an identifier that is not unique to the consumer and that is used by the person solely for the purpose of verifying the identity of the consumer; and

C. other information pertaining to a consumer that does not identify the relationship or experience of the consumer with respect to a particular creditor or other entity.

3. Information Regarding Inquiries

Except as provided in Section 609(a)(5), /fcra609.htm – (a)(5) fcra609.htm – (a)(5), a consumer reporting agency shall not furnish to any person a record of inquiries in connection with a credit or insurance transaction that is not initiated by a consumer.

d. Reserved

e. Election of Consumer to Be Excluded from Lists

1. In General

A consumer may elect to have the consumer's name and address excluded from any list provided by a consumer reporting agency under subsection (c)(1)(B) in connection with a credit or insurance transaction that is not initiated by the consumer by notifying the agency in accordance with paragraph (2) that the consumer does not consent to any use of a consumer report relating to the consumer in connection with any credit or insurance transaction that is not initiated by the consumer.

2. Manner of Notification

A consumer shall notify a consumer-reporting agency under paragraph (1)

A. through the notification system maintained by the agency under paragraph (5); or

B. by submitting to the agency a signed notice of election form issued by the agency for purposes of this subparagraph.

3. Response of Agency After Notification Through System

Upon receipt of notification of the election of a consumer under paragraph (1) through the notification system maintained by the agency under paragraph (5), a consumer reporting agency shall

A. inform the consumer that the election is effective only for the two-year period following the election if the consumer does not submit to the agency a signed notice of election form issued by the agency for purposes of paragraph (2)(B); and

B. provide to the consumer a notice of election form, if requested by the consumer, not later than five business days after receipt of the notification of the election through the system established under paragraph (5), in the case of a request made at the time the consumer provides notification through the system.

4. Effectiveness of Election

An election of a consumer under paragraph (1)

A. shall be effective with respect to a consumer reporting agency beginning five business days after the date on which the consumer notifies the agency in accordance with paragraph (2);

B. shall be effective with respect to a consumer reporting agency

    i. subject to subparagraph (C), during the two-year period beginning five business days after the date on which the consumer notifies the agency of the election, in the case of an election for which a consumer notifies the agency only in accordance with paragraph (2)(A); (e)(2)(A) e)(2)(A) or

    ii. until the consumer notifies the agency under subparagraph (C), in the case of an election for which a consumer notifies the agency in accordance with paragraph (2)(B); (e)(2)(B) e)(2)(B)

C. shall not be effective after the date on which the consumer notifies the agency, through the notification system established by the agency under paragraph (5), that the election is no longer effective; and

D. shall be effective with respect to each affiliate of the agency.

5. Notification System

A. In general: Each consumer reporting agency that, under subsection (c)(l)(B), furnishes a consumer report in connection with a credit or insurance transaction that is not initiated by a consumer shall

    i. establish and maintain a notification system, including a toll-free telephone number, which permits any consumer whose consumer report is maintained by the agency to notify the agency, with appropriate identification, of the consumer's election to have the consumer's name and address excluded from any such list of names and addresses provided by the agency for such a transaction; and

    ii. publish by not later than 365 days after the date of enactment of the Consumer Credit Reporting Reform Act of 1996, and not less than annually thereafter, in a publication of general circulation in the area served by the agency

        I. a notification that information in consumer files maintained by the agency may be used in connection with such transactions; and

        II. the address and toll-free telephone number for consumers to use to notify the agency of the consumer's election under clause (i).

B. Establishment and maintenance as compliance: Establishment and maintenance of a notification system (including a toll-free telephone number) and publication by a consumer reporting agency on the agency's own behalf and on behalf of any of its affiliates in accordance with this paragraph is deemed to be compliance with this paragraph by each of those affiliates.

6. Notification System by Agencies That Operate Nationwide

Each consumer reporting agency that compiles and maintains files on consumers on a nationwide basis shall establish and maintain a notification system for purposes of paragraph (5) jointly with other such consumer reporting agencies.

f. Certain Use or Obtaining of Information Prohibited

A person shall not use or obtain a consumer report for any purpose unless

1. the consumer report is obtained for a purpose for which the consumer report is authorized to be furnished under this section; and the purpose is certified in accordance with Section 607 /fcra607.htmfcra607.htm by a prospective user of the report through a general or specific certification.

(FTC Guidelines Regarding Prescreening for Insurance Transactions: The Federal Trade Commission may issue such guidelines as it deems necessary with respect to the use of consumer reports in connection with insurance transactions that are not initiated by the consumer pursuant to Section 604(c) of the Fair Credit Reporting Act, as added by subsection (a) of this section.)

g. Furnishing Reports Containing Medical Information

A consumer reporting agency shall not furnish for employment purposes, or in connection with a credit or insurance transaction, a consumer report that contains medical information about a consumer, unless the consumer consents to the furnishing of the report.

Section 605, 1681c. Obsolete Information Requirements Relating to Information Section Title Here Contained in Consumer Reports

h. Information Excluded from Consumer Reports

Except as authorized under subsection (b) of this section, no consumer reporting agency may make any consumer report containing any of the following items of information:

1. Cases under Title 11 or under the Bankruptcy Act that, from the date of entry of the order for relief or the date of adjudication, as the case may be, antedate the report by more than 10 years.

2. Civil suits, civil judgments, and records of arrest that, from date of entry, antedate the report by more than seven years or until the governing statute of limitations has expired, whichever is the longer period.

3. Paid tax liens which, from date of payment, antedate the report by more than seven years.

4. Accounts placed for collection or charged to profit and loss which antedate the report by more than seven years.

5. Any other adverse item of information, other than records of convictions of crimes, which antedates the report by more than seven years.

i.

The provisions of subsection (a) of this section are not applicable in the case of any consumer credit report to be used in connection with

1. a credit transaction involving, or which may reasonably be expected to involve, a principal amount of $50,000—$150,000 or more;

2. the underwriting of life insurance involving, or which may reasonably be expected to involve, a face amount of $50,000—$150,000 or more; or

3. the employment of any individual at an annual salary which equals, or which may reasonably be expected to equal $20,000—$75,000 or more.

j. Running of Reporting Period

1. In General

The seven-year period referred to in paragraphs (4) and (6) of subsection (a) shall begin, with respect to any delinquent account that is placed for collection (internally or by referral to a third party, whichever is earlier), charged to profit and loss, or subjected to any similar action, upon the expiration of the 180-day period beginning on the date of the commencement of the delinquency which immediately preceded the collection activity, charge to profit and loss, or similar action.

2. Effective Date

Paragraph (1) shall apply only to items of information added to the file of a consumer on or after the date that is 455 days after the date of enactment of the Consumer Credit Reporting Reform Act of 1996.

k. Information Required to Be Disclosed

Any consumer reporting agency that furnishes a consumer report that contains information regarding any case involving the consumer that arises under Title 11, United States Code, shall include in the report an identification of the chapter of such Title 11 under which such case arises if provided by the source of the information. If any case arising or filed under Title 11, United States Code, is withdrawn by the consumer before a final judgment, the consumer reporting agency shall include in the report that such case or filing was withdrawn upon receipt of documentation certifying such withdrawal.

l. Indication of Closure of Account by Consumer

If a consumer reporting agency is notified pursuant to Section 623(a)(4) /fcra623.htm – (a)(4) fcra623.htm – (a)(4) that a credit account of a consumer was voluntarily closed by the consumer, the agency shall indicate that fact in any consumer report that includes information related to the account.

m. Indication of Dispute by Consumer

If a consumer reporting agency is notified pursuant to Section 623(a)(3) /fcra623.htm – (a)(3) fcra623.htm – (a)(3) that information regarding a consumer that was furnished to the agency is disputed by the consumer, the agency shall indicate that fact in each consumer report that includes the disputed information.

n. Reinvestigations of Disputed Information

1. Reinvestigation Required

A. In general: If the completeness or accuracy of any item of information contained in a consumer's file at a consumer reporting agency is disputed by the consumer and the consumer notifies the agency directly of such dispute, the agency shall reinvestigate free of charge and record the current status of the disputed information, or delete the item from the file in accordance with paragraph (5), before the end of the 30-day period beginning on the date on which the agency receives the notice of the dispute from the consumer.

B. Extension of period to reinvestigate: Except as provided in subparagraph (C), the 30-day period described in subparagraph (A) may be extended for not more than 15 additional days if the consumer reporting agency receives information from the consumer during that 30-day period that is relevant to the reinvestigation.

C. Limitations on extension of period to reinvestigate: Subparagraph (B) shall not apply to any reinvestigation in which, during the 30-day period described in subparagraph (A), the information that is the subject of the reinvestigation is found to be inaccurate or incomplete or the consumer reporting agency determines that the information cannot be verified.

2. Prompt Notice of Dispute to Furnisher of Information

A. In general: Before the expiration of the 5-business-day period beginning on the day on which a consumer reporting agency receives notice of a dispute from any consumer in accordance with paragraph (1), the agency shall provide notification of the dispute to any person who provided any item of information in dispute, at the address and in the manner established with the person. The notice shall include all relevant information regarding the dispute that the agency has received from the consumer.

B. Provision of other information from consumer: The consumer reporting agency shall promptly provide to the person who provided the information in dispute all relevant information regarding the dispute that is received by the agency from the consumer after the period referred to in subparagraph (A) and before the end of the period referred to in paragraph (1)(A).

3. Determination That Dispute Is Frivolous or Irrelevant

A. In general: Notwithstanding paragraph (1), a consumer reporting agency may terminate a reinvestigation of information disputed by a consumer under that paragraph if the agency reasonably determines that the dispute by the consumer is frivolous or irrelevant, including by reason of a failure by a consumer to provide sufficient information to investigate the disputed information.

B. Notice of determination: Upon making any determination in accordance with subparagraph (A) that a dispute is frivolous or irrelevant, a consumer reporting agency shall notify the consumer of such determination not later than five business days after making such determination, by mail or, if authorized by the consumer for that purpose, by any other means available to the agency.

C. Contents of notice: A notice under subparagraph (B) shall include

    i. the reasons for the determination under subparagraph (A); and

    ii. identification of any information required to investigate the disputed information, which may consist of a standardized form describing the general nature of such information.

4. Consideration of Consumer Information

In conducting any reinvestigation under paragraph (1) with respect to disputed information in the file of any consumer, the consumer reporting agency shall review and consider all relevant information submitted by the consumer in the period described in paragraph (1)(A) with respect to such disputed information.

5. Treatment of Inaccurate or Unverifiable Information

A. In general: If, after any reinvestigation under paragraph (1) of any information disputed by a consumer, an item of the information is found to be inaccurate or incomplete or cannot be verified, the consumer reporting agency shall promptly delete that item of information from the consumer's file or modify that item of information, as appropriate, based on the results of the reinvestigation.

B. Requirements relating to reinsertion of previously deleted material:

    i. Certification of accuracy of information: If any information is deleted from a consumer's file pursuant to subparagraph (A), the information may not be reinserted in the file by the consumer reporting agency unless the person who furnishes the information certifies that the information is complete and accurate.

    ii. Notice to consumer: If any information that has been deleted from a consumer's file pursuant to subparagraph (A) is reinserted in the file, the consumer reporting agency shall notify the consumer of the reinsertion in writing not later than five business days after the reinsertion or, if authorized by the consumer for that purpose, by any other means available to the agency.

    iii. Additional information: As part of, or in addition to, the notice under clause (ii), a consumer reporting agency shall provide to a consumer in writing not later than five business days after the date of the reinsertion

        I. a statement that the disputed information has been reinserted;

        II. the business name and address of any furnisher of information contacted and the telephone number of such furnisher, if reasonably available, or of any furnisher of information that contacted the consumer reporting agency, in connection with the reinsertion of such information; and

III. a notice that the consumer has the right to add a statement to the consumer's file disputing the accuracy or completeness of the disputed information.

C. Procedures to prevent reappearance: A consumer reporting agency shall maintain reasonable procedures designed to prevent the reappearance in a consumer's file, and in consumer reports on the consumer, of information that is deleted pursuant to this paragraph (other than information that is reinserted in accordance with subparagraph (B)(i)).

D. Automated reinvestigation system: Any consumer reporting agency that compiles and maintains files on consumers on a nationwide basis shall implement an automated system through which furnishers of information to that consumer reporting agency may report the results of a reinvestigation that finds incomplete or inaccurate information in a consumer's file to other such consumer reporting agencies.

6. Notice of Results of Reinvestigation

A. In general: A consumer reporting agency shall provide written notice to a consumer of the results of a reinvestigation under this subsection not later than five business days after the completion of the reinvestigation, by mail or, if authorized by the consumer for that purpose, by other means available to the agency.

B. Contents: As part of, or in addition to, the notice under subparagraph (A), a consumer reporting agency shall provide to a consumer in writing before the expiration of the five-day period referred to in subparagraph (A)

i. a statement that the reinvestigation is completed;

ii. a consumer report that is based upon the consumer's file as that file is revised as a result of the reinvestigation;

iii. a notice that, if requested by the consumer, a description of the procedure used to determine the accuracy and completeness of the information shall be provided to the consumer by the agency, including the business name and address of any furnisher of information contacted in connection with such information and the telephone number of such furnisher, if reasonably available;

iv. a notice that the consumer has the right to add a statement to the consumer's file disputing the accuracy or completeness of the information; and

v. a notice that the consumer has the right to request under subsection (d) that the consumer reporting agency furnish notifications under that subsection.

7. Description of Reinvestigation Procedure

A consumer reporting agency shall provide to a consumer a description referred to in paragraph (6)(B)(iii) by not later than 15 days after receiving a request from the consumer for that description.

8. Expedited Dispute Resolution

If a dispute regarding an item of information in a consumer's file at a consumer reporting agency is resolved in accordance with paragraph (5)(A) by the deletion of the disputed information by not later than three business days after the date on which the agency receives notice of the dispute from the consumer in accordance with paragraph (1)(A), then the agency shall not be required to comply with paragraphs (2), (6), and (7) with respect to that dispute if the agency

A. provides prompt notice of the deletion to the consumer by telephone;

B. includes in that notice, or in a written notice that accompanies a confirmation and consumer report provided in accordance with subparagraph (C), a statement of the consumer's right to request under subsection (d) that the agency furnish notifications under that subsection; and

C. provides written confirmation of the deletion and a copy of a consumer report on the consumer that is based on the consumer's file after the deletion not later than five business days after making the deletion.

If the reinvestigation does not resolve the dispute, the consumer may file a brief statement setting forth the nature of the dispute. The consumer reporting agency may limit such statements to not more than 100 words if it provides the consumer with assistance in writing a clear summary of the dispute.

Whenever a statement of a dispute is filed, unless there is reasonable grounds to believe that it is frivolous or irrelevant, the consumer reporting agency shall, in any subsequent consumer report containing the information in question, clearly note that it is disputed by the consumer and provide either the consumer's statement or a clear and accurate codification or summary thereof.

Following any deletion of information which is found to be inaccurate or whose accuracy can no longer be verified or any notation as to disputed information, the consumer reporting agency shall, at the request of the consumer, furnish notification that the item has been deleted or the statement, codification or summary pursuant to subsection (b) or (c) of this section to any person specifically designated by the consumer who has within two years prior thereto received a consumer report for employment purposes, or within six months prior thereto received a consumer report for any other purpose, which contained the deleted or disputed information.

Section 616, 1681n. Civil Liability for Willful Noncompliance

Any consumer reporting agency or user of information which

a. In General

Any person who willfully fails to comply with any requirement imposed under this title with respect to any consumer is liable to that consumer in an amount equal to the sum of

1. any actual damages sustained by the consumer as a result of the failure;

   A. any actual damages sustained by the consumer as a result of the failure or damages of not less than $100 and not more than $1,000; or

   B. in the case of liability of a natural person for obtaining a consumer report under false pretenses or knowingly without a permissible purpose, actual damages sustained by the consumer as a result of the failure or $1,000, whichever is greater;

2. such amount of punitive damages as the court may allow; and

3. in the case of any successful action to enforce any liability under this section, the costs of the action together with reasonable attorney's fees as determined by the court.

b. Civil Liability for Knowing Noncompliance

Any person who obtains a consumer report from a consumer reporting agency under false pretenses or knowingly without a permissible purpose shall be liable to the consumer reporting agency for actual damages sustained by the consumer reporting agency or $1,000, whichever is greater.

c. Attorney's Fees

Upon a finding by the court that an unsuccessful pleading, motion, or other paper filed in connection with an action under this section was filed in bad faith or for purposes of harassment, the court shall award to the prevailing party attorney's fees reasonable in relation to the work expended in responding to the pleading, motion, or other paper.

Section 617, 16810. Civil Liability for Negligent Noncompliance

j. In General

Any person who is negligent in failing to comply with any requirement imposed under this title with respect to any consumer is liable to that consumer in an amount equal to the sum of

1. any actual damages sustained by the consumer as a result of the failure;

2. in the case of any successful action to enforce any liability under this section, the costs of the action together with reasonable attorney's fees as determined by the court.

k. Attorney's Fees

On a finding by the court that an unsuccessful pleading, motion, or other paper filed in connection with an action under this section was filed in bad faith or for purposes of harassment, the court shall award to the prevailing party attorney's fees reasonable in relation to the work expended in responding to the pleading, motion, or other paper.

Section 623, Sec. 623. Responsibilities of Furnishers of Information to Consumer Reporting Agencies

l. Duty of Furnishers of Information to Provide Accurate Information

1. Prohibition

A. Reporting information with actual knowledge of errors: A person shall not furnish any information relating to a consumer to any consumer reporting agency if the person knows or consciously avoids knowing that the information is inaccurate.

B. Reporting information after notice and confirmation of errors: A person shall not furnish information relating to a consumer to any consumer reporting agency if

   i. the person has been notified by the consumer, at the address specified by the person for such notices, that specific information is inaccurate; and

   ii. the information is, in fact, inaccurate.

C. No address requirement: A person who clearly and conspicuously specifies to the consumer an address for notices referred to in subparagraph (B) shall not be subject to subparagraph (A); however, nothing in subparagraph (B) shall require a person to specify such an address.

2. Duty to Correct and Update Information

A person who

A. regularly and in the ordinary course of business furnishes information to one or more consumer reporting agencies about the person's transactions or experiences with any consumer; and

B. has furnished to a consumer reporting agency information that the person determines is not complete or accurate, shall promptly notify the consumer reporting agency of that determination and provide to the agency any corrections to that information, or any additional information, that is necessary to make the information provided by the person to the agency complete and accurate, and shall not thereafter furnish to the agency any of the information that remains not complete or accurate.

3. Duty to Provide Notice of Dispute

If the completeness or accuracy of any information furnished by any person to any consumer reporting agency is disputed to such person by a consumer, the person may not furnish the information to any consumer reporting agency without notice that such information is disputed by the consumer.

4. Duty to Provide Notice of Closed Accounts

A person who regularly and in the ordinary course of business furnishes information to a consumer reporting agency regarding a consumer who has a credit account with that person shall notify the agency of the voluntary closure of the account by the consumer, in information regularly furnished for the period in which the account is closed.

5. Duty to Provide Notice of Delinquency of Accounts

A person who furnishes information to a consumer reporting agency regarding a delinquent account being placed for collection, charged to profit or loss, or subjected to any similar action shall, not later than 90 days after furnishing the information, notify the agency of the month and year of the commencement of the delinquency that immediately preceded the action.

m. Duties of Furnishers of Information Upon Notice of Dispute

1. In General

After receiving notice pursuant to Section 61l(a)(2) /fcra611.htm – (a)(2) fcra611.htm – (a)(2) of a dispute with regard to the completeness or accuracy of any information provided by a person to a consumer reporting agency, the person shall

    A. conduct an investigation with respect to the disputed information;

    B. review all relevant information provided by the consumer reporting agency pursuant to Section 61l(a)(2); /fcra611.htm – (a)(2) fcra611.htm – (a)(2)

    C. report the results of the investigation to the consumer reporting agency; and

    D. if the investigation finds that the information is incomplete or inaccurate, report those results to all other consumer reporting agencies to which the person furnished the information and that compile and maintain files on consumers on a nationwide basis.

2. Deadline

A person shall complete all investigations, reviews, and reports required under paragraph (1) regarding information provided by the person to a consumer reporting agency, before the expiration of the period under Section 61l(a)(l) /fcra611.htm – (a)(1) fcra611.htm – (a)(1) within which the consumer reporting agency is required to complete actions required by that section regarding that information.

Recommended Resources

Books

Bounce Back from Bankruptcy, by Paula Langguth Ryan, Pellingham Casper Communications, LLC, 1998.

Debt and Bankruptcy (Ask a Lawyer), by Steven D. Strauss, WW Norton & Co., 1998.

Debt Control, by Chris J. Richards, Emerald Ink Pub., 1998.

Discover the Wealth Within You: A Financial Plan for Creating a Rich and Fulfilling Life, by Ric Edelman, HarperCollins, 2002.

Everyone's Money Book, 3rd Edition, by Jordan Elliot Goodman, Dearborn Trade Publishing, 2001.

Fifty Simple Things You Can Do to Improve Your Personal Finances: How to Spend Less, Save More, and Make the Most of What You Have, by Ilyce R. Glink, Crown Publishers, 2001.

Honey, I Want to Start My Own Business, by Azriela Jaffe and John Gray, HarperCollins, 1997.

Kids, Money & Values, by Patricia Schiff Estess and Irving Barocas, Betterway Publications, 1994.

The Millionairess Across the Street: Women: Lessons to Change Your Thinking and Achieve Wealth and Success, by Jennifer Basye Sander and Bettina R. Flores, Dearborn Trade, 1999.

Money Demons: Keep Them from Sabotaging Your Relationships and Your Life, by Dr. Susan Forward and Craig Buck, Bantam Books, 1995.

Money Harmony: Resolving Money Conflicts in Your Life and Your Relationships, by Olivia Mellan and Warren Farrell, Walker & Co., 1995.

Overcoming Overspending: A Winning Plan for Spenders and Their Partners, by Olivia Mellan and Sherry Christie, Walker & Co., 1997.

The Penny-Pinching Hedonist: How to Live Like Royalty with a Peasant's Pocketbook, by Shel Horowitz, Accurate Writing & More, 1995.

The Pocket Idiot's Guide to Living on a Budget, by Jennifer Basye Sander and Peter J. Sander, Alpha Books, 1999.

Rich Dad, Poor Dad: What the Rich Teach Their Kids About Money That the Poor & Middle Class Don't, by Robert T. Kiyosaki and Sharon L. Lechter, Techpress Inc., 1999.

The Richest Man in Babylon, by George S. Clason, New American Library, 1997.

True Prosperity: Your Guide to a Cash-Based Lifestyle, by K. C. Knouse, Double-Dome Publications, 1996.

What You Need to Do Now, by Ric Edelman, HarperCollins, April 2003.

Websites

www.Forbes.com

www.Miserlymoms.com

www.Money.com

www.MrAllBiz.com

www.wsj.com

Glossary

401(k)   A tax-deferred retirement plan. The money contributed into the plan must remain in the account until you are 59 years old. If it is withdrawn early, a penalty will apply (except under specific circumstances defined by the law).

alimony   Money paid to an ex-spouse due to a court judgment.

annual fee   The amount owed and paid to a credit card company for the right to use the card for one year (or any amount paid each year).

arrears   Money that is overdue and unpaid. The term usually applies to support payments and mortgages.

automatic stay   The court order that issues automatically upon the filing of any bankruptcy. The stay suspends all collection activities aimed at the debtor during the case.

bankruptcy   A federal court action designed to give debtors relief from indebtedness and a fresh start.

budget   A plan that allows you to allocate your financial resources where they can be best used.

Chapter 7   The most common type of bankruptcy, a Chapter 7 normally allows a debtor to wipe out (discharge) all unsecured debts.

Chapter 13   A bankruptcy that centers on a repayment plan.

child support   Money paid from one parent to another for the benefit of the child.

collateral   Property that is pledged as security for the satisfaction of a debt; property subject to a security interest.

collection agency   A business that attempts to collect a debt that the original creditor has deemed uncollectable.

credit   The ability of a person or business to borrow money, based upon credit payment history.

credit report   The report that details your credit history and bill-paying habits.

creditor   A person to whom a debt is owed.

debtor   A person who owes money to creditors; also, someone who files bankruptcy.

discharge   The order of the bankruptcy court that releases the debtor from his legal obligation to repay dischargeable debts.

entrepreneur   A person who takes a risk with money to make money, usually by starting a business.

equity   The value of property once all debts have been subtracted from its worth.

Fair Credit Reporting Act   Federal law that regulates credit bureau activity.

Fair Debt Collections Practices Act   Federal law that regulates collection agencies.

first meeting of creditors   Also known as a 341 hearing, this is a meeting that all people who file bankruptcy must attend. During this meeting, the debtor will be questioned about his assets and debts.

foreclosure   An action whereby a secured creditor forces the sale of the collateral that was used to secure the loan.

garnishment   A court-ordered method of debt collection whereby the debtor's wages are withheld to pay the debt.

home equity loan   A home loan that provides the debtor with a loan amount equal to the equity in his property and sometimes even more.

indebtedness   The total amount of money you owe. Also, being in debt.

introductory rate   An interest rate, often a very low one, offered to entice you to choose one credit card over another.

judgment   The official and final decision of a court.

late fees   The fees charged when payment is received after the due date.

levy   The legal process whereby property is seized and sold or where money has been attached.

lien   A claim upon property used to secure payment of a debt. After the debt is paid, the lien is removed.

minimum payment   The least you must pay to avoid any other fees. Paying the minimum will ensure that, over the course of the repayment period, you will pay the maximum.

overspending   Going into debt by spending more money than you have. Often, compulsive overspending is treated as an addiction.

personal property   All property you own other than real estate.

principal   The amount you actually borrowed. If you charged a $300 plane ticket, that is your principal.

repossession   The action taken by the creditor to reclaim the property after a debtor defaults on a loan.

secured credit card   A credit card that is tied to a savings account.

Small Business Administration   The federal program that is intended to help small businesses succeed. The SBA guarantees loans, among many other activities.

sue   To commence a legal proceeding intended to recover monetary damages.

teaser rate   A very low, and short-term, interest rate offered to entice you to choose that credit card.

transfer balances   To move your balance from one credit card to another—hopefully from one with a higher interest rate to one with a lower interest rate.

unsecured debt   Debt not associated with any sort of collateral.

Index

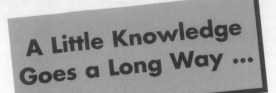
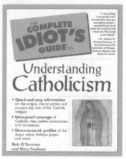

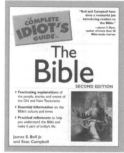

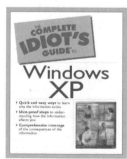